FRESH-RUN SILVER SALMON
(INSET: SEA LOUSE)

FEMALE IN SPAWNING COLOURS

MALE IN SPAWNING COLOURS

KELT (NOTE PRESENCE OF FUNGUS ON MANY KELTS)

THE COMPLETE
SALMON
FISHER

VOLUME ONE:
The Life of the Salmon

THE COMPLETE
SALMON
FISHER

VOLUME ONE:

The Life of the Salmon

MALCOLM GREENHALGH

BLANDFORD

A Blandford Book

First published in the UK 1996 by Blandford, a Cassell Imprint
Wellington House
125 Strand
London
WC2R 0BB

Distributed in the United States by Sterling Publishing Co. Inc.
387 Park Avenue South, New York, NY 10016-8810

Distributed in Australia by Capricorn Link (Australia) Pty Ltd
2/13 Carrington Road, Castle Hill, NSW 2154

British Library Cataloguing-in-Publication Data
A catalogue record for this book is available from the British Library
ISBN 0-7137-2544-3

Printed in Great Britain by Hartnolls Limited, Bodmin, Cornwall

Jacket illustration by Denys Ovenden

CONTENTS

CONTENTS

INTRODUCTION

Whenever I go fishing and spend some time nattering with other anglers, or when I go to angling clubs and talk on the subject of salmon, it is clear that the majority of anglers know relatively little about their quarry. This is in spite of the fact that more is known about the salmon than perhaps any other fish. It seems sad that so many anglers know so little about the salmon, for there is no doubt that, like the wildfowler who understands the behaviour and movements of ducks and geese and the deer-stalker who knows the daily and yearly routine of the red deer, an angler who knows the salmon well as a wild animal will catch more than one who knows little.

It has been said that the angler who can think like a fish will catch more than one who can do no more than handle a fishing rod. This is so true! Angling is a form of applied natural history; we apply our knowledge of what the fish are up to when we are trying to catch them. How can we use our knowledge if we have none?

It might be argued that ignorance is bliss, but when it comes to the vast army of salmon anglers, ignorance is highly dangerous. For it is imperative that all salmon anglers are aware of the problems facing salmon and salmon rivers.

Some years ago, Rod Sutterby and I produced our book *The Wild Trout* in which, with my words and Rod's paintings, we highlighted the remarkable nature and the sad plight of wild trout in Britain and North America. That book had an impact, for it made many anglers aware that wild fish and wild rivers and lakes need careful protection. We were highly honoured when our book was put in the final list for the coveted annual Conservation Book Prize (our equivalent of the Booker Prize), and that through the book I was invited to talk, on television and radio, of the problems faced by wild trout. It was our intention to follow up *The Wild Trout* with a similar volume on salmon, but unfortunately other pressures prevented Rod from contributing. This first volume presents the wild salmon, a remarkable species of fish that has been lost from many rivers and its populations brought to an all-time low in others. Although it is not threatened with extinction as a species, mankind's stupidity and mismanagement has brought present-day salmon stocks under pressure

7

from many quarters: excessive commercial fishing, pollution, the damming of rivers, damage to rivers by lumbering, water abstraction, land drainage, pollution and so on.

Sadly, it would appear that the conventional natural history lobby cares little for fish populations. As far as the run-of-the-mill naturalist or layman is concerned, fish are merely food for furry creatures such as otters and seals or feathered creatures such as kingfishers and herons. Natural history or conservation charities are greatly concerned if the population of a species of bat, or moth, or bird suddenly declines, or when a woodland or patch of marshland becomes threatened by development. If numbers of seabirds die from pollution, or seals from disease (as happened in 1992 in the Wash), then the matter becomes a major item in the national news. A river or lake, or its finny inhabitants, rarely make the headlines.

Television and radio natural history programmes, with their herds of wildebeest sweeping majestically across the Serengeti, and with gorillas and pandas and other spectacular birds and mammals, encourage people into believing that these are what conservation is all about – that slimy fish are of little importance as wildlife unless they are pretty coral-reef fish or man-eating sharks.

You think that I am exaggerating? On p. 184 I describe a pollution incident that I witnessed on a salmon river. It received scant notice in the national press and nothing on national TV or radio. Yet had this pollution caused the death of puffins, or seals, or a pod of whales, I believe it would have been front-page news and a lead item on national news programmes.

Many conservationists and naturalists care little about our rivers, lakes and fish. They leave it to us, the anglers, to look after them. Fish are not, as far as the public are concerned, wildlife! If you doubt this, go into your local library or bookshop and look for books on fishes. Almost always they are there with angling books and not in the natural history section.

This puts a great responsibility on the shoulders of anglers – a responsibility to care for our rivers and lakes and the animals and plants living in the water. We should not treat angling solely as a sport. It is a sport, of course, and one of the greatest, but angling also brings with it the duty to be guardian of the water and of the fish that we hope to catch. *If we do not care for and tend our rivers and lakes, no one else will!*

ACKNOWLEDGEMENTS

Although many observations in this book are my own, much information has been gleaned from scientific reports, papers and textbooks.

First I must pay tribute to that vast army of scientists who have done so much to help in our understanding of the beast: Dr R.G.J. Shelton, Ross Gardiner, Alastair Thorne and the Freshwater Fisheries Laboratory at Pitlochry and the F.B.A. at Ambleside for library facilities; also the two greatest students of salmon biology, Dr Derek Mills and W.M. Shearer, whose papers and books (especially Mills's *Ecology and Management of Atlantic Salmon* and Shearer's *The Atlantic Salmon*, essential reading for the salmonologist) are a mine of information. Mention must also be made to all those scientists whose work is referred to, to Runar Warhuus, Thorbjorn Tufte, Hans Odegard, Per Olav Moum, Ian Davis, Thorgeir Gustaven and other Norwegian friends who have shown me their rivers and given information, to the Ontario Federation of Hunters and Anglers, and the Fishery Departments of the provinces of Nova Scotia, Newfoundland and Quebec for their information. Thanks are due to Lords Home and Leicester for letting me have some of their records.

I thank Denys Ovenden for producing some wonderful paintings specially for this book, Alan Davies for other artwork, and Colin de Chair for some of the photographs. Photographs 34–38 are reproduced by kind permission of the Earl of Leicester and the trustees of the Holkham Hall Estate.

I must also thank my fishing pals who give me much moral support in my writings: Alan Davies, Dave Evans, Geoff Haslam, Paul Stanton, John Todd (fount of Irish knowledge), and my son Pete.

Finally, thanks also to Hugh Falkus and Yvonne for their support. When I gave up my lecturing job on my fortieth birthday to write and fish, Hugh summoned me to Crag Cottage. 'I am pleased to hear that you have seen sense and stopped going out to earn a living!' said he. 'I will tell you something. You will be very happy. You will never be wealthy, but very happy!'

Yvonne goes out to earn a living, pays the bills and then tolerates a houseful of fishing books, tackle and fly-tying rubbish. Without her I would never get a single article or book written simply because I would not be able to find anything in my chaotic office!

Conversion table

1 inch = 2.5 cm
1 foot = 30.4 cm
1 yard = 0.9 metre
1 mile = 1.6 km
1 sq foot = 0.09 sq metre
1 sq yard = 0.8 sq metre
1 acre = 0.4 hectare
1 ounce = 28.3 g
1 pound = 0.4 kg
1 ton = 1.01 tonnes

$$°F = \frac{9 \times °C}{5} + 32$$

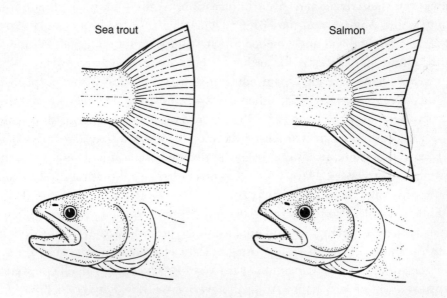

It is easy to confuse large sea trout with small salmon. In the sea trout the tail is square; in the salmon it is forked. In the sea trout the jaw extends beyond the rear of the eye, but in the salmon it extends no further back than the rear of the eye.

Fig. 1 – Characteristics to separate salmon and sea trout

CHAPTER 1

THE KING OF FISH

... anyone who has not seen a wild salmon
has not seen what a fish should be ...

W.M. SHEARER, *The Atlantic Salmon*, 1992

An Atlantic salmon that has just run into fresh water after a year or more at sea is the most perfect of fish. Its shape is the apotheosis of a fish: the ultimate of streamlining; a torpedo of hard, finned muscle. Its coloration is stunning and well summed up by the cliché, 'like a bar of silver'. For the angler it is the ultimate prize; because it does not feed in fresh water, it is difficult to hook and, because it is a powerful fish, not easy to land after it has been fooled into taking the hook. As Lee Wulff stated in his book, *The Atlantic Salmon*, 'Atlantic salmon fishing represents, in all likelihood, the highest development of individual angling ... To fish for Atlantic salmon is to accept a difficult challenge ... '

Part of this challenge is the mystery of the fish. In 1950 nobody knew where the salmon went once it had swum down the river to the sea. Nor where it had been when it returned. One suggestion, by Arthur Ransome, was that it went out to the Sargasso and fed its way back across the Atlantic on young eels or elvers. Today, almost half a century later, we know a good deal about the salmon at sea, where it goes to and what it eats. But there are still gaps in our knowledge. Yet no matter how much we learn, the arrival back of a shoal of fresh-run salmon from the tide into a great salmon pool is, and will ever remain, a source of wonder for the angler wading waist deep in the swirling current.

The salmon is good to eat. Whether smoked or poached, it is as rich a fish as one can find. Eat and enjoy it once a month or, at most, once a fortnight – not more, for it is so rich. I can understand the revulsion felt by London apprentices or the navvies driving the LMS railway through the Lune Gorge in 1840–6 (the tale is now apocryphal) that resulted in their refusing to work until the salmon on their menu was reduced to less than four days a week!

But what is a salmon? Where and how do they live? That is the subject of this chapter.

Classification of Salmonidae

The Atlantic salmon is a member of a great family of fish, the Salmonidae, characterized by a slender, streamlined body and the presence of a small, rounded adipose fin on the back, between the dorsal fin and the tail fin. The Salmonidae are divided into four separate groups or subfamilies: the Thymallinae, Coregoninae, Osmerinae and Salmoninae.

Grayling are in the subfamily Thymallinae. These have very large scales, very small teeth in their jaws, a noticeably underslung mouth and a huge dorsal fin. One species occurs commonly in Europe, the European grayling *Thymallus thymallus*, one species in North America, the arctic grayling *T. arcticus*, and four species in central Asia. The grayling are the only members of the salmon family that are wholly freshwater fish. None of them can tolerate sea water and none of them spend any part of their lives in the sea.

Whitefish are in the subfamily Coregoninae. These have large scales and very small mouths with toothless jaws. As their group name suggests, they are very pale, almost white, fish. Several species of whitefish occur throughout northern Europe, Asia and America, including the houting *Coregonus oxyrinchus*, vendace *C. albula* and powan *C. lavaretus*. Because of the similarity between the different whitefish species and the amount of individual variation within each species, the classification of this group remains confused and far from complete.

Smelts are in the subfamily Osmerinae. Superficially they resemble small, slender, almost translucent whitefish, but they can be distinguished by their very short lateral line, which extends back to just beyond the pectoral fins. In other members of the salmon family the lateral line extends the whole length of the body. Several species of smelts are numerous along the coasts of northern Europe, Asia and North America.

We now come to the subfamily Salmoninae, of which the Atlantic salmon is a member, all of which have very tiny scales and toothed jaws. This subfamily is divided up into six genera:

- *Hucho*, which includes the huchen, *H. hucho*, of the River Danube system and the taimen, *H. taimen*, of northern Siberia.
- *Brachymystax*, which includes the lenok, *B. lenok*, of eastern Siberia.
- *Salvelinus*, or chars, which include the circumpolar arctic char, *S. alpinus*, as well as three North American species, the great lake trout, *S. namaycush*, the dolly varden, *S. malma*, and the brook trout, *S. fontinalis*.
- *Onchorhynchus*, a Pacific genus that includes the rainbow trout, *O. mykiss*, cut-throat trout, *O. clarkii*, and six salmon species, the chinook, *O. tschawytscha*,

sockeye, *O. nerka*, coho, *O. kisutch*, humpback, *O. gorbuscha*, dog or chum, *O. keta*, and the cherry salmon, *O. masou*. This genus of salmonids occurs naturally in rivers draining into the Pacific from the United States and Canada west of the Rockies, and Asia from northeastern Russia south to Japan and Korea. Some species, however, have been introduced to eastern North America and to Europe.

• *Salmothymus*, whose sole member is the Adriatic salmon, *S. obtusirostris*. This is thought to be a land-locked relict of the Atlantic salmon from glacial times 10,000 and more years ago (see below).

• *Salmo*, which includes just two species, the brown trout, *S. trutta*, and the Atlantic salmon, *S. salar*. The latter is the subject of this book.

Readers can hardly fail to notice the varied, and somewhat confusing, use of the names 'salmon' and 'trout' in this account of the classification of the Salmonidae. We have, for instance, *Onchorhynchus* trout, *Salvelinus* trout and *Salmo* trout, and we also have *Onchorhynchus* salmon and *Salmo* salmon.

The popular or common names which we give to the creatures around us may be a convenient way of describing them but they often have little or nothing to do with the scientific relationships of the different species. In the case of the Salmonidae, the use of 'trout' or 'salmon' is historical. When the New World was first settled, the European colonists set about describing the animals that they found there, using familiar names based on their experience of the European fauna.

So, in the eastern USA and Canada they found a trout-like fish living in the creeks which they called the brook trout, and a big trout-like fish living in the lakes which they called the lake (or great lake) trout. Today we classify these fish as char species and use the more appropriate alternative names of speckled char and lake char respectively.

Similarly, when the United States and Canada west of the Rockies was explored and then colonized by Europeans in the late eighteenth and nineteenth centuries they found two species that lived in lakes and rivers and called them rainbow trout and cut-throat trout – 'rainbow' because of the fish's iridescent coloration (an early scientific name for this was *irideus*) and 'cut-throat' because of the red slashes on the fish's throat. To other fish, which ran to sea and returned to the rivers to breed, they gave the name 'salmon' because they are migratory and generally bigger than trout.

Even science became confused. Until 1989–90 the two Pacific trout were classified with the European brown trout and Atlantic salmon in the genus

Salmo, the rainbow trout as *S. gairdneri* and the cut-throat trout as *S. clarkii*. On the other hand, the Pacific salmon was not lumped with the Atlantic salmon, but put into its own genus *Onchorhynchus*. This was in spite of the fact that the rainbow and cut-throat are clearly far more closely related to the Pacific salmon than to the Atlantic salmon, while the Atlantic salmon is more closely related to the brown trout than to the Pacific salmon. It is, therefore, only by accident of history that to the honorary titles of trout and salmon have been conferred on the Pacific fish. The only true salmon is the Atlantic salmon, *Salmo salar*, the one king of fish!

Evolution

This classification is borne out by our knowledge of the evolution of the salmon family (Fig. 2). The first salmonid fossil showing an adipose fin, called *Protothymallus*, comes from the beginning of the Eocene Period, some 70 million years ago. We are not sure when, but it was probably soon after this that the smelts separated from the line that gave rise to the rest of the salmon family. Smelts have only about half of the amount of the genetic material DNA in their chromosomes than do all the other salmonids, indicating that they are more distantly related to other salmonids than other members are to each other. It is likely also that the forerunner of the modern grayling separated from the line that would eventually give rise to the Atlantic salmon about this time.

Unfortunately, fossil evidence from the Eocene is sparse, though several fossils called *Eosalmo* from the late Eocene, some 45 million years ago, suggest that by this date all the other subfamilies had become separated, including the whitefish, chars, and the forerunners of the Pacific salmon and trout and of the Atlantic salmon and trout.

That the separation of the Atlantic and Pacific salmons and trouts (which gave rise to the two genera *Onchorhynchus* and *Salmo*) from one common stock must have occurred during the Eocene is clear, for it was during this period that the Atlantic Ocean finally separated Europe from North America, isolating the two populations that eventually evolved into the Old World and New World trouts and salmons.

We are now left with three species: the Adriatic salmon, brown trout and Atlantic salmon. It is not clear when these three separated. Some have suggested the Miocene (11–25 million years ago), others as recently as the Pleistocene (in the last two million years). For instance, one theory suggests that the Adriatic salmon *Salmothymus obtusirostris* is more closely related to the

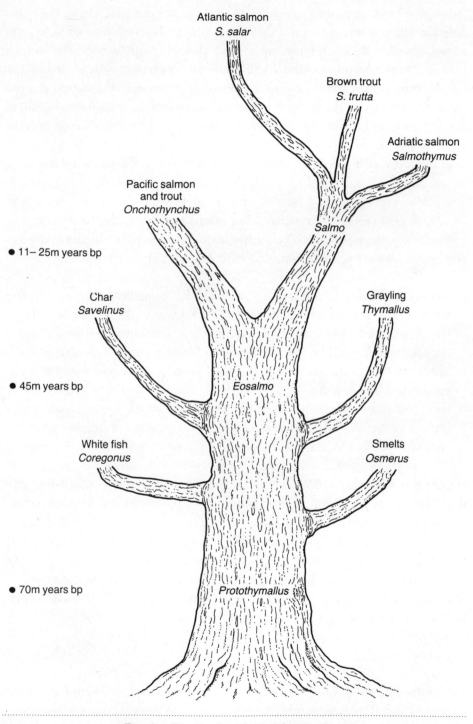

Fig. 2 – Family tree of the Atlantic salmon

Atlantic salmon than is the brown trout, despite the fact that brown trout and Atlantic salmon are put into the same genus. During one of the great Pleistocene Ice Ages, the argument goes, the icing up of northern Europe forced salmon south into the Mediterranean. After the retreat of the ice, salmon moved back north leaving a remnant population in the Mediterranean basin. However, the Mediterranean became too warm for migrating salmon, so this remnant population remained trapped in some rivers and evolved into the tiny Adriatic salmon.

It is not surprising that, despite much recent research, the family relationships of the Salmonidae are still incompletely known, for it is only in the last 150 years or so that there has been full agreement amongst fishery scientists as to what is or is not an Atlantic salmon. For instance, many early scientists argued strongly that the parr (p. 64) was a species in its own right. In the *Edinburgh New Philosophical Journal* of June 1835, Sir William Jardine wrote:

> Among the British *Salmonidae*, there is no fish whose habits are so regular, or the colours and markings so constant . . . It takes any bait at any time with the greatest of freedom; and hundreds may be taken when no Trout, either large or small, will rise, though abundant among them. That part of its history only which is yet unknown is the breeding. Males are found so far advanced as to have the milt flow on being handled; but at that time, and indeed all those females which I have examined, had the roe in a backward state; and they have not been discovered spawning in any of the shallow streams or lesser rivulets, like the Trout.

Jardine was supported by William Yarrell in 1836 who noted, in his monumental *A History of British Fishes*, 'By the kindness of various friends, I have received Parrs from several rivers on the east, south, and west shores; and from close comparative examination of specimens from distant localities, and these with the young of other *Salmonidae*, I believe the Parr to be a distinct fish.' So Yarrell named it the samlet or parr, *Salmo salmulus*. It was only after one J. Shaw carried out rearing experiments at Drumlanrig Castle, by the River Nith, that parr were finally confirmed to be juvenile salmon.

Genetic studies

In recent years much work has been carried out on the classification of salmon using the technique of starch gel electrophoresis or genetic fingerprinting. This technique identifies certain proteins in the blood of salmon. These proteins are formed under the influence of genes, the material that is passed on from one generation to the next in the egg and the sperm. One such blood protein is called transferrin, and transferrin can occur in seven forms: TF1, TF2, TF1/TF2, TF1/TF3, TF1/TF4, TF3/TF4 and TF4.

In a report published in *Nature* in 1971, a team of scientists led by R.H. Payne described how the British and Irish salmon population had three of these transferrins, TF1, TF2 and TF1/TF2, while salmon from eastern Canada had five transferrins, TF1, TF1/TF3, TF1/TF4, TF3/TF4 and TF4. Notice that only one genetically controlled transferrin was common to both populations (TF1). From this Payne and his team concluded that the Atlantic salmon species consists of two genetically distinct subspecies which, though they mix together in their oceanic feeding areas, rarely if ever interbreed. These they called *S. salar americanus* and *S. salar europaeus*.

This work was confirmed by a team of scientists led by O.L. Nyman, who found other genetic differences between the eastern North American and European salmon populations and were able to use these differences to identify the subspecies of individual salmon caught feeding in the Atlantic. More recent studies have shown that, besides these chemical differences between the Canadian and European subspecies, there are also subtle structural differences in the structure of scales, fins, vertebrae, gill rakers, and measurements of pelvic and pectoral fins and body depth:length ratios. These structural differences can be seen only through complex statistical analysis of many individuals from each population.

Several scientists, amongst them E. Verspoor and N.P. Wilkins, have analysed further the subspecies of salmon, using genetic fingerprinting. It seems that the eastern Canadian and USA subspecies is fairly homogenous. The European subspecies, however, can be separated into three distinct genetic races, a southwestern or 'celtic' race (which breeds in Iberia, France, the extreme south of Ireland, Wales and western England), a northern or 'boreal' race (which breeds throughout the rest of the British Isles and northern Europe), and a Baltic race (which breeds in rivers draining into the Baltic Sea). It is likely that the celtic and boreal races became separated during the last major Ice Age, which ended about 14,000 years ago, and that the Baltic race separated from the boreal race after the retreat of the last Ice Age from the Baltic about 10,000 years ago. The three races remain distinctly separated even though there is some overlap between their ranges.

For the angler whose interest is restricted to catching salmon, these genetic studies may seem a trivial scientific game. Nothing, however, could be further from the truth! Ongoing genetic studies are accumulating evidence that we do not have just two subspecies of salmon, one of which has three distinct races. There is an increasing wealth of evidence that each river has its own particular genetic strain of salmon and that, in larger river systems, each tributary might have its own genetic strain. Experienced anglers have suspected this for many years. Take, for instance, my local river, the Ribble and its tributary the Hodder. The Ribble fish are long and slender; the Hodder fish short and deep. The difference is so marked that we can catch a salmon below the Hodder and Ribble confluence and say, with confidence, which river that salmon would have run had it reached the confluence. It is pleasing for science to confirm our long-held views!

One such piece of evidence was described in the 1991–2 Annual Review of the Freshwater Fisheries Laboratory at Pitlochry, Scotland: 'Studies carried out to date provide compelling evidence that the salmon of most, if not all, Scottish rivers belong to different genetic populations or stocks.' The report continues, 'The work further suggests that salmon in larger rivers such as the Dee, Tay and Spey are divided into a number of substocks, each associated with a different part of the system. The existence of multiple stocks within rivers is indicated by the strong tendency of spawners to home to their natal streams and the occurrence of significant genetic differences among juvenile salmon from different tributaries within these river systems.'

The report then illustrates this with work done on the Scottish Dee that shows significant genetic differences between the salmon spawning in the main river, those spawning in the Baddock, those spawning in the Girnock, those spawning in the Gairn, those spawning in the Feugh, and those spawning in the Sheeough: one river with five tributaries, six genetically different stocks. It follows that each genetic population has evolved, over the last 10,000 years, to become adapted to its own river or tributary. But what would happen should some catastrophe wipe out one of these specially adapted populations? The usual response would be to restock with fish from another river. But they will not be as well adapted to living in the river as the original population. They are unlikely to produce as many progeny to the adult salmon stage (i.e. the quarry sought by anglers) as the natural population would have produced.

Another serious and growing problem is that of salmon farm escapees running the rivers and interbreeding with wild salmon stocks. The 1987–8 Freshwater Fisheries Laboratory Annual Review highlighted this: 'The effects of the interbreeding of native and non-native fish or the replacement of native fish with the progeny of non-native parents may be to reduce viability. Hybrids or non-native fish may not respond appropriately to the particular selective pressures of their new environment.' It is plain that if anything should ruin the natural genetic salmon population of a river it is likely that the population will crash. This has already happened to many once productive salmon rivers. We will return to this topic in Chapter 6.

Never say, as an angler, that fine detail of salmon classification is irrelevant. We anglers go out to catch the Atlantic salmon *Salmo salar*. Those of us fishing in Canadian rivers will be seeking one subspecies, *S. s. americanus*, those of us fishing European rivers another subspecies, *S. s. europaeus*. Those of us fishing a European river will be seeking one of three races. But we will all be fishing a particular river or tributary stream: the salmon that we are trying to catch are unique to that river or stream. They are irreplaceable. And it is the responsibility of anglers to help conserve these special stocks.

Salmon – the leaper

The scientific name of the Atlantic salmon, *Salmo salar*, is derived from the well-known habit of the salmon to leap powerfully from the water, for the Latin *salire* means 'to leap'. This trait was first noted by Hector Boece, in 1527, in *History of Scotland*: 'Because many of the Waters of Scotland are full of waterfalls, as soon as they come to a fall they leap. Those that are strong or leap well, get up through the fall, and return to the place where they were bred, and remain until their breeding season.'

Often salmon that for most of the day lie lethargically on the river bed will suddenly leap high from the water for no apparent reason. It has been argued that they do this to rid themselves of parasites such as sea-lice (p. 180), but as sea-lice fall from the skin of the fish after a few days in fresh water the argument cannot explain why salmon that have been in a river for several weeks still make occasional leaps. One theory, put forward by many cynical anglers over the years, is that these salmon that have been resident in a pool for a long time (and unlikely to take the anglers' lures) make the occasional defiant leap as a form of mockery: 'I'm here . . . try to catch me!'

Curiously, the sight of a leaping stale salmon certainly goads anglers into action. There they all are, the unlucky anglers, sitting on the bank and bemoaning the lack of salmon in the river. But then a fish leaps. Seconds later they are in the water with lures hurtling out in the direction of the leaping fish. But if they thought about it, these anglers would realize that, firstly, the leaping fish was stale and 'potted' and thus virtually uncatchable and, secondly, in most rivers fish that are more likely to take the lure are those that are not leaping out of the water.

Of course, a salmon that has been hooked frequently leaps from the water in an attempt to free itself from the hook and line. Smaller fish (up to about 10lb) are the most acrobatic, with the much larger ones (say, in excess of 20lb) usually boring deep, close to the river bed. Sometimes the leaping ruse is successful; the hookhold fails and the fish swims freely away. But there have been occasions where the leap of a hooked fish has greatly shortened the battle between salmon and angler in the latter's favour. In her *Fish Tales*, Billee Chapman Pincher recounted the experience of an angler who, on his first ever cast on his first ever day's fishing for salmon, from a boat on Scotland's Loch Stack, hooked a fish that immediately leapt from the water into his lap!

Some years ago I had a similar experience one summer's evening on the River Lune, but this time the salmon leapt twice. The fish took my fly, a size 8 double Silver Stoat's Tail, and immediately forged across to the shingle beach where I was standing. Hurriedly I tried to reel in the slack line as the fish approached. As the fish reached the shallows it leapt – and landed at my feet on the dry shingle, about three feet from the water's edge. I stared with astonishment. Then I hurriedly bent down to pick up my prize. But too late. The fish flicked its tail and leapt again, the hook fell from its jaw, and it landed back in the river and swam away.

The most spectacular of salmon leaps are where the fish must jump over obstacles such as weirs and waterfalls if they are to progress on their upriver migration. For centuries this has been a source of wonder. Three hundred years ago, in his *The Compleat Angler*, Izaak Walton noted that:

> Camden mentions in his Britannica the like wonder to be in Pembrokeshire, where the river Tivy falls into the sea; and that the fall is so downright, and so high, that the people stand and wonder at the strength and sleight by which they see the Salmon use to get out of the sea into the said river: and the manner and height of the place is so notable, that it is known far by the name of the Salmon-Leap.

How high can a salmon leap?

There are some quite wild claims which, if carefully analysed, fail to hold water! Where, for instance, the obstacle is a long, high cataract rather than a single vertical fall the salmon may pass through in stages, resting in a relatively slack piece of water in between leaps. The highest recorded single leap, to surmount a vertical waterfall, is 11ft 4in (the distance from the water level in the pool below the fall to the water level of the pool above the fall). This was up the Orrin Falls on the river Orrin in Ross-shire, Scotland, but only about 5 per cent of leaps there are successful.

Frequently a salmon must make several attempts before it successfully leaps a waterfall of even moderate height. This can lead to many would-be leapers dying in the attempt. There are reports of fish, falling back after a failure, being injured by striking rocks or bouncing from boulders away from the river. Of course, man has not been slow to take advantage of these struggling leapers. North American Indians and European poachers used (and in some rivers, still use) all sorts of contrivances, including net and gaff, to take the leapers. A salmon leaps, and immediately a long-handled net is swung around and under the waterfall. Should the salmon fail to make a successful leap then it falls back into the waiting net.

Perhaps most ingenious exploiter of failed leapers was Lord Lovat who, in the nineteenth century, had 'a salmon leap where, in consequence of the local conformation, a kettle of boiling water can be so placed that the fish literally jump into it and are boiled' (H. Cholmondley Pennell, *Salmon & Trout*). Fresh salmon, caught and cooked simultaneously. How convenient! Perhaps that is the origin of the terms 'convenience food' and 'poached salmon'!

How do salmon leap over obstacles?

This is a question that has produced some quite fascinating answers. The poet Michael Drayton (1563–1631) came up with one of the most incredible in one of his verses in *Polyolbion*:

> Here, when the laboring fish does at the foot arrive,
> And finds that by his strength he does but vainly strive;
> His tail takes in his mouth, and, bending like a bow
> That's to full compass drawn, aloft doth throw.
> Then springing at his height, as doth a little wand,
> That, bended end to end, and started from man's hand,
> Far off itself doth cast; so does the Salmon vault.

In other words, when the salmon finds that it cannot simply jump over a high waterfall, it takes its tail into its mouth (rather like we may bend a springy stick), thus flexing the body, and flicks itself up by the sudden release of the tail from its mouth. This rather far-fetched explanation, completely lacking in direct observation, persisted into the nineteenth century. A similar, ancient explanation was that the salmon took its tail in its mouth and rolled, like a wheel, up the waterfall.

21

A later theory was that the fish swims to the bottom of the plunge pool below the waterfall and then accelerates upwards with powerful sweeps of the tail, generating the necessary velocity to propel itself vertically up the waterfall. Added to this was a further suggestion that, when in mid-leap, the fish could gain further impetus by flapping its tail and 'pushing' against the air. Again, this lacked accurate observation of leaping fish.

It is true that, in order to leap a high weir or waterfall, the salmon must begin in a deep pool at the foot of the obstacle. However, this is not because the fish must swim from great depth at the start of the leap. Watch fish just before they leap: they will swim around the plunge pool at the foot of the waterfall, close to the water surface, looking up to the target of their leap which is the crest of the weir or waterfall. If they did start their leap from deep in the pool, they would be unable to see their target because of the swirling mass of bubbles above their heads. There is then a sudden acceleration – with the fish still just below the surface – followed immediately by a leap that, if it is successful, will take them to the lip of the top of the weir or waterfall. It is nothing more than the sudden burst of energy – sheer muscle power – over a split second that propels the fish in its leap. Then, as the salmon lands in the water at the top of the fall, powerful sideways flicks of the tail force it on through the fast water into the slower pool beyond.

It has long been known that, although salmon will enter the fresh water of a river from the sea when the river temperature is close to freezing, they will not leap weirs or waterfalls, or force their way through cataracts or extensive stretches of white water, unless the water temperature is at least 40°F. The reason for this is that at very low temperatures they do not have sufficient energy. Being cold-blooded creatures, the body temperature of salmon is always very close to the temperature of the surrounding water. The higher that temperature, the more energy can be generated in nerves and muscles. When water temperatures are very low, the fish cannot generate enough energy to leap; a sudden rise in temperature and they have sufficient energy to do so.

Why then, if the salmon takes off on its leap close to the water surface, must the take-off pool be deep? This is a matter of hydrodynamics. Look at a waterfall. Water pounds vertically down into the plunge pool beneath. The falling water sweeps down as a strong current through the pool. Some of this current is then deflected from the bottom of the pool and moves downstream, but some circulates around and passes back upstream through a wave that lies close to where the waterfall hits the pool. It is from this stationary wave, which runs across the plunge pool close to the foot of the waterfall, that salmon make

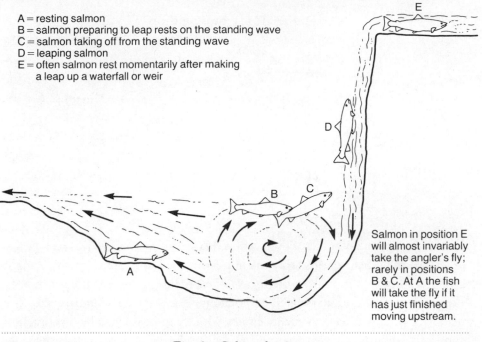

A = resting salmon
B = salmon preparing to leap rests on the standing wave
C = salmon taking off from the standing wave
D = leaping salmon
E = often salmon rest momentarily after making
    a leap up a waterfall or weir

Salmon in position E
will almost invariably
take the angler's fly;
rarely in positions
B & C. At A the fish
will take the fly if it
has just finished
moving upstream.

Fig. 3 – Salmon leaping

their leaps. This stationary wave provides the tail of the salmon with sufficient purchase to propel the fish upwards (Fig. 3).

If the plunge pool is too shallow, then this stationary wave will be broken or non-existent. There are many instances where boulders have fallen into a plunge pool, broken the stationary wave, and turned a passable obstacle into an impassable one. There is no doubt that access to many river headwaters could be made easier to spawning salmon simply by clearing plunge pools of large boulders.

If the weir or waterfall is not vertical then the stationary wave – the salmons' take-off board – will be further downstream of the obstacle. Salmon will still make their leap from the wave but, because they must now leap in a sloping trajectory to reach the crest of the obstacle, the height that they can attain is much reduced. Again, many river headwaters could be opened up to spawning salmon by ensuring that weirs are constructed with vertical faces, and by judicious altering of sloping waterfalls to give a vertical rock wall.

The ability of salmon to leap high over waterfalls is one of the wonders of nature – but there are limits to this ability. So often rivers that formerly held salmon have been rendered salmon-less by the construction of dams and weirs over which no salmon could ever leap. The solution now depends on constructing artificial salmon passes.

The anatomy of a salmon

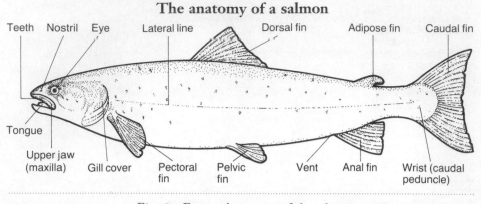

Fig. 4 – External anatomy of the salmon

In order to get the best out of this section, I suggest that the reader treats it as a practical study. Instead of simply reading from the book, take a freshly caught salmon or buy a salmon from the fish market, making sure that it has not been cleaned. Lay it on the kitchen table and examine it as you read. Compare what you read with what you see on your specimen. Much can be learned by this practical approach, and what you learn will add to your understanding of the fish and, consequently, make your angling days more fascinating and perhaps more productive.

Scales

The first thing to notice is the scales that cover the entire body save for the head. These scales are oval in shape, with the front edge embedded in the skin under the rear edge of the scale in front. In this way the overlapping scales add to the streamlining of the body and, at the same time, they provide a protective cover that reduces the risk of infection by pathogenic fungi and bacteria. Because scales are easily dislodged by careless handling, anglers should endeavour not to use knotted nets or dry hands when landing salmon that they wish to release alive to the water. As we shall see in Chapter 4, scales can teach us a great deal about the life of our salmon.

Notice the lateral line scales. Running along the sides of the body is a single line of scales that is sufficiently distinct from all other scales to merit the term 'lateral line'. The lateral line scales have very tiny pores. Water flows freely and continuously from outside the salmon's body, through these pores, and into narrow canals in the skin where it passes over a series of sensory organs. Some of these organs can detect very slight changes in water temperature, others detect changes in water pressure, and others detect subtle chemical changes in the water surrounding the fish. The pressure sensory organs are possibly the most important from the angler's point of view.

24

It is these that can tell when a clumsy, heavy-footed angler approaches along the bank: the heavy footsteps cause minute vibrations to pass out from the bank into the water where they are picked up by the lateral line system. It is these that urge the salmon to flee when an angler wades carelessly down the river. It is these that can detect the splashy fall of a badly cast fly line on to the water. (See also Ears, below.)

Colour

Salmon are beautiful creatures. The silver sheen of a fresh-run (or farmed) salmon is caused by the deposition on the scales of an iridescent, white, light-reflecting chemical called guanine. This is deposited under the influence of a hormone called thyroxine, produced by the thyroid gland in the neck of the fish, as the parr become smolts and prepared for life at sea (see p. 68). The guanine completely hides the underlying river coloration. When the salmon returns to fresh water it is still bright silver, but slowly the guanine is broken down to reveal a drabber coloration which, in the male fish, develops into a red breeding dress.

Out of the water salmon are very conspicuous, yet when they are in the water they can be very difficult to see. This is because the coloration that has developed in the skin of the salmon has evolved to give the best camouflage. In the sea, the dark steel-blue back of the salmon makes the fish less likely to be spotted by a potential sea bird predator flying overhead. The white and silver belly and sides also act as a camouflage against the background of light sky and help to protect it from larger fish, killer whales or seals swimming underneath. In the river the drabber coloration helps the salmon blend into the dark boulders and peat-stained water. It takes a trained eye (ideally aided by polaroid glasses) to spot salmon lying in the depths of a river pool.

Fins, tail and movement

Our examination of the salmon that is lying on the kitchen table now moves to the fins and tail. But because these are involved in movement we must also include an examination of the skeleton and muscles. These latter are best examined when we come to eat our salmon, adding a little more interest to the meal!

Salmon are swimming machines, with a highly streamlined body that can accelerate rapidly, stop suddenly, and twist and turn at speed. How fast can it go? One estimate suggested that the maximum speed of a fast-swimming salmon may be in the order of 6–9 m.p.h.; another suggested that a large salmon may be able to accelerate to about 19–22 m.p.h. But these speeds would only be possible for very short periods, just enough to catch a prey item or flee from a predator. Salmon migrating upstream rarely exceed 2–3 m.p.h.

The problem faced by salmon that are swimming flat out for anything other than a few minutes is that they tire rapidly. We see this when we are playing them. After a few very rapid bursts of speed the fish yields. Why? During its normal leisurely swimming speed, or during very short bursts of very fast speed, the salmon muscles produce sufficient energy by burning up glucose fuel in the muscle cells with oxygen carried from the gills by the blood. In a prolonged period of fast swimming, as when we play a fish, the blood cannot supply sufficient oxygen to the muscle cells to maintain that high speed. Instead the muscle cells obtain some energy from the glucose by breaking it down to lactic acid. This is an emergency source of energy: it may give the salmon that little bit more time in which to escape from the hook, or to evade a predator. But lactic acid is a chemical that, as it accumulates in the muscle, debilitates and eventually prevents the muscle from functioning.

That is why, when you have landed a fish (especially a large one), the fish will often lie motionless in the landing net or on the shingle. Furthermore, if you are going to release a fish that you have caught, always hold it in the water, head pointing upstream, so that the fish can take in oxygen from the water to burn up all the lactic acid before it swims away.

The power for swimming, then, comes from muscles which are arranged in tight muscle blocks. When you eat your salmon these muscle blocks are most conspicuous, arranged in a quite regular pattern that gives maximum power. These muscle blocks work in conjunction with the skeleton. Again you will see this when you eat your fish: the muscles are attached, by tendons, to the vertebrae comprising the backbone and to spiny bones that extend out from the backbone. When muscle and skeleton work in harmony in fish like the salmon they produce the characteristic S-shaped motion of the swimming fish. The bulk of the power used to thrust the body forwards comes from the large muscle blocks of the tail (the body immediately behind the anus), which cause the large caudal (or tail) and anal fins to push against the water. It is this force of fin against water that propels the salmon forwards.

The rest of the fins are used primarily in manoeuvring the body as the fish swims. To take an aircraft as an analogy, the tail and caudal and anal fins are the engine, while the other fins are the rudder and flaps and reverse thrust.

Immediately behind the gill cover is the pair of pectoral fins. These are used to prevent sideways rolling, or fore-and-aft pitching; they can be held out to assist braking; they can be moved slowly to allow the fish to swim slowly backwards; they can be used independently of each other for turning.

Low on the belly, between the pectoral fins and the anal fin, is a pair of pelvic (sometimes called ventral) fins. These can be held out to assist in braking; they can also be used together, or independently of each other, to produce vertical movements.

On the back of the salmon are two fins. The rear one is the adipose fin. This is functionless and is sometimes cut off, without any apparent detriment, to mark salmon parr or smolts that have been raised in hatcheries and released into the river, to distinguish them from wild-bred fish.

The forward, and much larger, back fin is the dorsal fin. This is entirely a stabilizer, used to prevent the salmon rolling from side to side as it swims, and in this function it is assisted by the anal fin.

The eyes and sight

Although the eyes of the salmon have features in common with ours, there are some important differences. The first is that the salmon cannot close its eyes, neither can it contract the pupil on bright, sunny days to reduce glare. Thus, in clear water and in bright sunshine, when the sun is shining down a pool, it is very difficult to attract a salmon to the fly as the sunlight will dazzle the fish and prevent its seeing the fly clearly. Salmon lying in the shade of trees or in

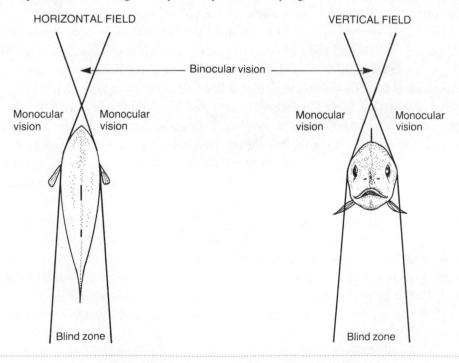

Fig. 5 – Monocular and binocular vision in salmon

fast riffles will be easier to catch, for the shade and the broken, bubble-filled turbulent water will reduce the glare in the fish's eyes.

The eyes are positioned at the side of the head and set slightly forwards and upwards. Each eye has an independent almost cone-like optical angle of approximately 78°. With two eyes, therefore, the fish has two zones of monocular vision (one to each side), a cone of binocular vision to the front (where the cones of vision from each eye overlap) and blind zones immediately below, behind and on top of the fish (see Fig. 5). This enables the fish to see much of the surrounding underwater scene. It will be able to see potential food or predators or an angler's fly approaching from a wide radius using its monocular vision – though it may not be a perfect image, lacking precise detail of the distance and size of the object. It will certainly be enough to warn the salmon of an approaching predator or attract its attention to prey and our fly and, hopefully (in the latter case), cause the fish to make a head-on approach. Then, when the prey or our fly is in the cone of binocular vision in front of the snout of the fish, it will be able to see clearly, judge size and distance perfectly, and either intercept it or turn away.

In clear water, and from a good vantage point, we can see this behaviour. For instance, once on the Lune a friend watched from a bridge as I cast a Peter Ross over three newly arrived salmon. One fish moved up through the water when the fly was about 5yd away, to the right. It had noticed the fly in the monocular vision of its right eye. But then, as the fly passed in front and slightly above the salmon's nose, it sank back. It had rejected the fly after scrutinizing it with its binocular vision. Of course, as I was standing some 22yd upstream I could not see this. I had to rely on the commentary from the bridge. The same fly produced no further response. Then I changed fly for a Stoat's Tail two sizes smaller. Again the same fish began to move when the fly was some distance away, in the monocular cone of the right eye, and it followed the fly as it swung across the stream with the fly firmly fixed in its binocular vision in front of its nose. After following the fly for about 2yd it took.

I have seen this behaviour several times: the salmon was attracted to the fly at a distance by its monocular vision, but the decision of whether or not to take was made after scrutiny with its binocular vision. It has often been recommended, should a salmon swirl at the fly, to change fly for one a size smaller. Sometimes it does work. Unfortunately, when we are fishing down a pool we do not know how many salmon have examined our fly and turned away – unseen!

On four occasions I have watched salmon spot an approaching slow-moving fly with monocular vision and then follow it with their binocular vision. As the fly came to rest below the angler one of them took the fly, and the other three turned away. On three other occasions the same thing happened but the angler stripped in line, causing the fly to accelerate upstream, instead of letting the fly stay motionless 'on the dangle'. On all three occasions the pursuing salmon took the accelerating fly. Binocular vision was not enough in these cases to goad the salmon to take the slowly moving fly. Extra speed was. (We will reconsider such observations in Volume Two, *Salmon on the Fly*.)

We must now consider the phenomena of the salmon's 'window' and 'mirror' (Fig. 6). Most anglers will have heard of the former, for through it a fish can see an angler who cannot see the fish. You, too, can experience the window and mirror phenomena by visiting a swimming pool, holding your breath (or taking a snorkel), sinking below the surface and looking up. Light rays passing from air into water are refracted (or bent) at the air–water interface. You see this when you hold a stick in water; the stick appears to bend as it enters the water. Only light rays striking the water at angles greater than 10° enter the water. At angles of less than 10° the light rays are deflected from the water surface (rather like a flat stone will skim off the surface when thrown from a low angle).

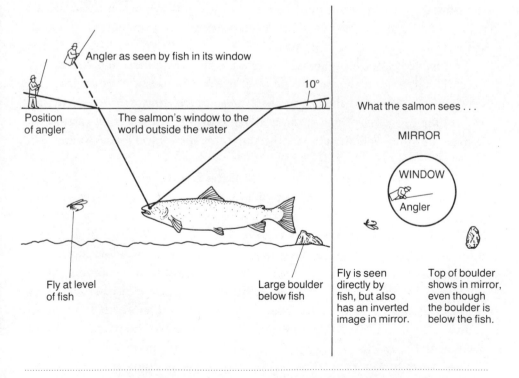

Fig. 6 – Salmon's mirror and window

A fish looking up to the surface will see those light rays that penetrate the water surface as an inverted cone of light. The angle at the cone base is 97°. The circular top of the inverted cone is at the water surface: this is the salmon's window because it is only through this restricted circle that it can see objects out of the water. As the salmon swims forwards, sideways or backwards, the window moves with it. As it rises through the water the window becomes smaller in area, and as it sinks deeper the window becomes larger in area. The rest of the water surface, around the window, appears, to the fish, as either a silver or blackish mirror. Anything above that mirror, provided that the angle between it and the edge of the window is less than 10°, will be invisible to the fish. For instance, an angler kneeling down or wading deep may be invisible in the window, but the same angler standing up high above the water surface may be visible in the window.

Anything below the surface film will be reflected in the mirror, including the river bed. Anything that is lying at or above the level of the salmon (such as our wet fly) will from the start be visible (in monocular vision) both directly and as a reflection in the mirror. As the salmon moves to take that fly, it will be moved from out of the mirror (so that the reflection will vanish) and into the front of the salmon's window and it is in this position when the fish takes it (in binocular vision). When we are fishing the wet fly, just before it takes, the salmon has a splendid view of our fly.

The mirror is not hard; its surface is the soft surface film. Suppose that an insect is standing on the surface film, on the mirror, some distance from the window. It will be invisible to the fish *except where it touches the surface film*. Where the feet and, perhaps, the underside of the insect's body rest on the surface film they will show up in the mirror as dark speckles surrounded by pin-points of light.

When fishing a dry fly for salmon, that is the first thing that the fish will see of our fly – a moving silvery splodge of light on the dark mirror if we are using a Bomber pattern, a moving mass of light speckles if we are using a heavily hackled fly. As the fish approaches our dry fly (or the dry fly drifts directly over the fish) the pin-points of light approach the edge of the window, and the fly suddenly appears in the front of the salmon's window. For a split second the salmon has its best view of all of the fly. But it remains an indistinct fuzzy view because it keeps the fly in the front edge of the window so that the image comes to its eyes from a very low angle. At the edge of the window the rays striking and entering the water are very oblique, and the image is somewhat blurred with colour fringes caused by dispersion of light at the air–water interface at the window edge. Thus, when we are fishing a dry fly for salmon the fish never gets a very good view of the fly – mostly it sees just the light spots or splodges on the dark mirror and then, just before it takes the fly, a blurred, distorted view of the fly. Again, we will consider the significance of this when we discuss the design and fishing of salmon flies in Volume Two.

Like us, salmon have two sorts of light-detecting organs in the retina at the back of the eye: cones and rods. Cones can detect colour, rods work in monochrome.

It has been said or implied by many writers that, because salmon and trout (like us) have blue, green and red colour-detecting cones in their retinas, they see colour just as we see colour. The first part of this is true but a gross over-simplification; the second part is not entirely true! Salmon do have these three sorts of cone in their eyes, but it is thought that they also have a fourth sort (which we do not have) that absorbs ultra-violet light rays. This means that, whereas we cannot see ultra-violet, salmon can. It follows that some objects that we see as black might be, to the fish, visible as ultra-violet.

If white light is passed through a prism, it is split into its component parts: the red, orange, yellow, green, blue, indigo and violet bands that we see in a rainbow. We can discern these bands because they are wavelengths of light that our three sorts of cone can absorb. Salmon are able to see the extra band of ultra-violet wavelength. But that is not all. Scientists measure wavelengths of light in a unit called the nanometre (nm). We can contrast salmon and human colour vision by using these units:

HUMAN COLOUR VISION:

	Blue cones	Green cones	Red cones
Peak absorption	419 nm	513 nm	558 nm

Visible colour spectrum range
   violet—indigo—blue—green—yellow—orange—red

SALMON COLOUR VISION:

	U-V cones	Blue cones	Green cones	Red cones
Peak absorption	360 nm	447 nm	526 nm	619 nm

Visible colour spectrum
   u-v—indigo—blue—green—yellow—orange—red—far red

From this it is clear that the salmon and trout can see more shades of red than we can, although Dr J.N. Lythgoe informs me that the ability of brown trout to see 'far reds' (which we cannot see) is reduced in summer. Some things that are black to us may appear a distinct 'far red' to the salmon. For instance, some burglar alarm beams that are invisible to us will be distinctly far red to salmon and trout, especially in autumn, winter and spring. And some fly tying materials that appear black to us may appear far red to the salmon. Imagine setting out all your black salmon flies and fly tying materials and having a fish look at them. 'But they are not all black!' exclaims the salmon. 'Those are black, but *those* are ultra-violet and *those* are red!'

The cones in our eyes, which not only detect colour but also give us quite precise and detailed vision, require quite high light intensities to function. As the sun goes down at dusk, light levels eventually fall below the point at which the cones can detect light. We cannot see colour; we find it difficult to perform jobs that require precision. Our vision now depends solely on the other light-detecting cells of our retina – the rods. These can detect light in monochrome, but they lack precision and so we cannot see detail with them. Anglers out fishing in the dark will have noticed this. Before the sun has finally set and we can still see in colour we can easily thread the leader through the hook eye and tie a good knot. And we can easily climb up a bank at the water's edge. Later, when our colour vision no longer functions though there is still enough light to see leader and hook eye we have difficulty threading the line though the eye and tying the knot. When we come to climb the bank, we tend to stumble because we cannot judge distance correctly.

It is the same with salmon, although the functioning of their system is more marked. As light fades the colour-detecting and precise-observation cones are physically withdrawn into the retinal tissues. Through the night, the salmon can see, but only indistinctly and in black and white. The fly that we are using may have a yellow wing and blue hackle. If we turn on a torch we can see this, but if we showed our fly to a salmon in torchlight it still would only be able to see the fly in shades of grey because its cones have been packed away until dawn.

Wild salmon live in water that contains dissolved mineral salts, planktonic organisms and breakdown products from plant material known as 'yellow substances' because of their colour. Rivers and lakes surrounded by peat moorland often have a permanent peaty tinge of humic acids and other chemicals drained from the peat. Following a spate, a river (or lake) might have silt or clay particles in suspension. All these absorb light as they pass through the water. Yellows and greens are absorbed quickly and do not penetrate far down through the water (the more contaminants in the water the less deeply do they penetrate). Blue penetrates a little deeper. Reds and infra-reds penetrate furthest. So whilst we have considered salmon vision under experimental conditions in clean water, we must not forget that in its natural environment the state of the water will affect what colours are present and what colours the salmon can see. This too has a great bearing on the colours we use in our salmon flies – something that we will again turn to in Volume Two.

Mouth and gills (Fig. 7)

Lay a salmon down on its side on the kitchen table and take a pair of stout scissors. Look at the bony gill cover. Some refer to this as the gills, but that is incorrect. What you see is the protective gill cover or operculum over the gills. Lift this gill cover. When the fish was alive, water continuously streamed out through the gap that you can see. Now take the scissors and carefully cut away the gill cover without damaging the underlying red gills. Start at the top (dorsal side) and cut towards the snout of the salmon. Then start again at the bottom (ventral side) and cut away the whole gill cover (see Fig. 7). You should now have exposed the gills.

Now take a pencil and look at the mouth. Unlike ours, the lower and upper jaws of the salmon are very loosely hinged so that the mouth can be opened very wide to accommodate very large prey. Along the edge of both jaws there was (in wild salmon) or is (in farmed salmon) a line of short, sharp, backward-pointing teeth. Wild salmon lose these teeth when they return to the river (see p. 81). In addition to the teeth in the jaw the salmon also has teeth in the roof of the mouth. Running the length of the mouth, down the centre, is a narrow bone called the vomer, and running around either side of the roof of the mouth, parallel with the edges of the upper jaw, are the palatine bones. Both carry tiny, sharp, backward-pointing teeth. Salmon do not chew their food; they swallow it whole, and these backward-pointing teeth are there to prevent a large, wriggling prey from escaping from the mouth.

Open the jaws wide and insert the pencil. Push it straight down through the mouth and you will be able to see it by-passing the gills as it travels into the next part of the food tract, the oesophagus, which leads to the stomach. Slowly withdraw the pencil.

The inside of the mouth of the salmon has sensory organs that can taste food. Many anglers have confused the senses of taste and smell in fish; the nasal organs are used for smell (see Nostrils, below) and the mouth is used to taste. So, when a natural food is in the mouth of the salmon the fish can taste it. If the potential food tastes good, then the salmon will swallow it by reflex. Our salmon flies and spinners do not taste of food so the salmon will not

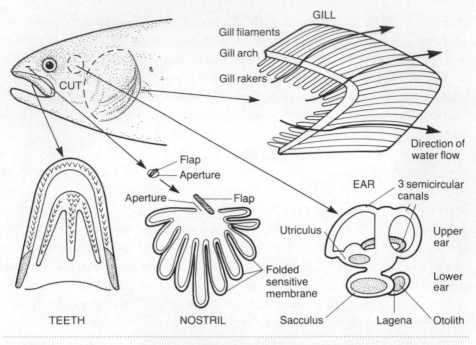

Fig. 7 – The salmon's gills, ears, feeding teeth and nostrils

swallow them. Bait anglers, however, especially those fishing worm, will often find that the salmon will swallow a bunch of worms even though it is neither hungry nor feeding (see p. 136). It will take the bait as it does a fly or spinner, but the taste buds will cause the salmon to swallow the bait.

If you now feed a piece of bendy wire through the mouth of the salmon and out through the gills you can see the route by which water carries oxygen to the gills. The passageways are very large and it is essential that food items are not washed out through the gills instead of being passed into the oesophagus. It is also essential that other solids that may be in the water, such as grit, are filtered away from the fine, fragile gills. This control is performed by structures attached to the gills called gill rakers. To see these it is essential to remove an entire gill.

There are four gills on each side under the gill covers. With a pencil it is possible to raise the first of the U-shaped gills from where you have already removed the gill cover. You will see that it is attached at two ends, top and bottom. With scissors snip away the gill at either end. When the fish was breathing, water passed from the inside of the U and on this inner surface, attached to the bony gill arch, are stout filaments called gill rakers. It is these that filter the water before it passes through the fine gill filaments on the outside of the U-shaped gill arch. If the gill rakers become clogged with debris then they can be cleaned by the salmon momentarily reversing the water flow and expelling the waste through the mouth. The gill rakers ensure that food items end up in the digestive tract and are not washed away through the gills.

Compared with the gill rakers, the gill filaments are long, feathery, fragile structures. Blood is pumped directly from the heart to these filaments, where it off-loads waste carbon dioxide and absorbs oxygen which it then carries to the other organs of the body. Because they have a very thin membrane and large blood supply the gill filaments are easily damaged. If a salmon is to be returned live to the water make sure you do not touch the gills when removing the fly and handling the fish.

Nostrils (Fig. 7)

At the front of the snout are a pair of tiny openings, the nostrils. Unlike ours, these do not connect with the back of the mouth. Instead they end in large nasal sacs that fill the bulk of the salmon's snout. Here water is continuously being passed over delicate folded membranes that can detect (smell) the presence of, or fluctuations of, chemicals dissolved in the water. It is with these organs that salmon are able to detect the 'smell' of their own rivers when still far out at sea (see p. 82). Recent experiments have suggested that they may also be capable of smelling the presence of predators (including man) in the water. So sensitive are the nasal sacs that they are capable of detecting incredibly low concentrations of substances (perhaps individual molecules) in the water. To reduce the possibility of a salmon rejecting a fly because it smells of *Homo sapiens* many anglers now rub their flies in waterside mud or vegetation before use.

Ears (Fig. 7)

As we examine our salmon we notice that there are no ears and therefore conclude that the salmon cannot hear! This is wrong. They do have ears, though they lack external ears. The outer ear that we see on ourselves and other mammals is simply a means of gathering sound waves and passing them into the inner ear where they are registered as vibrations. We need outer ears because sound waves travel slowly and for only short distances in air. By contrast, fish do not need outer ears, simply because sound waves travel five times as quickly and five times as far in water as they do in air.

The salmon's ears are situated beneath the bone and skin at the side of the head just behind the eyes. They are divided into two parts: the upper ear and the lower ear. The upper ear consists of three connecting semi-circular canals, each arranged in a plane at right angles to the other two. By the movement of fluids in these canals the salmon's brain is constantly being fed with information on the orientation or position of the fish in the water. Should the fish accidentally tilt sideways, backwards or forwards, this is detected by the semi-circular canals, a message is sent to the brain, and the brain causes an automatic movement of the appropriate fins to bring the fish back into the correct position. They are thus organs that control balance in the fish.

The lower ear is used to detect sound waves or vibrations. This part of the ear has three chambers (the utriculus, sacculus and lagena) each of which has a tiny stone (called an otolith) in its centre. Vibrations in the water cause the otoliths to vibrate and this vibration stimulates nerves to the brain. It is certain that fish cannot hear anglers talking on the riverbank or in a boat. But they can hear the crunching noise made by the feet of a wading angler on gravel, and the rapping of a metal-tipped wading staff against boulders, or the dropping of a fly box or anchor on the bottom of a boat. Many salmon escape being caught because most anglers imagine that they cannot hear!

We have completed our investigation of the outside, head, mouth and gills of the salmon. Now for its inner workings (Fig. 8).

Digestive system

Start to gut your fish, but, after cutting through the body wall between anus and gills, instead of ripping out its innards, slowly tease them from the body cavity with minimal damage.

The first and most obvious structures to examine are the parts of the gut or alimentary canal. This is quite easy to follow. Leading from the back of the mouth is the short oesophagus, a muscular, folded tube that is capable of carrying very large prey items to the J-shaped stomach. The first part of the stomach – the long arm of the J, sometimes called the cardiac region because it lies close to the heart – stores food and pours digestive enzymes on to it. The partly digested food then passes into the second part of the stomach, the short arm of the J-shape, sometimes called the pyloric region. Here the stomach wall is very muscular, and by rapid contractions of these muscles the food is churned to a semi-liquid pulp. In this state the food is passed into the intestine.

At the junction between stomach and intestine are lots of fine, hollow, finger-like projections. These are called pyloric caeca: salmon have 55–80 of them. These produce enzymes that digest proteins and which they pour into the intestine.

Whilst examining the caeca, a loose, diffuse fatty tisse may be noted. This is the pancreas. This, too, pours digestive juices into the intestine and, as in humans, it is also responsible for the regulation of sugar level in the blood through its two hormones insulin and glucagon.

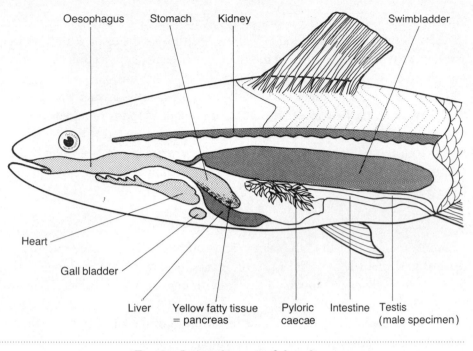

Oesophagus   Stomach   Kidney   Swimbladder

Heart

Gall bladder

Liver   Yellow fatty tissue   Pyloric   Intestine   Testis
         = pancreas   caecae   (male specimen)

Fig. 8 – Internal organs of the salmon

Lying alongside the stomach and extending down the body to the intestine is a large red-brown gland, the liver. Look carefully in the liver and you will notice a small grey-green sac called the gall bladder. This produces a green fluid called bile which is poured, via the bile duct, into the intestine. The bile neutralizes the acidic food released from the stomach and aids in the digestion of fats and oils. Later, many of the products of digestion – sugars and amino acids (the breakdown products from proteins) – are absorbed by the liver.

Once digested, the food is absorbed through the gut wall into the bloodstream. Finally, any indigestible material is passed out of the gut through the anus as faeces.

The heart and blood system

As you carefully remove the liver and front portion of the stomach in the area between the pectoral fins, you will expose the heart. The salmon's heart is quite different from ours. The human heart has four chambers: the right atrium and right ventricle and the left atrium and left ventricle. The atria gather blood into the heart, which is then pumped out again by the ventricles. In humans and other mammals, the right ventricle pumps blood to the lungs (where it is oxygenated) and the blood flows back to the left atrium. From there the blood enters the left ventricle which pumps the oxygenated blood through arteries to all parts of the body. The blood is then passed through veins back to the right atrium which passes it, in turn, to the right ventricle. So, for each full circulation our blood passes twice through the heart.

In the salmon heart there are only two chambers: one atrium that gathers the blood and one ventricle that pumps the blood. Blood is pumped through arteries from the ventricle to the gills, where it is oxygenated. The blood then flows from the gills in another set of arteries around the entire body before being passed through the vein system to the atrium at the start of the next circuit.

Reproductive system

Carefully remove the gut of the salmon and you will see clearly the reproductive organs. In the female these are a pair of ovaries, held by a fine membrane to the back of the body cavity, in which the large orange eggs are visible. The eggs are carried down fine membranous oviducts and released through the urinary pore in the urino-genital papilla, just in front of the anus. In the male the reproductive organs are a pair of soft, white, flattened testes, again held by a fine membrane to the back of the body cavity. These produce sperm in a white, cloudy fluid called milt that is carried from the body through semi-transparent sperm ducts that again reach the outside via the urino-genital papilla.

Swimbladder

Remove the ovaries or testes and, if you look very carefully at the back of the body cavity, you may see, running alongside a large red-brown blood vessel-like structure, a near-translucent air-filled tube. This is the air bladder or swimbladder. I say 'may see' because you are unlikely to see one in a salmon taken from the deep freeze – it will have burst; it can be difficult to find even in a freshly killed fish in spite of the fact that it may occupy up to 7 per cent of total body volume.

The swimbladder is a buoyancy aid, used to regulate the density of the body so that it can remain stationary at one particular depth without having to swim to keep position. The swimbladder has a valved entrance at the front of the oesophagus. By gulping in air at the surface, the swimbladder can be filled. When the salmon has taken up the depth at which it wants to lie, it simply expels sufficient air to keep the body at a neutral density at that level. The fish will then neither sink deeper nor float higher in the water. This buoyancy aid saves much energy expenditure. Fish lacking a swimbladder, such as sharks, must swim constantly if they are to avoid sinking to the bottom.

Kidney

Many anglers will have noted the large blood vessel that lies at the back of the body cavity, immediately under the backbone. This is, in fact, not a blood vessel but the kidney. Unlike our own, the salmon kidney is a very primitive organ. It is important in maintaining body fluid composition by excreting water and mineral salts. But it cannot excrete nitrogenous wastes such as ammonia and urea. These are excreted through the gills.

Maintaining body fluid concentration (Fig. 9)

This is one of the major problems faced by fish like the salmon that live in both fresh water and the sea.

In fresh water, water automatically enters the body through the skin, gills

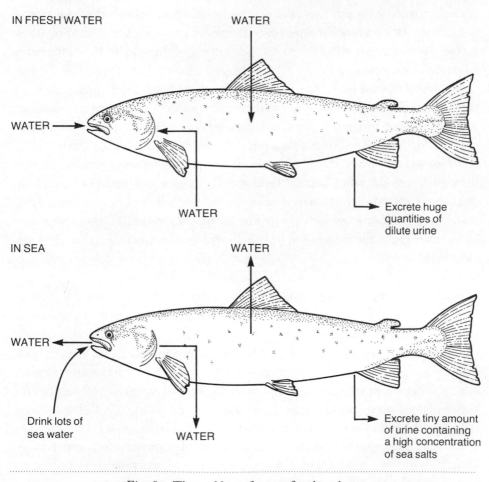

Fig. 9 – The problem of water for the salmon

and the inside of the mouth by the process of osmosis. If this continued for any length of time, cells in the body would rupture, body fluid concentrations would fall to lethally low levels and the salmon would die. To make matters worse, important salts are constantly being lost through the skin by the process of diffusion. Again, if these salts were to fall below a certain concentration, the fish would die.

To overcome these problems, the salmon in fresh water is constantly excreting huge amounts of very dilute urine (to rid itself of the water taken up by osmosis) and its gills work hard to absorb salts from the surrounding water (to compensate for the salts lost by diffusion).

In the sea the salinity of sea water causes water to pass out from the salmon body through osmosis from the skin, gills and mouth. The danger now is one of dehydration. To overcome this the salmon constantly drinks sea water. But there is now another problem: the accumulation of sea salts in the body of the fish. So the salmon now excretes tiny volumes of very concentrated urine (thus saving the water that it has drunk but getting rid of the salt) and the gills work to pump out excess salts.

A salmon leaving fresh water and entering the sea must rapidly switch from the freshwater system to the seawater system of body fluid regulation. And when it returns to fresh water it must switch back rapidly to the freshwater system. Studies have shown that some fish on their way back to fresh water from the sea may make several attempts to pass through the estuary, but have to drop back into salt water because their regulatory mechanisms are not ready to change over. It also seems that if salmon that have changed over from a salt-water to a freshwater system are unable to run immediately into fresh water (perhaps because the river is too low in a summer drought) mortality rates are very high.

Such is the anatomy of the salmon. It is an animal perfectly adapted for life in rivers, lakes, estuaries and the sea. But now it is time to cook and eat your salmon! And what makes salmon so appealing on the table is the red colour of the flesh and its rich flavour. The intensity of red in the meat (muscle) of a salmon is due to the quantities of crustaceans in the diet. The argument goes along these lines: crustaceans contain a high concentration of carotenoid pigments (the pigments that make a cooked lobster or crab red), and thus those fish (like the salmon) that eat most crustaceans will have most red in the skin and meat. Though there is some truth in this argument, it is a gross over-simplification of the situation. First of all, there are many species of fish that include a high proportion of crustaceans in their diet but that have white flesh and no red in their skin colour: for instance, in fresh water the grayling and barbel, and in the sea the herring. Secondly, at sea salmon do not eat only crustaceans. They also eat a lot of smaller fish (see p. 74). This suggests that salmon have the ability to retain the orange carotenoid pigments, unlike other fish that may feed exclusively on crustaceans and yet excrete all these orange pigments.

Distribution of the salmon

The Atlantic salmon is a fish of the North Atlantic basin, spawning in rivers that flow down to the Atlantic, Baltic and Arctic Oceans and feeding and growing to sexual maturity in the sea. There have been arguments as to whether the salmon evolved from a saltwater species that later developed into a freshwater breeder, or whether it is a freshwater species that later developed the habit of feeding out at sea. Each of these has some scientific support. However, the fact that the eggs of the salmon will not hatch in sea water and that young salmon (parr) die in full-strength sea water makes the latter theory the more likely. This section examines the freshwater distribution of salmon; distribution at sea is described in Chapter 2.

The salmon is a cold-water fish. During the last Ice Age, when much of northern Europe was covered with deep ice and snow and the rivers were inhospitable to fish, its population was forced southwards, with a northerly limit in the eastern Atlantic certainly to Portugal and probably to the Rhine and waters of northern France. During this period, between 70,000 and 10,000 years ago, salmon fed in the Mediterranean and ran the rivers draining into the Mediterranean. Subsequently the Mediterranean became too warm for the salmon and the species moved northwards to colonize the rivers that had become free of ice. Just one remnant of the glacial Mediterranean population survives, the Adriatic salmon, which is now confined entirely to a life in rivers (see pp. 14–16). Much of the present-day distribution of the salmon is thus less than 10,000 years old.

There is no real northern limit of the sea range of the salmon, for it has been reported from under pack ice and could therefore penetrate to the North Pole. Its northerly breeding limit is controlled by the ability of the eggs to hatch in the river: the colder the water the longer the eggs take to hatch and the longer the fry will take in growing to a stage in which they can survive the winter.

The limit is probably rivers where the water temperature averages about 35.5°F through the winter and spring when the eggs are developing. Salmon eggs (laid in autumn) hatch in 114 days (just over 3½ months) at 36°F. The hatched salmon then remain in their gravel nest continuing development and feeding on their own stored food supplies. The colder the water the longer this will take. After that the fry need to feed in order to prepare for the oncoming winter. If the river is too cold, there will not be enough time before the onset of the following winter for eggs to hatch and fry to build up enough food reserves to survive the winter. Again, another lower temperature limit has been suggested: a water temperature of at least 50°F for about 100 days (three months) in summer. A lower winter water temperature will greatly retard development of the eggs and their in-built food supply will be exhausted before they have hatched. A lower summer water temperature will retard the development of the fry and they will have failed to reach a stage in which they can survive the following winter. In the most northerly arctic salmon rivers fry emerge from the gravel nests and begin to feed in July: that appears to be the limit, giving them barely two months to prepare for the onset of the long winter.

On the map opposite we can see the effects of the two factors, winter and summer river temperatures, on the general breeding distribution of the salmon. On both sides of the Atlantic the southernmost streams in which salmon spawn are at fairly similar latitude: 41°N on the American side (Long Island Sound), 38°N on the European side (Tejo River, Portugal). But the northern limits are quite different. In Europe, the salmon spawns as far north as there are rivers: to 71°N (4½ degrees north of the Arctic Circle). On the western side of the Atlantic, however, the northerly limit is reached at rivers draining into Ungava Bay: to 60°N (6½ degrees south of the Arctic Circle).

Eleven degrees' latitude difference is significant. The reason is that the coastline and climate of northern Europe are greatly affected by the warm North Atlantic Drift that brings warm sea currents and air to the continent from the Gulf of Mexico. By contrast, the coastal regions of the north-eastern USA and Canada are affected by sea currents and weather originating in the arctic. So whilst the Ungava Bay region has a mean January temperature of -13°F and July temperature of 50°F, the most northerly point of the European mainland, North Cape in Norway, has a mean January temperature of 23°F and July temperature also of 50°F. Even though Ungava Bay is 900 miles south of the latitude of North Cape, it has colder winters and similar summer temperatures to the northernmost salmon rivers of Europe. On the western side of the Atlantic the salmon spawns at a higher latitude than Ungava Bay, in the Kapisigdlit River of Greenland (latitude 64°N), though this is still 7 degrees to the south of the northernmost European salmon river. Here, mean January temperature is 14°F, July mean 50°F: warmer than Ungava Bay in winter though further north.

Present-day salmon distribution is, however, only partly related to marine and river temperatures. The explosion of the human population in countries bordering the North Atlantic during the nineteenth and twentieth centuries has resulted in a reduction of the breeding range of the salmon, for in these two centuries many rivers have been polluted and dammed so that spawning salmon are unable to run them. Over-fishing has contributed to the problem, though there is no case of a river losing its entire salmon stocks simply through over-fishing. We will return to such problems in Chapter 6, but here we will describe two distributions: the natural distribution and the current distribution. There is a problem, however. Whilst the natural distribution may change over thousands of years, as the natural environment slowly changes, the actual distribution may change rapidly as salmon rivers become dammed or so polluted that they lose their stocks or formerly polluted rivers become cleaned and salmon return. Happily the latter is the increasing trend today.

On the east side of the Atlantic the southern limit of the salmon's natural distribution is in Portugal, the River Tejo (or Tagus) which rises in the Serrania de Cuenca mountains and flows for about 625 miles through central Spain before reaching the sea at Lisbon. The Douro river system, which drains the northern Spanish plain from the Cantabrian mountains in the north, the Sierra de la Demanda in the east, and the Sierra de Guadarrama in the south, and flows through Old Castille before passing into Portugal and entering the sea at Oporto, is also a salmon river. Probably the shorter Mondego and Lima rivers are also salmon rivers. Alas, all these Portugese salmon rivers lost their

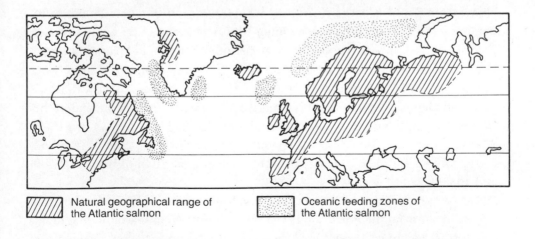

Natural geographical range of the Atlantic salmon

Oceanic feeding zones of the Atlantic salmon

Map 1 – Breeding and marine feeding distribution of the Atlantic salmon

stocks in the dim and distant past. Records are very few, and part of literature rather than scientific records. For instance, a seventeenth-century poem by Tirso de Molina tells of Lisbon, on the Tejo estuary, where:

> Citizens, when they are at table
> Can buy great loads of fish
> And most from their own doors are able
> To catch as many as they wish.
> And from the nets where salmon flounder
> It's scarce a stone's throw to the dish.

A modern poet might respond

> Don't go to Lisbon
> To see a salmon
> For they are gone!

Spain has many salmon rivers and can boast the earliest legislation to conserve salmon stocks. The world's first close season for fishing for salmon was established in 1258 by Alfonso; in 1435 Juan II prohibited the taking of salmon by adding poisons to the river; and in the late 1500s Philip II prohibited the use of temporary weirs to trap the fish and regulated the use of nets so that there would be enough salmon left at the end of each season to perpetuate the stocks. The consequence of this was that Spain had, in the north and north-west provinces, at least 50 salmon rivers which, up to the end of the eighteenth century, produced a harvest of up to 900,000 salmon per year. Subsequent damming of rivers resulted in the salmon stocks of many rivers being lost and that of others decimated. Today there are 21 salmon rivers in Spain: in Galicia the rivers Minho, Verdugo, Lerez, Umia, Tambre, Mandeo, Eume, Sor, Landro, Oro and Masma; in Asturias the rivers Eo, Navia, Canero, Narcea, Sella and Deva-Cares; in Cantabria the rivers Nansa, Pas and Ason; and in the Basque Region the River Bidasoa. Recent statistics (by C.G. de Leanis and J.J. Martinez) indicate that five of these, the Sella, Deva-Cares, Narcea, Pas and Ason, account for over 70 per cent of the total annual catch of between 2500 and 10,000 fish.

Every river flowing to the north and north-west coast of France was once a salmon river, from the great Adour and the 450-mile-long Garonne that drain the northern Pyrenean slopes and the Loire and Seine that flow through the northern French countryside from sources in the Massif Central and Plateau de Langres, to shorter rivers of Brittany and Normandy: rivers like the Aulne, Elorn, Douron, Trieux, See and Bresle. These rivers were prolific salmon rivers. According to Louis Roule the harvest from the Brittany rivers in the 1700s amounted to 9 million pounds weight of salmon per year, the short River Aulne producing 4000 fish annually up to 1789. Pollution and damming of the rivers, together with over-fishing following the French Revolution, saw a rapid decline in salmon stocks, the only rivers having a reasonable run of fish today being a few Brittany rivers (including the Aulne, Elorn, Odet), the Bresle and Loire (where work is being carried out to improve the runs of fish), and the Gave d'Oloron, a tributary of the Adour, with a total national catch of barely 5000 fish.

Two salmon rivers flow eastwards from France. The headwaters of the Meuse rise on the Plateau de Langres and Vosges and the river flows north, through Lorraine, and then passes through the Ardenne region of Belgium before entering the Rhine delta as the River Maas and the sea on the coast of the Netherlands. The Meuse is one of Europe's biggest rivers, 580 miles long excluding a maze of tributaries. The second is the Mosel, a river that rises in the Vosges, flows 330 miles north-eastwards from France through Luxembourg and on to Koblenz in Germany where it joins the Rhine.

The Rhine itself is one of Europe's biggest rivers, rising in the Swiss Alps and flowing 820 miles northwards through the length of Germany and the Netherlands before it reaches the North Sea. Both the Meuse and Rhine river systems were once great salmon rivers, but damming (with inefficient fish passes or no fish pass at all) and pollution exterminated their salmon runs. The Meuse run collapsed after the Dutch constructed the first weirs across the river in 1925; although the river has no salmon now (1994) attempts are being made to reintroduce salmon to the river. Salmon used to run the Rhine in vast numbers as far as the Rhine Falls below Lake Constance, a distance of about 600 miles. How big was the pre-industrial population we can only guess, but in 1885 three estuary netting stations took 82,000 salmon with an average weight of over 17 pounds. And at that time fish were being taken throughout the Rhine and its tributaries. In the first half of the twentieth century pollution, canalization of the river and the building of dams in the upper reaches caused the demise of the Rhine salmon, the river losing the last of its runs in the early 1950s. There are rumours, however, that salmon are again prospecting the Rhine system. Will this mighty river become a major salmon river again?

Further east in the Low Countries are rivers that must once have had a salmon population, though precise information is lacking for the Ijssel, Ems and Weser. The 706-mile-long Elbe certainly had good runs of salmon into the nineteenth century, but not today. Several of Denmark's sluggish rivers have good runs of big sea trout though only one, the Guden, which rises in central Jutland and enters the Kattegat at Randers Fjord, is recorded as once being a salmon river. Once – but not today.

Earlier we noted that the Baltic has its own genetic race of salmon (p. 17) that feed in the Baltic and spawn in rivers that enter the Baltic. The Oder rises in Moravia and flows north-westwards through Poland to the German border at Frankfurt an der Oder and then northwards to its estuary below Szczecin, a distance of 560 miles. The Vistula rises in the Carpathians and meanders for about 680 miles through Poland before entering the Baltic in Gdansk Bay. Both were once major salmon rivers, though statistical records are not available for the important years from 1939 (important for it was probably after 1939 that the last major salmon runs occurred in these rivers) when this part of eastern Germany was involved in the Second World War and subsequently controlled by the secretive German Democratic Republic. The Oder is reported to have lost its run, perhaps consequent to the canalization (through the years 1874–1941) of the river from Wroclaw downstream, though the Vistula apparently still has a small run of fish. Details for the rivers of the three Baltic States of Lithuania, Latvia and Estonia are similarly difficult to trace for they, too, were part of the secretive USSR until 1990. The 600-mile-long Neman and Venta of Lithuania, the 640-mile-long West Dvina and Gauja of Latvia, and the Narva of Estonia are salmon rivers.

Finland and Sweden now have the major and most productive Baltic salmon rivers though damming for hydroelectric power schemes, together with pollution and damage to the rivers through land drainage and logging operations, has exterminated the salmon populations of some rivers and reduced them in others that still have a run of fish. Of 47 Finnish rivers that once had a run of salmon, 15 had been completely destroyed by 1966 (Seppo Hurme) and by the mid-1970s, out of a total of 17 rivers still having a run of salmon, only the Torne and Ii continued 'to contribute substantial numbers of smolts to the Baltic' (A. Netboy). Since then, attempts have been made to remedy the loss of natural runs by releasing hatchery-raised fry, parr and smolts to the rivers. The 1975 report of the International Council for the Exploration of the Sea into Baltic salmon stocks identified about 40 salmon rivers in Sweden. Many have had their runs reduced through damming, land drainage and the lumber industry. However, natural spawning in the most prolific rivers – such as the Morrum, Dal, Kalix and Torne (the border river between Sweden and Finland) – together with the annual release of large numbers of hatchery-raised smolts, makes Sweden the greatest contributor to the Baltic salmon stocks.

Norway has long been famous as one of the premier salmon fishing countries in the world. And unlike many countries, which have allowed their salmon stocks to suffer as a consequence of industrialization, the Norwegians have carefully conserved their stocks. Not that they are without problems. Acidification through acid rainfall from elsewhere in Europe (see pp. 186–9) has damaged several rivers in the south of the country. Escaped farmed salmon are threatening the wild stocks of some rivers (see p. 200). Hydroelectric power systems have damaged some streams (see pp. 214–15). Nevertheless, the 1992 survey by Naturforlaget AS, *376 Norske Laks- og Sjooerretelver*, tells of 376 salmon rivers throughout the country with substantial runs of salmon, including the mighty Namsen, Gaula, Orkla, Alta and Tana, the Lapland river that separates northern Norway and Finland.

Norway continues to be a honeypot for salmon anglers and so too, increasingly, are several arctic Russian rivers. The Kola Peninsula has five great salmon rivers, the Tuloma, Kola, Iokanga, Varzuza and (most visited by foreign anglers) the Ponoy. To the east, and draining into the White Sea, are the Onega, Pinega, North Dvina (a massive river, over 630 miles long) and Mezen (530 miles), while further east the 1100-mile-long Pechora is the longest Atlantic salmon river in the world and considered by some writers as the eastern limit to the range of *Salmo salar*. However, this record probably belongs to the relatively short 130-mile Kara River which reaches the Arctic Ocean via the Kara Sea at longitude 65°E, where Europe meets Asia.

Like Norway, the British Isles has a long history of salmon and salmon angling. All the rivers of these islands were probably once salmon rivers. However, the Industrial Revolution resulted in a loss of salmon stocks in many, especially those in the south and east of England: the Thames, the Trent and Yorkshire Ouse systems, the Tees and Tyne. Some in lowland Scotland likewise suffered, for instance the Clyde. When the state of British salmon rivers was at its worst, in about 1950, there were still many great salmon rivers: amongst the most famous, in Wales the Wye, Usk, Dovey and Conwy; in England the Lune, Derwent and Eden; and amongst a host in Scotland, the famous four Spey, Dee, Tay and Tweed. Since 1950, and especially since 1970, great efforts have been made to clean up many formerly polluted rivers – with great success. Salmon have returned to the Thames. The Tyne, whose runs had virtually been exterminated, is probably now England's most prolific salmon river. The Tees estuary was, up to the late 1980s, a filthy sewer; today it is clean enough for salmon to pass, and fish are spawning in the Tees headwaters.

Ireland has not suffered from industrialization to anywhere near the same extent as the rest of Europe, and is still a great salmon country. Some formerly great salmon rivers, such as the Shannon (at 315 miles, the longest salmon river in the British Isles) and Erne, have been spoilt by hydroelectric power schemes whilst damming has reduced the runs of others. Some rivers are grossly over-fished, such as the Foyle, where legal nets take up to 80,000 salmon each year and many illegal nets an unknown number more. Nevertheless the salmon has survived in even these rivers. What makes Ireland unique as far as salmon are concerned is the large number of tiny rivers that have good runs of small fish.

To the north of the British mainland are two small archipelagos, the Shetlands and Faroes. The Shetlands has small streams that have always had a run of salmon. By contrast the rather similar Faroes appears not to have had a salmon river in living memory, though the River Laksa on the island of Eysturoy may have once been a salmon river, for 'Laksa' suggests the Norse *laks* or salmon. The problem on the Faroes is a lack of good deep river pools in which the fish can shelter before entering the spawning streams. In Shetland the salmon streams invariably have freshwater lochs in which the salmon can shelter. However, since 1947 attempts have been made to introduce the salmon to Faroese streams, Sanda on Sandoy, Fjardara on Eysturoy, and Leynara, Dalsa and Stora on Streymoy.

Iceland has about 70 salmon rivers, most of them very short but some so prolific that they are a mecca for anglers from North America and Europe. The effects of industrialization have not touched Icelandic rivers; they are now carefully protected as an important natural resource. Most famous and productive are the Ellidaa, the two Hvita Rivers, Laxa i Kjos, Laxa, Blanda, Midfjardara, Vididalsa and Vatnsdalsa.

To continue our survey of Atlantic salmon distribution we must now cross the ocean to North America and the states of Connecticut, Massachusetts and Maine. When the European settlers arrived here over 300 years ago they found all the rivers from Long Island Sound northwards full of salmon. They trapped and netted huge numbers, and salted and exported them back to Europe. Unfortunately, during the nineteenth century the expanding cities polluted many of the rivers, and dams were constructed across the rivers that prevented salmon passing upstream to their spawning redds. Consequently the salmon stocks crashed. Nevertheless, many salmon rivers still exist in the north-eastern United States, and attempts are being made to enhance stocks and reintroduce salmon in rivers that have lost them: Connecticut and Housatonic Rivers in Connecticut, Merrimack River in Massachusetts, and

Androscoggin, Dennys, Kennebec, Machias, Narragaugus, Penobscot, Pleasant, St Croix and Sheepcot Rivers in Maine.

The St Lawrence River and Lake Ontario (together with Lake Champlain in the states of New York and Vermont) had a large salmon population but this was exterminated at the end of the nineteenth century (the last dated record being 1896). To provide sport for anglers, alternative species were introduced from western (Pacific) Canada to Ontario and the other Great Lakes, including rainbow trout and coho salmon. These have thrived. In recent years the Atlantic salmon has also been reintroduced to Ontario with some success, under the auspices of the Ontario Federation of Hunters and Anglers. The species is now spawning successfully in some Ontario feeder streams and the record fish caught to date scaled 23lb. The original salmon stocks of this system, and the reintroduced stocks, do not run to sea. Instead the smolts run into Lake Ontario where they feed on whitefish before making their spawning runs into their natal streams. The St Lawrence–Ontario–Champlain salmon stocks could therefore be described as 'land-locked' (see below).

All rivers flowing to the coasts of New Brunswick, Nova Scotia, Quebec and Newfoundland–Labrador (north to Ungava Bay) are salmon rivers – many of them great salmon rivers. The Cascapedia, Eagle, Humber, Miramichi, Moisie, Restigouche, Romaine and Saint John are familiar names to most salmon anglers. But what of Labrador's Adlatok and Ujitok, or the Serpentine, or a host of almost unknown prolific rivers in this vast wilderness? Although the runs of fish were greatly reduced in many of them during the nineteenth and twentieth centuries, salmon rivers they continue to be. And stringent conservation measures are slowly returning them to their former glory.

Our survey of the Atlantic salmon rivers ends in Greenland, for here is the northernmost New World salmon river, the Kapisigdlit.

Land-locked salmon

Not all Atlantic salmon migrate to salt water to feed and grow. Some remain in fresh water for all their lives. We have seen this already with the salmon population of Lake Ontario (area 7500 square miles). But there are other populations that are referred to as being 'land-locked', a term that really means that the salmon remain in fresh water. Russia's Lake Lagoda (with a surface area of 7100 square miles) and Sweden's Lake Vanern (2150 square miles) have salmon that spawn in the lakes' feeder streams. In Vanern the *blanklax*, as they are called, grow fairly large, reaching 8lb by the time it comes for them to run the rivers and spawn. Much smaller, running to half a pound in weight, are the parr-like *smablank* of the Namsen. These are restricted to the river above

Fiskemoss waterfall, an impassable barrier for the Namsen's stocks of migratory salmon. Another small Norwegian land-locked salmon called the *blege* is found in Lake Byglandsfjord through which the River Otra flows. There are several populations of land-locked salmon on the North American side of the Atlantic. In Lake St John they are called *ouananiche*. In the lakes of Nova Scotia, New Brunswick and New England the same fish are called *sebago*.

Some taxonomists have suggested that these land-locked salmon are worthy of subspecific status, to separate them from the usual migratory populations. *Ouananiche* and *sebago* salmon have thus been referred to as *Salmo salar sebago*. However, other studies have suggested that they are not sufficiently separate from the migratory stocks to merit this classification, differences in size, general shape and the heavy spotting on land-locked fish being a consequence of where they live, and not based on major genetic differences.

CHAPTER 2

BIRTH AND DEVELOPMENT
IN RIVER AND SEA

When the frosty nights of autumn set in, and the leaves begin to fall,
the fish are impelled to the exercise of their reproductive functions.

A.H. CHAYTOR, *Letters to a Salmon Fisher's Sons*, 1910

Hugh Falkus and I were talking, one November lunchtime, on the current state of salmon stocks and whether the salmon could really be described as an endangered species. Suddenly Hugh came out with a simple, obvious, but classic statement: 'The salmon river is simply a smolt factory. If it is functioning at 100 per cent then it can do no more. If it is, then there will be enough adult salmon returning to perpetuate this production and to produce a surplus crop to be shared between anglers and commercial fisheries. The problem is that very few rivers are producing all the smolts that they are capable of producing.'

Let us consider Hugh's metaphor of the river being a factory manufacturing smolts. What are the basic factors that can affect the productivity of this factory?

The first factor is the mating salmon that will produce the basic raw material, fertilized eggs. If there are insufficient salmon to produce the optimal number of eggs, then the factory is not working at 100 per cent efficiency.

The second is a nursery stream that has clean water and that contains enough food to produce maximum growth rate for the maximum density of young salmon that the river can sustain. If water cleanliness and food production are not perfect then the factory is not working at 100 per cent efficiency.

The third is the extent of the factory; the area of suitable gravel for spawning and the area and structure of the river and river bed for the growing young salmon. For instance, if a tributary of one river is blocked by an impassable weir then one workshop of the factory is effectively shut down and production reduced by that amount. Similarly, if a naturally impassable waterfall is by-passed with a fish pass so that adult salmon can proceed upstream into formerly salmonless water, then the factory is enlarged and its potential

51

production increased. These are obvious. But there are less obvious, easily overlooked ways in which factory size is reduced – ways in which the effective area of the river is reduced without the apparent size of the river being reduced. The silting up of redds and exposure of huge shingle banks that were formerly never exposed to the air, due to water abstraction and land drainage, are common examples (see p. 172). Reduce the size of the factory and production will be cut.

The fourth is a loss of either eggs or young, or adult salmon that are ready to produce the fertilized eggs, by natural predation or disease. Usually, however, in any natural system, predators do not significantly damage the eventual production, and mortality by disease is of minor importance, other than when an outbreak of a virulent disease such as UDN breaks out (see p. 178).

The fifth factor affecting productivity of the smolt factory is excessive cropping by man. The salmon should be harvested, whether by anglers or commercial fishermen. However, the crop that is taken should be regulated so that the numbers of salmon remaining are sufficient to keep the factory working at maximum output. Which links back to the first factor.

Today, anglers often blame high seas or coastal netting for the decline of salmon stocks. Such losses at sea are important. However, they are minor, as far as the survival of the salmon is concerned – trivial if the river factory is 100 per cent effective. That commercial netting has contributed to a decline in the numbers of salmon returning to our rivers is not in dispute. But the chief problem is that the rivers, the smolt factories, have not been working efficiently.

This has been no more strikingly illustrated than on that famous salmon river, the Aberdeenshire Dee, where matters have been brought to a head in 1994. This river was one of the greatest, most famous, of spring salmon rivers. To fish the Dee between February and May, when the river was full of bright silver springers, was expensive. Fishing on the best beats was almost impossible to obtain, for they were booked by the same anglers who came back year after year to enjoy this bounty. But then the spring runs began to decline, alarmingly. By the mid-1980s anglers were looking downstream to the netting station in the estuary and accusing the netsmen of taking too many fish. Then, following the setting up of the Atlantic Salmon Conservation Trust in 1985, the nets were bought off, leaving the salmon free passage into the river and to the waiting anglers. But the Dee spring runs continued to decline. Frank Casson, a regular visitor to the Dee in spring, expressed the situation in a quite honest way by declaring that, in the old days, when the estuary nets were catching a lot of fish, so did the anglers. When the nets were not catching a lot of fish, neither did the anglers. He concluded, 'Now the nets catch no fish, for there are no nets. Anglers catch hardly any fish, for there are hardly any fish!'

The problem on the Dee is not netting at sea, or anglers taking too many fish. It is due almost entirely to the fact that the Dee is not functioning at 100 per cent efficiency as a factory to produce the smolts that return to the Dee as spring salmon. It is so easy to blame netting on the high seas (most of which has been bought off (see p. 192)), or inshore waters. Less easy to blame the decline of stocks on the river itself.

Mating and the production of eggs

It is 8 December, a bright frosty early winter morning, and I am sitting on the banks of the River Hodder, a clearwater salmon stream in the Bowland Fells of Lancashire. The cool breeze is stripping the last of the autumn leaves from the overhanging oak trees and they are floating down the sluggish flow. The weak sun glints through the stark branches of riverside alders. All is still and quiet except for the metallic song of displaying dippers, the occasional chatter of jays and the yaffle cries of green woodpeckers. A roebuck tiptoes its way through the wood behind me without making one autumn leaf rustle.

From July to the end of October I visited this river many times with the salmon rod. But now the fishing season has been finished for seven weeks and I have come to watch, not catch, salmon. I have chosen my vantage point carefully. Below where I am perched, on a rock ledge four feet above the river, is a slow pool and streamy riffle about three feet in depth. The water is so crystal clear, though with the slightest of peat tinge, that each pebble can be seen distinctly. A big moss-covered boulder juts out of the water some eight yards away, and tight up besides the boulder lies a dark shadow, a hen salmon, ripe with spawn. She is a big fish, perhaps weighing 15 or 16lb. Just downstream of her is another dark shadow, this time of a cock fish. Judging from the length of his shadow he is smaller, but not that much. Perhaps 10 to 12lb.

I have been here since first light and the only action has been when both fish left their lie and cruised round and round the pool slowly, the cock slightly behind his hen. And off they go again, unhurriedly cruising on a circular route through the pool neck and riffle. After seven minutes of wandering they return to the lie by the big rock. But then the hen fish moves upstream into the slightly faster water and quickly the cock sidles alongside her. They lie there motionless for 11 minutes. Suddenly the hen salmon moves forward, quickly flips over on her side and vigorously flaps at the gravel surface with her tail and caudal fin. Silt, sand and small fragments of gravel are disturbed, both by the direct action of her tail and by the violent swash created, and washed downstream. Her exertions last no more than two or three seconds. She drops back downstream to the big boulder, followed by the cock. The only evidence of their presence in the faster riffle is a small but conspicuous bright patch of white pebbles on the dark, algal-stained river bed.

Over an hour passes and the pair move once more upstream, the hen leading. Once more they make a tour of the riffle but quickly they come to rest, side by side though with the hen slightly in front, just downstream of the bright gravel patch where she made her first tentative cut. The cock fish moves forwards, close by her, and his body clearly quivers or vibrates. This seems to urge on the hen, for she moves forwards over the bright patch and crouches low. What she was doing, although I could not see this from my vantage point, was testing the depth and quality of the slight hollow with her anal fin. As she crouches, the body of the male again quivers. After a very few seconds she moves slightly upstream, flips over on her side, and again cuts down on the gravel with vigorous flappings of her tail. Once more a cloud of silt and sand and some larger stones are carried downstream, leaving a slightly larger bright depression in the river bed. She slides her body back, over the hollow and crouches low – again testing for depth with her anal fin. Apparently not satisfied, she makes another series of violent cuts, rights herself, and slides back in position over the hollow. Now the male, who has been waiting about three feet away, moves alongside her, his body quivering and mouth wide open.

Suddenly the climax is reached. The hen, with mouth and gill covers wide open, releases eggs into the nest. The male, also with mouth and gill covers wide open, sheds a cloud of sperm-bearing milky milt. Orgasm, egg laying and milt shedding, takes only four or five seconds.

Now the hen fish moves forwards and, slightly upstream of the egg-bearing nest, makes another series of violent cuts on the river bed. Silt and sand are washed away but, through my binoculars, I can see larger pebbles falling back, over the nest, covering the eggs. Then she moves quietly back to the lie beside the big boulder. The cock fish makes one solitary circuit of the riffle and he, too, moves back to the boulder lie.

From my bag I take a pack of smoked salmon sandwiches. As I enjoy their delicate, rich flavour, a thought passes through my mind. I caught the salmon that I am eating in that lie by the big boulder. In four or five years' time I might be similarly enjoying a salmon that I saw being born this chilly December morning.

These notes describe a typical act of spawning. But observations of many spawnings are essential to piece together the whole of the salmon's courtship.

Maturing of eggs and sperm

Having returned from the sea, salmon rest before the time comes for them to court and spawn. In spring-run fish (p. 101) the time of waiting may be the best part of 10–12 months, in autumn-run fish perhaps a month or even less. During this time the eggs slowly develop in the ovaries of the hen salmon, eventually filling the body cavity. The testes of the male salmon also enlarge to become a pair of large soft white sacs, running the length of the body cavity. The external appearance of the salmon also changes. The silvery sheen of the salmon fresh from the sea quickly fades to a pewter-grey. In the females this darkens to a dark grey or bronze-grey, the colour of a big bream. In the male the coloration brightens; copper-red patches develop on the gill covers and spread across the entire body to produce an autumnal tartan effect. The skin thickens considerably, embedding the scales more firmly in place; scales are easily dislodged from a silver fresh-run salmon but must be scratched or gouged out of the skin of a fish that has been long in the river.

As salmon make their long journey back from their oceanic feeding grounds, they stop feeding and their teeth are shed. A fresh-run salmon will usually have toothless gums or the odd tooth left. As they come into breeding condition so other teeth, which have been hidden in the tissues of the jaw, develop and, in the male, the upper and lower jaws elongate to produce the characteristic, often grotesque, kype. At the same time as the fish cease to feed, there is an atrophy of the gut; this shrinks to a fraction of its previous size, allowing extra space for the development of the ovaries or testes.

Rapid enlargement of the ovaries and testes, as well as the other changes in body structure, and the energy necessary to swim up the river and complete the arduous task of spawning cannot come directly from the digestion and assimilation of food, for the salmon does not feed after it leaves the sea. Instead the essential nutrients come from a recycling of materials already stored in the body's tissues. Salmon are oily fish; they have a high level of oils stored in their muscles (unlike many other fish, such as the cod, which store oils in their livers). They have red flesh due to the pigment carotene stored in the tissues and their flesh is rich in protein. The longer the fish has been in the river instead of feeding at sea, and the further advanced the alterations to the body (including development of ovaries and testes), the lower the oil, carotene and protein levels of the flesh. The muscles turn from being a bright red, firm, highly nutritious and delicious meat to a drab, soft, watery, washed out grey-pink mass.

It is obvious, therefore, that the best salmon to eat are those straight up from the sea, whose meat quality has not deteriorated. Best of all are fresh spring-run salmon, which have a higher quality of meat than fresh autumn-run fish. In the former the ovaries and testes have barely started to develop when they arrive back in the river, full development occurring in the long months that the fish wait in the river until spawning time. By contrast autumn-run salmon arrive back with ovaries and testes well developed and the flesh quality of these autumn fish is that bit poorer.

Because salmon that have been in the river for some time, and can be recognized as such from a rapid examination, are relatively poor on the table, they should not be killed. Indeed, in many areas it is illegal to do so, for the fish are 'stale' in angling jargon and 'ripe' in legal jargon. Only recently, in the British Isles, have such laws been enforced: in autumn 1992 a gillie on the Aberdeenshire Dee was prosecuted for 'being in possession of ripe salmon'. But why kill a fish of poor table quality? Far better that the fish spawn successfully and add to the egg production of the smolt factory. *Any salmon that is not bright silver should not be killed.* Instead it should be held in the water, head upstream, until it has regained enough strength to swim away. If the fish is badly hooked, cut the line close to the hook eye and let the fish swim off with the fly.

'It's a bit red, but it will smoke!' This is an excuse often given by anglers who have killed stale salmon. I take salmon to be smoked to Mr Price at Glasson Dock on the Lune estuary, for Mr Price produces the best smoked salmon! When I first approached him about having some fish smoked he warned me: 'Only bring silver, fresh-run fish! No stale, potted ones!'

I went to collect some from him and he reminded me of his warning. 'Look at this!' he exclaimed, opening up the smoker. 'That was a fish that was going red, but not too bad.' We compared the two. The fresh-run smoked salmon was bright orange-red; the stale stuff a pale dull orange. The fresh-run smoked salmon was tender, juicy and absolutely delicious; the stale stuff dry, chewy and of poor taste.

A friend, in his early days of salmon fishing on the Spey, took several stale fish home and had them smoked. They were so poor that he buried them. What a waste of eggs and milt!

Egg laying and fertilization

Each female salmon produces approximately 650–700 eggs (occasionally up to 800) per pound of her body weight. Some counts also suggest that females that run the river in spring produce 20–40 per cent fewer eggs than those of similar size running in autumn and that the eggs of spring-run salmon are smaller than those of autumn-run fish. This can be explained by the fact that most egg development in spring-run fish occurs during the many non-feeding months in the river, whereas egg development in autumn-run fish is rapid, in a short period of time just after sea feeding has ceased.

Not all eggs are released simultaneously in the one redd. As we shall see in many aspects of salmon natural history, nature rarely puts all her eggs into one basket. The bigger the female the more redds. Thus a small salmon weighing 3–5lb will usually cut two (sometimes one) redds; a fish weighing 10lb will usually cut three redds; and a big salmon weighing 40lb or more may divide her eggs amongst six or more redds. The size of the redd also varies depending on the size of the female salmon: a 5lb salmon will dig a redd that is only 6in deep whereas a 30lb fish will cut one 1ft deep. The depth is a function of the depth of the anal fin, for the fish uses the anal fin to measure depth and check for gravel quality at the bottom of the redd.

In the act of mating, and triggered by the redd and the close proximity of a 'quivering' male salmon, the eggs are released from the thin transparent ovary sac into the body cavity and then expelled from the body via the urino-genital papilla of the vent. When still in the body of the female and immediately after release the eggs are soft and pliable, but they rapidly swell and become firm and rounded. The eggs are also somewhat sticky, a feature that helps them hold together in one mass and on to the stones in the excavated redd.

Although the number of eggs produced by one salmon may seem large to us, it is, in fact, not particularly so. A 20lb salmon may produce 14,000 eggs; but a cod of the same size may produce three million! And a 4lb perch 100,000! However, the cod and perch do not hide their eggs in a nest deep enough to protect them from predators, as does the salmon. Nevertheless it is important that no chances are taken when it come to ensuring that the eggs are fertilized. Firstly, the numbers of sperm produced by male salmon are vast, perhaps a million for every egg produced by the female. This ensures a great chance of each egg being fertilized. But there is often (not always) a back-up. In Chapter 1, I described how some earlier writers described the parr as a separate species, and noted that they had found them producing milt. These mature or 'precocious' parr are a natural insurance policy against the older males not fertilizing all the eggs. During late summer the testes of a proportion of male parr begin to develop, and from November to January (in British rivers at least) they are capable of producing milt and the milt is capable of fertilizing salmon eggs.

The first description of parr fertilizing eggs released by female salmon into a redd was by J.W. Jones in his book *The Salmon* (1959). It had long been known that salmon parr are frequently guests at salmon marriages, but before Dr Jones's study the motives of the parr were considered anything but beneficial. A.H. Chaytor's grandfather was a careful observer, Chaytor using his notes to describe the mating of a pair of salmon, the cock with a conspicuous white nose, in *Letters to a Salmon Fisher's Sons*, which was published in 1910 (the observations probably dating back to the nineteenth century). He described how the eggs were released but then noted, 'Suddenly a small fish, which had been close to the edge of the water and directly under my feet, rushed in behind white nose's mate, and instantly fell back. This manoeuvre, evidently for the purpose of getting the ova, was repeated every time the spawning fish "threw" [shed eggs].' We now know that the little parr dash in as the eggs are shed and themselves release milt which mixes with that from the old cock, thereby increasing the chance of fertilization.

It has been estimated that in some rivers up to 25 per cent of salmon eggs are fertilized by sexually mature parr. For instance, in a survey of Girnock Burn (a Dee tributary) it was discovered that between 1.4 per cent and 25.2 per cent (mean 12.3 per cent) of eggs had been fertilized by parr and not adult male salmon.

There are very few instances of female parr becoming mature and contributing to the egg production of salmon rivers. One example was caught in the River Elorn, France. Weighing 5.3oz and measuring nearly 9in, she had produced 256 viable eggs.

Territorial and courtship behaviour

Besides the mechanics of producing eggs and sperm into a redd, the process of spawning involves quite elaborate behaviour patterns: pair formation and territoriality. This is what makes the watching of mating salmon so exciting, for salmon are not placid creatures. A male will fight off other males trying to seduce his mate, and females will defend the area of gravel that they have chosen for cutting redds against intruding females.

In *The Borders and Beyond* (1929) Abel Chapman described, in his flowery Victorian style, a December morning battle between cock salmon in a small spawning burn:

Two gallant Palladins were locked in mortal combat on a battlefield not six yards across and in water barely two feet deep. The rivals were cock-fish of 12 and 15lb. respectively, and their methods of attack varied and savage. Now, for several seconds it resembled a regular wrestling-bout, the pair driving shoulder to shoulder, and then – by hurling his bulk full

full broadside across the enemy's bows – to 'drown' him. Both combatants at intervals became exhausted, the smaller fish the more so, though clearly full of fight. Then, for brief seconds, the protagonists rested – lying parallel a foot apart – till the Fury that first recovered his wind, turned in a lightning flash and RAMMED his rival full amidships. The impact sent the water flying and 'midst turmoil and spray, one's eyes caught glimpses of great crimson and coppery broadsides writhing, revolving, and rushing athwart the troubled stream . . . For a solid hour – probably more – the Furies had fought thus . . .

It may be, in a densely populated stream, where males outnumber females, that a great deal of fighting does occur between males attempting to gain mates. However, in rivers where the sex ratio of salmon is about equal, all males can obtain mates (in theory at least). On the rivers where I have watched spawning salmon, the Esk, Lune, Hodder and Tyne, even where several males are in occupation prolonged physical violence between males seems rare. Unmated males entering the territory of a mated pair will usually flee downstream as soon as the occupying male swims towards it. I have occasionally watched an intruding male approach a pair of salmon that were close to spawning. The approach has always been from downstream. It seems that these unattached males can detect ripe females, presumably by smell or taste carried downstream by the flow, and so are attracted upstream. The resident male has turned on the intruder, with mouth gaping and gills flared, and pursued the intruder away downstream. Sometimes the chase has involved several laps of the pool before the intruder has fled. Once the resident cock barged the flank of an intruder who was slow to leave. Never has the female taken any part in the pursuit. Of course such tactics are far better than actual physical combat which may damage or fatigue both males to the point at which neither are capable of mating successfully. Cold war and not cold blood!

I suspect that the reputation of the salmon spawning ritual to be a bloodbath comes partly from the huge, ferocious-looking kyped mouth and teeth of the cock salmon. It has, for instance, been said that the kype is used in the battle to grasp other males by the tail because that is what the kype appears to be designed for. But, as in all male animals, these grotesque secondary sexual characteristics are there for threat far more than for action.

I have watched territorial behaviour between female salmon on four occasions. In one of these a lone female moving upstream stopped on a patch of gravel where a resident female had already prospected. When the newcomer arrived the resident female was resting to one side of the gravel patch. Immediately the latter shot rapidly across the pool and barged the flank of the intruder with her shoulder. The intruder then continued her journey upstream. That is the only physical contact I have noted between female salmon; on the other three occasions the resident female swam up behind the intruder and shepherded her upstream.

The primary feature of sexual behaviour in the male salmon is the 'quiver', where mouth and gill covers open, pectoral, pelvic and dorsal fins are erected, and the body visibly quivers with short waves of ripples extending from head to tail. Quivering can clearly be seen in clear water, especially if binoculars are being used. Before quivering the male usually darts forward to the side of the female, but with his head between one-third and two-thirds of her body length behind her snout. Quivering is used by male salmon when they are courting a hen salmon. Quivering is a stimulus that encourages the hen fish to cut a redd in the gravel. And quivering is the stimulus that results in both male and female orgasms. Should the female not respond she may be threatened by further quivering and nudging of her body by the quivering male. If she continues to ignore his quivering she may be attacked by being chased round the pool or being barged by the frustrated male. J.W. Jones also noted other quivering situations. A male salmon may quiver against another male salmon; if the latter does not leave then it will be forced out. In this way the quiver is used as a threat. I have seen this only once. Dr Jones also observed male salmon quivering against boulders, sometimes in the open away from any other fish or boulders. The function of these latter quiverings is unknown.

The pair bond between pairs of mating salmon is a weak one and the fact that one female mates with one cock when she cuts her first redd and sheds her first batch of eggs does not necessarily mean that she will mate with the same cock when she cuts her next redd. One one occasion, on the Lune, I watched a female preparing to dig her second redd but the male seemed not to be able to stimulate her. His quivering ceased just before she made a second cut in the gravel and after lying stationary for about 20 minutes she moved across the river into slacker water. The male then dropped downstream. Just before dusk another, much smaller, male joined her and she completed her second redd with him. Perhaps her first mate was spent, having previously mated with another female. On another occasion, also on the Lune, two canoeists came down the river directly over a pair that were preparing to spawn in a second redd. Both salmon fled. A quarter of an hour later the female returned with another, larger, cock fish. In both these cases the females spawned twice in one day. However, observations using radio-tagged females have shown that some females may have a gap of two or more days between spawnings. In these it is quite likely that they mate with different males.

Sexually ripe male salmon appear to be quite promiscuous. This is some-thing that is difficult for the amateur salmon-watcher to see, but it is readily observed by the fish scientist using radio-tagged fish. John Webb and A.D. Hawkins described their radio-tagging observations of several fish in the Girnock Burn in *Scottish Fisheries Report* No. 40. Here they found that tagged females spawned once or twice. One cock fish spawned five times in 13 days (presumably with at least three different females) and was still sexually active enough to court three spent female salmon (kelts) over the next week before dying of exhaustion. Another was seen paired with a maiden hen fish three times in four days before spawning (presumably) with her. The next day he obtained another mate and spawned twice with her. He quickly obtained yet another mate but icy conditions seemed to bring an end to this relationship for later that week he was recorded trying to court a spent female kelt. He then moved downstream and courted another kelt before moving back upstream where he courted and spawned with another maiden hen fish. Over the following nine days he attempted to court yet another female kelt before dying.

Hen salmon will cut a redd and mate only if they have eggs to release. It seems clear, however, that male salmon will continue courting and mating until they are close to death – even, perhaps, if they have little milt remaining. It would be a waste of eggs if nature allowed eggs from later matings to go unfertilized. Hence the insurance of having sexually mature male parr whose milt will fertilize eggs that the old spent males might be unable to fertilize. There is also an advantage in spent males mating with maiden hen salmon, especially if there are surplus females. As we saw earlier, the sexually mature male parr cannot sexually arouse a female. But a spent male can. Thus by the old male arousing the female to cut a redd and shed her eggs which are then fertilized by a male parr, the eggs of a hen salmon who cannot find a fertile adult partner are not wasted.

After spawning, the return to the sea

After spawning virtually all spent males and most female kelts die, with about 10–35 per cent of kelts attempting to return downstream to the sea. Why do so many die? From the time a salmon stops feeding and enters the river to the time when it is a spent kelt, it will lose up to about 45 per cent of its body weight. Those that are at the upper limit of this loss, 40–45 per cent, are beyond the physiological point of no return, for very few animals can sustain that weight loss and survive. The survivors are those whose weight loss is not at that high level, say 30–40 per cent loss. Autumn-run fish, fish running short rivers, and females that do not continue in the exertions of courtship and mating after their eggs have been shed will lose less weight and have a higher kelt survival rate than spring-run fish, or those that have to make long upstream and downstream river journeys, or cock fish that have several sexual partners.

The fish's attempt to swim down the river immediately after spawning is not always completed. Some reach the sea by late December. However, many remain in the river up to as late as the end of April, occasionally to mid-May. Although kelts will not feed until they reach the sea they are often caught accidentally by anglers who are fishing for fresh-run spring salmon; kelts certainly seem to take a fly far more readily than when they were fresh-run salmon. It is essential that these kelts are identified as such and returned speedily to the river, for a proportion of kelts do return to spawn and add to later egg production.

Kelts are recognized by their long slender body, the belly and back being virtually parallel. The belly is soft, the vent usually enlarged and often inflamed. The head appears disproportionately large; the fins are often slightly ragged. If the gill cover is lifted, small gill maggots will be seen on the red gill filaments. The colour of the kelt is no guide, for many quickly lose the drab spawning colour and regain a silver coloration (these silver fish are referred to as 'well-mended' kelts). If you are doubtful, put it back! For there will be no doubt at all if the fish is a fresh-run spring salmon.

Occasionally, female salmon that should have spawned but failed to do so are caught in spring. These are called 'baggots'. They are not as thin as the kelt and so are much more likely to be mistaken for fresh-run salmon. The first clue to the identification of a baggot is that the belly, still holding the mass of large eggs, sags. And when the fish is lifted by the tail, the distorted belly holding the egg mass will slurp forwards towards the head. Gill lice will be present on the gill filaments.

At one time it was thought that kelts that made it successfully back to sea remained feeding in the estuary or nearby inshore waters before making a second spawning run. This is now known to be not necessarily true, for tagged kelts have been recorded from distant oceanic feeding areas. Some of these may spend only a few months feeding at sea, returning to spawn in the autumn after their previous spawning. Others remain at sea for a full year, returning to spawn in the second autumn after their previous spawning. Others may stay out even longer, returning to spawn in the third autumn after their previous spawning. A very few salmon may spawn more than twice. There was one famous fish, aged 13 years old when it was finally captured on Loch Maree, that had already spawned four times and was making its fifth spawning run. And some salmon from short Canadian rivers have been recorded as spawning five or six times.

Many anglers ask if it is possible to tell a previous spawner from a virgin fish. The only sure way is by scale reading (see p. 97). However, two clues come from coloration, the previous spawner having more black spots on the back and the gill covers, and being not so brightly silver (more of a gold-silver) as a virgin fish. Then, if the gills are checked and gill maggots are found, the fish is almost certainly a previous spawner.

The proportion of fish running a river in one year that are previous spawners is generally very small, variously estimated at between 3 and 8 per cent for most rivers but as high as 30–34 per cent in some short Canadian rivers. They are, however, an important component in egg production in the river smolt factory.

From egg to smolt

We left the eggs lying in their gravel nest, protected from predators such as the dipper, eel, caddis larva and big stonefly nymph, and constantly supplied with clean, well-oxygenated water. Development is fairly slow, for its rate depends on water temperature and water temperatures are low during the winter months: in arctic rivers the water temperature may be only 36°F for 114 days, 43°F for 90 days and 46°F for 70 days. This means that in rivers of the British Isles, France and Spain, the eggs hatch sometime in March or April, whereas in more northerly waters and the rivers of eastern Canada, which are iced over through the winter, hatching is delayed to May or June, after the melt.

Development and hatching

The first signs of development are the appearance, in the orange egg, of a pair of dark eyes: hatcheries refer to this stage as being an 'eyed ova'. Then, slowly, a little slender fish begins to form, and when development is complete the egg membrane ruptures and out wriggles the alevin, an embryonic fish about 1/3–1/2in long, with a large food-bearing yolk sac attached to its underside. This yolk sac provides the alevin with all the food that it will need for about a month, for the alevin does not feed, remaining hidden in the gravel. To prevent alevins from moving up through the gravel where they would risk being devoured by predators or washed away by the current, they have an inbuilt 'negatively phototropic' mechanism: they automatically move away from light. Should a piece of gravel be washed away from the surface of the river bed, allowing a chink of light to fall upon them, they will immediately burrow deeper into the gravel.

Fry

Once the yolk sac is exhausted the little fish is called a fry – initially, because it does not feed, an unfed fry. The water flowing through the gravel carries tiny particles of food. These enter the mouth of the unfed fry with water; the water passes out through the gills and the food particles are strained out by the gill rakers and passed back into the stomach. Having had its first meal the little fish is now a fed fry. The negatively phototropic response of the alevin is replaced by three new responses. The first is that the fry becomes positively phototropic: it moves towards the light. So it now swims up through the gravel, arriving at the surface in spring or early summer at the time when the populations of small invertebrates are at their peak in the river. The fry thus has an abundance of food. But the fry cannot lie anywhere in the river. It must lie on the bottom, so that it is not swept away by the current, and with its head facing into the current, so that oxygenated water can enter its respiratory system. So two other responses develop before the fry swims up, one to keep it on the bottom and one to keep it facing into the flow.

The fry now disperse in shoals, mostly downstream of the redd. W.M. Shearer found, on the North Esk, that four weeks after swim-up the fry from one redd were distributed from 175yd upstream of the redd to 812yd downstream. The deep open river contains many predators of tiny fry (goosanders, trout, miller's thumbs, and even large invertebrates), and so through the summer they tend to seek quieter shallows. On the middle Dee in August 1994, for instance, almost each shallow puddle at the edge of the river had a shoal of fry.

Fry are initially a pale sandy grey and scaleless; their scales slowly develop from primitive scale-buds when they have reached about 1in in length. These are the scales that it will have when it is a mature salmon, though some might be lost and replaced. So as the fish grows the scales enlarge; the number stays the same throughout its life.

Parr

As the fry grows so coloration changes, with dark mottling developing on the back and sides. At this stage between eight and eleven dusky grey oval markings develop along each side of the body. These are parr marks. The fry is now a parr, the main river-feeding stage.

Unlike the fry, the parr is an independent, solitary fish. The fry shoals break up as each parr becomes territorial, taking its own niche or station on the river bed. Any parr that cannot obtain a station will be chased away by those that have a station and thus the number of possible parr stations in a length of river limits the population of parr. The parr stage is thus the most critical in determining the number of smolts produced by a river: if all parr stations are occupied the river can produce no more, no matter how many eggs were laid or how many fry swam up from the redds. This territoriality is based on sight, neighbouring parr resting on their riverbed stations being unable to see each other. Thus, where the river bed is a mass of boulders parr densities can be very high; parr stations might be only a few inches apart, the boulders providing sight-boundaries. But where the river bed consists of flat, very fine gravel the parr can see further; consequently territories are larger and the parr density in the river much lower. Therefore, if a flat riverbed can be broken up it will hold more parr – or, to go back to the Falkus smolt factory metaphor at the beginning of this chapter, the greater is the size of the factory.

An illustration of this is the effect of three weirs that Bowland Gamefishing Association constructed on their Paythorne beat on the River Ribble. There was a length of about 250yd of shallow flow where the bottom was largely very fine gravel, sand and silt – dead water for angling. After taking advice, the Association constructed three weirs which concentrated flow in midstream. The river did the rest: deep channels were formed and the downcutting washed away fine sediments and exposed some larger boulders. The pools thus formed provided good fishing, for that was the aim of the exercise, but it also increased the parr-holding ability of the water. Formerly parr were very sparse in that stretch of river; now they are abundant. In Chapter 6 we will consider other ways in which a river might be managed to increase smolt production.

Studies of rivers in New Brunswick, Quebec and Scotland have shown that in summer the parr select territories in shallow, fast riffles and pool necks and tails, whereas in winter they tend to seek deeper, slower pools (in Quebec parr movements to summer shallows occur when the water temperature has risen to 45°F, movements back into winter quarters occurring when the water temperature falls below 45°F). Studies in Scottish streams have also shown that, in their first year of life, parr tend to occur in shallower water than parr in their second year.

From these observations it follows that the greater the variety of depth and flow rate, and the more broken the river bed, the more parr a length of river can support. Many surveys of parr densities have confirmed this. For instance, a survey of the Tweed by D.H. Mills and A.T. Tomison showed that in the upper reaches of the Tweed, where there are extensive boulder-strewn shallows and riffles separating deeper pools, parr density was very high: an average of 0.21 parr per sq. yd of river bed. Density was lower in the middle Tweed, at 0.12 parr per sq. yd, where there were fewer boulder-strewn shallows; in the lower Tweed, where the river was deep and slow, density was very low at 0.02 parr per sq. yd. Two rough, rocky feeder streams of the Tweed were also surveyed, the Ettrick and Teviot. In these the parr densities were the highest on the Tweed system at 0.49 and 0.24 per sq. yd respectively.

Parr feed on a wide variety of river invertebrates and also on land-bred insects that happen to fall on the water. These include small caddis, midge and blackfly larvae in deep pools, stonefly and mayfly nymphs in riffles and hatching mayflies, midges, backflies and caddis-flies from the water surface. I have watched them pulling large daddy-long-legs and the big *Ephemera danica* mayfly duns under the water by their legs and tails. In late spring I have watched them taking moth caterpillars, descending from trees on silk threads, as soon as they touched the water. In high summer I have watched them rising to take a whole variety of insects that have fallen on to the water: ants, wasps, small grasshoppers, black gnats and so on. In autumn I have seen them feeding frantically on huge numbers of aphids (greenfly) that have fallen from waterside trees. They are thus opportunistic feeders, grabbing anything that passes in front of their noses or through their surface window (see p. 29).

Very little of their food is grubbed from the river bed (25 per cent at most according to one Scottish study), most of the food being insects that are drifting downstream in the flow. This behaviour is well known to the fly fisherman, for parr will grab at any wet fly or dry fly intended for trout and even at salmon flies that bear no resemblance to real food. To take maximum advantage of any drifting food, parr prefer lies or stations that are at the boundary between bands of different flow rate, resting in the slacker flow and taking food at the edge of the faster flow. We have already seen that parr territory size is based on their not being able to see their neighbours, and that the more broken the river bed the greater the parr density. Such broken water also has the greater variety of flow rates and more creases (the conveyor belts along which drifting food items are carried) than slow deep pools with a flat bottom.

It was once thought that parr stop feeding in winter, when they leave the shallows and take lies in deeper water. This is not so. If food is available the parr will continue to feed, although less food is available in the depths of winter. This was demonstrated as long ago as 1940, when K. Carpenter analysed a series of parr stomachs taken throughout the year:

VOLUME OF FOOD IN THE STOMACH (cm^3)

Jan	Feb	Mar	Apr	May	Jun
0.52	2.2	1.9	2.01	2.49	1.45

Jul	Aug	Sep	Oct	Nov	Dec
1.59	negligible	1.86	0.65	–	0.35

The negligible amount recorded in August is curious and perhaps either a consequence of sampling techniques or due to the fact that, in the very warm water, digestion was so rapid that food remained only a short time in the stomachs. Certainly this table should not be read as suggesting that parr in late winter and early spring are eating more than they are in summer. They are not. It simply illustrates the fact that the food taken in cold water early in the year stays in the stomach much longer than the food taken in the warm water of summer. In summer a parr might fill its stomach several times in the day; in winter it cannot because it takes so long to digest a stomachful of food. But the table does demonstrate that parr may feed throughout the year.

Growth rate parallels feeding and digestion rates. Several studies have shown that, in their first year, parr grow rapidly from early April (ice-melt in northern rivers) to mid-August, slowly from mid-August to late October, and that there is no growth through the winter. In their second year of life parr recommence growing rapidly in early April (or after ice-melt in northern rivers), but growth slows in late July and from late October there is no growth. Although they will feed from November to March, digestion and assimilation of food is so slow that it is insufficient for growth.

Besides the spring and autumn movements between deeper and shallow water, parr may travel some distance along the river. Studies in Newfoundland have shown that precocious parr will migrate upstream to the spawning redds, while parr that will run to sea as smolts the following spring may start their seaward journey by moving downstream in autumn. Other studies have demonstrated the ability of parr to 'home' back to their territories (one homed quickly over a distance of 220yd), larger or older parr being better homers than smaller or younger parr. Parr that are displaced downstream of their territories home much better than those displaced upstream. This is an interesting observation, for it suggests that displaced parr use the scent of their territories, carried downstream by the current, as a guide. That parr might be able to recognize one small patch of river bed by its smell or taste, over quite long distances, is incredible!

Smolt

When a salmon parr attains about 4in in length it is ready to become a smolt and go to sea. The whole series of processes that change parr to smolt take time, probably about 50 days. In early spring, external factors (increased daylength is probably the most important, though warming of the water may also be a trigger) stimulate the tiny pituitary gland at the base of the brain to produce hormones. These hormones stimulate the thyroid gland in the neck which produces thyroid hormones. These hormones prepare the body of the parr for migration to and life in the sea; they turn parr into smolt.

The most obvious changes are external ones. The body becomes more slender and streamlined, with a rapid increase of length to 4.5–6in. A chemical called guanine is laid down in the skin. This masks the underlying parr coloration, turning the drab brown parr into a bright silver smolt. And the kidney–gill system becomes prepared for life in salt water instead of fresh water (see pp. 39–40).

Beginning in April (in more southerly rivers) or as late as June or July (arctic and Canadian rivers) the smolts move to the sea, dropping downstream tail-first in faster water and swimming actively through slow pools and lakes. Reports suggest that early in the smolt run, up to May, most smolt migration occurs at night, from mid-May onwards by day. Estimates of the rate: of down stream migration vary tremendously, from as low as about 0.1 mile to over 12 miles per day. Such variation may partly be a function of flow rate: in faster water the descent may be quicker. But shoals of smolts will often tarry for several days in one river pool to feed on the big hatches of spring flies. In 1992 and 1994 on the Ribble and Hodder it took 25 and 17 days respectively for the smolt shoals to move to below their confluence, and a further five days for the shoals to clear out of the 6 miles below the confluence. Observations on the North Esk suggest that while 55 per cent of parr are male, only 36 per cent of smolts are male. This may be a consequence of high mortality in precocious male parr (pp. 57–8). Observations have also shown that most female smolts migrate before male smolts and older smolts migrate before younger ones (see below).

The age of smolts

The age at which parr become smolts and migrate to sea is, like so many of the anatomical, physiological and behavioural features of plants and animals, genetically controlled. Like most genetic systems, more than one pair of genes is involved. This gives rise to several possible ages at which parr might become smolts. But again, as in many genetically controlled features, the environment interacts with the genes and modifies their influence.

The further north or, rather, the colder the river, the older are parr when they become smolts. Thus in the salmon rivers of France and Spain and the chalk streams of southern England about 90 per cent of parr become smolts when they are only one year of age (in their second summer), the other 10 per cent a year later. In the rivers of south Wales up to 5 per cent of parr become smolts when they are one year old, up to 90 per cent at two years old, and up to 7 per cent at three years old. In northern England barely 1 per cent of parr become smolts when they are one year old, up to 85 per cent at two years old, and up to 15 per cent when they are three years old. In Scotland most smolts are two or three years of age: on the Aberdeenshire Dee 67 per cent and 31 per cent respectively, with about 1 per cent each of one and four year olds; in the Grimersta system of the island of Lewis about 60 per cent of smolts are three years old. In southern Norway most smolts are two to four years of age: in the Evanger 33 per cent two year olds, 61 per cent three year olds and about 6 per cent four year olds, with about 0.3 per cent five year olds. In Iceland and western Norway smolts are usually aged three or four or five years old, in Lapland between three and seven years, and in the rivers draining into Ungava Bay in north-east Canada the average age of smolts is five years, with a range of four to eight years. The variation in each region is genetically controlled; the tendency for smolts to be older farther north is a consequence of environmental effects.

The higher the temperature of the water and the longer the spring, summer and autumn the more time there is for feeding and growing. Thus in southern rivers the parr have a longer feeding and growing period than those farther north (where the river may be frozen through five months of the year) and thus they reach the size for smolting more quickly.

Within one river there is variation of the age at which parr become smolts, which is related to variation of parr growth rates. For instance on the Welsh Dee, J.W. Jones found that parr that had reached 2.9in in length at the end of their first year migrated as smolts the following spring at a length of 5 in. Those parr that were averaging only 2in in length at the end of their first year migrated one year later (as two year olds) at a length of 5in. And those parr that averaged only 1.6in at the end of their first year migrated as smolts yet another year later (as three year olds) at a length of 6.5in.

This is another instance (and we have seen several in this chapter) of nature not putting all her eggs into the one basket! By having parr from the same year's egg production go to sea as smolts over two, three or more years there is less chance of a catastrophe wiping out the entire year's production. So off they go to sea from the smolt factory.

Life at sea

In 1953 the Danish fishery scientist Jorgen Nielsen examined some salmon that had been caught by cod fishermen off the west coast of Greenland. It had been known for several years that these cod fishers caught some salmon, but they had never been examined properly, for it was assumed that they would be from Greenland's only salmon river, the Kapisigdlit. However, scale reading revealed that these fish had spent between one and three years in the river as parr. This meant that they could not be Kapisigdlit fish, Nielsen argued, for parr remained in that arctic river for four or five years. They must have originated from salmon rivers farther south, perhaps from Canadian or European rivers.

It was not long before Nielsen's supposition was supported by hard evidence. In 1955 an adult salmon that had been stripped of its eggs was released into Loch na Croic in Ross-shire. Eleven months later, in October 1956, that salmon was recaptured near Maniitsoq, west Greenland. In 1960 a smolt was tagged in Canada's Miramichi estuary. It was recaptured in precisely the same place as the Scottish fish. These were the first of many tagged fish recovered in their feeding areas, out in the Atlantic. Such information was too late for Dr J.W. Jones to include in his classic *The Salmon* (1959); at that time he could only comment that 'We have scarcely begun to solve the problems of where the Salmon feed in the sea.'

It had been known for many years that salmon use the scent or taste of their own river to find their way home. How they do this, and other methods of navigation that they might use, will be described in Chapter 3. One earlier theory of where salmon feed was that they remain, not too far offshore, in waters that kept them, through taste or smell, in constant contact with their home river. In other words, they had to remain within smelling range of home and if they wandered further they would become lost. This theory had several problems. Firstly, with the exceptions of major rivers that discharge an immense amount of scent-holding water into the sea, the smell of the home river will quickly be dissipated and mixed with the scents of other rivers. Secondly, despite much effort, very few salmon were caught feeding close to the river estuaries. A modification of this theory suggested that some salmon remained in the sea close to their natal river and returned after one year as grilse. Others might go further afield, but it would take these much longer to find their way back home, so they would return after two or more years (depending on how far they had wandered) as larger salmon.

Another theory was that salmon headed south-west across the Atlantic, perhaps as far as the Sargasso Sea where eels spawn. They would drift back in the Gulf Stream with the developing young eels, feeding on the larval eels as they went. Their last meal before entering the river would be elvers, the form of eel that enters our rivers from the sea. As Arthur Ransome put it in *Mainly about Fishing* (1959): 'What was the very last creature the salmon was likely to have tasted before and even after coming up the estuaries and losing temporarily his powers of digestion? There is no need to hesitate over the answer. The answer of an elver was, for several reasons, a taste that the salmon was likely to remember with affection.'

It was on this basis that Arthur Ransome invented that deadly salmon fly, the Elver Fly. But the fly's effectiveness has nothing to do with what salmon eat nor where they have been, for they do not eat elvers nor do they spend time in the ocean where elvers might be found. It is just a damn good fly!

It is now known that salmon smolts generally move away from their natal rivers very quickly and head for fairly specific feeding areas. There are still gaps to fill in to complete the picture, for instance the routes they take and possible stopping-off locations where they may feed intensively before moving on. Further work is required on possible undiscovered sea feeding areas in the east side of the Atlantic, perhaps in the northern North Sea and off the coasts of northern Norway and Russia, for most research has concentrated on feeding areas on the New World side of the Atlantic (off Labrador and Greenland), around the Faroe Islands and in the Baltic Sea.

Map 1 (p 43) shows the feeding areas and breeding areas of the Atlantic salmon.

The first point is that the Atlantic salmon from rivers throughout their range (with the exception of the Baltic population) become mixed together once they are at sea. So tagged fish from Russia, Norway, Iceland, the British Isles, France and Spain have been found in the Faroe and Greenland feeding grounds along with salmon from Canada and the north-eastern USA.

The second point is that in their feeding grounds the salmon do not remain in shoals according to their place of origin. Thus, smolts from, say, the Spey do not migrate together, remain together as they feed, and return together, as a unit separate from the fish of other rivers. A long-liner or drift net out on the feeding areas will take, on one day and from one feeding area, fish that come from a variety of rivers.

Salmon that have moved to the Faroe feeding areas may feed there before returning home the following summer as grilse: this is the origin of perhaps the majority of grilse running European rivers. Instead of returning home after one winter at sea, some of the fish feeding around the Faroe Islands may either remain there for another year or head west to the feeding grounds off Greenland in Davis Strait or the Irminger Sea. Both of these groups would return as two- or more sea-winter salmon. As far as those feeding for a second year around the Faroe Islands are concerned, there is some separation between them and those that were there in their first year of sea feeding.

In 1988 S.H. i. Jakupsstovu described how the 40°F sea isotherm forms a boundary between feeding areas used by salmon that have been at sea for less than a year and those that have been there for over a year and that will return to the river as multi-sea-winter salmon. In other words, the larger and older (as far as sea age is concerned) fish will feed in colder water.

A study by D.G. Reddin (1988) suggests that the same also appears to be the case in the salmon's feeding grounds on the west side of the Atlantic. Smolts that will return to Canadian and US rivers do not head off to Greenland. Instead they remain in inshore waters, in the Bay of Fundy and in the Grand Bank and the shallow Flemish Cap area off Labrador. Here those fish that will eventually return to rivers as multi-sea-winter salmon remain for the winter before striking northwards to Davis Strait and the Irminger Sea. The warmer the sea the further they will travel: when average sea temperatures around Greenland are greater than 35°F they will penetrate the fjords of the Greenland coast, when less than 35°F they remain farther out at sea in deeper, slightly warmer water.

Multi-sea-winter fish may thus spend their second sea summer feeding off Greenland. Later in the year they all return to more southerly waters to over-winter (Canadian and US fish off Labrador, European fish off the Faroes and perhaps elsewhere) before the bulk of them run the rivers the following year as two-sea-winter salmon. A small proportion may instead move back, the following summer, to the Greenland feeding areas, then overwinter again off the Faroes or Labrador, before returning to their rivers as three-sea-winter salmon.

The following table illustrates this pattern with fish that all use the Faroes, some of them Greenland also, as feeding grounds:

THE AGE OF SALMON RETURNING FROM THEIR FEEDING GROUNDS

	Those returning as one-sea-winter grilse	Those returning as two-sea-winter salmon		
Spring	all migrate to sea as smolts			
Summer				
Autumn	all migrating to and feeding around Faroes			
Winter				
Spring	complete feeding and return to river	remain round Faroes	OR	go to feed off Greenland
Summer				
Autumn				
Winter				return to Faroes
Spring		complete feeding and return to river		
Summer				
Autumn				

Marine foods

It appears that salmon are opportunistic feeders, taking what is available from the productive, rich arctic and subarctic waters. However, they also tend to concentrate on whatever is most abundant. Some studies have shown that the stomachs of most feeding fish will contain only one prey species and that rarely are more than three prey species found in any one stomach. Studies by J.W.J. Wankowshi, J.E. Thorpe and, in the Baltic, F. Thurow have revealed that the prey is selected on the basis of size, the maximum size (diameter) of prey that a salmon can swallow being related to the gape of the mouth and the spacing of the gill rakers. This works out at about 2.5 per cent of the salmon's body length so that a smolt of 8in would be able to swallow prey with a diameter of about 0.2in (smolts caught feeding off western Scotland soon after entering salt water were found to be feeding on sand-eels up to 2.4in in length and the optimum diameter of 0.2in). It is likely that the ability to find an abundance of food of a suitable size in the first few weeks of marine life determines the later growth rate of the fish and the size that it will have reached when it finally returns to the river – the speed at which it grows determines subsequent sizes of prey that it can eat and the amount that it can eat (gape, gill raker spacing and stomach capacity increasing proportionally with overall size). It also seems that the ability to find an abundance of prey of appropriate size has a great effect on smolt survival in the first few weeks at sea: once the smolts have grown so that they can take significantly bigger prey then they are likely to be able to exploit a wider range of prey species.

Fish have often been shown to be the dominant component in the diet of the salmon. Food species include capelin *Malotus villosus* (up to 86 per cent by weight of food taken off Greenland), sand-eels *Ammodytes* sp., herring *Clupea harengus*, young cod *Gadus morhua*, whiting *Gadus merlangus*, lantern-fish species such as *Benthosoma glaciale* (one study reported finding this species in 83 per cent of stomachs and up to 28 of these little fish per salmon stomach in March), sprats *Sprattus sprattus*, pearlsides *Maurolicus muelleri*, Norway pout *Trisopterus esmarkii* and barracudina *Paralepis coregonides*.

Crustaceans are also a major component of the diet with two groups dominating, amphipod and euphausid shrimps: one study from the north-east Atlantic revealed euphausids (mainly *Parathemisto* species) in one-third of stomachs with 500 or more shrimps crammed into each stomach. Several species of squid have also been found in salmon stomachs, including the species *Brachioteuthis riisei* and *Gonatus fabricii*.

I have finished writing this chapter on Christmas Eve 1994. My mind (like that of most obsessed salmon anglers) frequently wanders off in winter out into the ocean where the salmon are seeking their prey in the cold black depths. Somewhere off the Faroes, or perhaps off Newfoundland, there are a few salmon that I will meet this coming year, or perhaps in 1996. My mind now moves forwards to those encounters, with salmon that have fattened on the richness of the high seas, that have made their way around the oceans and returned home, back to the rivers that I will fish when this dank, cold winter is over. What a series of mysterious and wonderful experiences salmon angling can give!

CHAPTER 3

RETURN FROM THE SEA

> . . . it is still quite impossible to imagine how fish distributed
> over a vast area of open sea and moving about it for a couple of years,
> still can emerge towards the place where they first entered sea water.

B. CARLIN, *Swedish Salmon Research Institute, LFI Meddelande*, 1969, **4**: 14–21

Homing

One of the most fascinating features of salmon behaviour is that they can find their way unerringly from the vastness of the Atlantic Ocean to the river of their birth. And not only the river, but the very tributary of their birth. This has been common knowledge since at least the mid-seventeenth century, for in his sixth edition of *The Compleat Angler*, published in 1676, Izaak Walton noted that:

And as I have told you that Sir Francis Bacon observes, the age of a salmon exceeds not ten years; so let me tell you next, that his growth is very sudden; it is said, that after he is got into the sea, he becomes from a samlet not so big as a gudgeon, to be a salmon, in as short a time as a gosling becomes to be a goose. Much of this has been observed by tying a ribbon, or some known tape or thread, in the tail of some young salmons, which have been taken at weirs as they have swimmed towards the salt water, and then by taking a part of them again with the known mark at the same place at their return from the sea, which is usually about six months after; and the like experiment hath been tried upon young swallows, who have, after six months' absence, been observed to return to the same chimney, there to make their nests and habitations for the summer following: which has inclined many to think, that every salmon usually returns to the same river in which it was bred, as young pigeons taken out of the same dovecote have also been observed to do.

During the twentieth century many extensive tagging experiments have confirmed this behaviour, provided some insight into how the fish detect their own river, and shown also that some do not succeed in homing but stray to other rivers. The first of these was carried out by P.D.H. Malloch, who marked smolts in the River Tay and subsequently found that 1.7 per cent of those marked smolts returned to the Tay, though a very few were also recaptured in other rivers.

A neater experiment was that of B. Carlin. He took eggs from the Swedish river Angermanalven and reared them for two years to smolt stage in a hatchery. The smolts were then taken and held in cages in the River Ume for a month, then the River Lule for one week. Half of these tagged smolts were then released into the Lule, the other half 40 miles away in the River Kalix. The smolts migrated to sea from these rivers. Of those released into the Lule, 150 were subsequently recaptured as salmon in the Lule, but one strayed to the Kalix and six to the Ume. Of those released into the Kalix, 74 were caught as salmon in the Kalix, but three strayed to the Lule and three to another river, the Torne, 30 miles away. In another experiment eggs from the River Indaal were raised and the smolts released in Poland's River Vistula. Fifteen of these were later recaptured as salmon; all returned to the Vistula and none to the Indaal.

W.M. Shearer described a similar experiment involving some Scottish rivers. Fertilized eggs were taken from the River Conon and raised in a hatchery through which water from the Inverness-shire river Garry flowed. When they became smolts they were taken to the River North Esk, tagged and released along with some smolts raised in the North Esk. All these smolts migrated quickly down to the sea. Salmon from both batches of smolts were caught over the next three years in (or at sea just off) the North Esk and none were recorded from either the Conon or Garry.

In yet another experiment smolts were released, not in the river but at sea. These did not return as salmon to their natal river, but on returning from the sea scattered to several rivers.

These, and other similar tagging experiments, have demonstrated that the home river is firmly imprinted in the sensory system of the young salmon just before it leaves the river, as a smolt, for the sea. It is not inherited, nor slowly imprinted in the year or more spent in the river as fry and parr. It is as though the smolt running down the river to the sea, takes a lingering look at the river and says 'I will return'. Take a smolt to a new river and it will return to that new river, not the one in which it grew up. Release smolts out at sea and they will not be imprinted with a home river; on their return from the sea they will wander into any river.

And yet some salmon, a small proportion, do not return to their natal river.

Why not? Surely they are failures? That a small proportion do apparently get lost and wander into other rivers is an advantage to the survival of the salmon as a species. Rivers that have no salmon, but are capable of supporting a salmon population, are colonized by these wanderers whose offspring will later return to the newly colonized river and establish a permanent stock there. That is how, when the last great Ice Age retreated from northern Europe and from the north-eastern USA and Canada some 10,000 years ago, freeing almost all of the present-day Atlantic salmon rivers from permanent ice, these rivers were colonized. Had there been no wanderers then most of our present-day salmon rivers would have no salmon. That will be how, should global temperatures rise, rivers that currently have no salmon in Greenland and northern Canada may be colonized by salmon. That is how formerly polluted rivers, such as the Thames and Tees, acquired a run of salmon once their estuarine pollution was cleared sufficiently to allow some wanderers to pass upstream. That is how rivers such as the Rhine, Meuse, Mersey and Trent will become colonized once pollution and dams are cleared to allow wanderers to move upstream: even now wanderers are constantly trying to enter these rivers.

Of course we attempt to accelerate the process by artificially stocking rivers, but there is no real need to do so. If the river is suitable, the wandering salmon can do the job quite efficiently. Indeed, to say that some returning salmon become lost is wrong. It is much better to say that some fish will not 'home', but are deliberate colonizers of new rivers.

Often salmon are faithful not only to the river system, but also to one part of a river system such as a tributary. I see this in the salmon river closest to my home in north-west England, the Ribble. The Ribble has a major tributary, the Hodder, their confluence being about 15 miles above the tide and the salmon spawning (almost) entirely in the Ribble and Hodder above the confluence. The Ribble salmon run begins as early as February and reaches a peak in August and September. By contrast salmon rarely enter the Hodder before May and the run peaks in October and November. Ribble salmon are quite long, slender fish, whereas Hodder fish of equal weight are shorter and deeper. So different are these two populations that an experienced angler fishing below the confluence can say, with great confidence, 'This fish would have run the Ribble,' or 'This is a Hodder salmon.'

The Ribble system has two other tributaries. One, the Douglas, flows into the south side of the estuary; the other, the Calder, enters the Ribble about two-thirds of a mile below the Hodder–Ribble confluence. Both of these rivers flow through industrial Lancashire and they have been dreadfully polluted throughout this century. So much so that they have frequently been responsible, by offloading excessive amounts of pollutants into the main river, for the deaths of huge numbers of salmon destined for the upper Ribble and Hodder. Since 1980 pollution entering the Calder has been significantly reduced; there has also been some decline of pollutants entering the Douglas. Consequently salmon are now running the Calder and have been reported spawning in its headstreams. Occasional salmon are also attempting to run the Douglas. Where did these colonizing salmon come from? They are wanderers or colonizers, some of that tiny proportion of fish that do not home to their natal rivers – perhaps they are from Hodder or Ribble stock.

Finding their way

A salmon may use one of three possible systems to find its way from river to marine feeding areas, from one marine feeding area to the next, and then back to its home river.

The first of these is homing (also called piloting), where the fish follows some sort of scent signal produced by its home river, rather as an aircraft pilot will use radio and radar signals sent from his destination airport to guide him into land. That salmon do home is well known, for they can detect their own river by its scent (see below). Such a signal is, however, of limited use, functioning only when the salmon has already come within reach of the homing signal and already close to home.

The second system that a salmon might use is orienteering, where the fish finds its way around the ocean using a map, compass and landmarks (more correctly, seamarks), just as orienteers follow a previously unknown course. If salmon do orienteer, the question that we need to answer is, what compass, what map and what seamarks do they use?

The third method is navigation. Navigation is the method used by ocean-going yachtsmen who, when far out at sea, use a compass, a calendar to give precise date, a watch to give precise time and the position of the sun and stars to fix their precise position. This position is plotted on the chart, and the following day another series of readings used to give the next 'fix'. Distance travelled, estimated time of arrival, and compass bearing that must be taken to remain on course can then be computed. If salmon do navigate, the question we need to ask is, again, what compass, what chart or map, what calendar and watch? And can salmon measure the position of the sun and, perhaps, stars?

We tend to think of the Atlantic Ocean as being a uniform, featureless mass of water. And it is when we stand on the deck of a ship or fly over it in an aircraft. But to creatures living in or on the sea is it not. The North Atlantic is a complex system of currents. The best known of these is the North Atlantic

Current or Drift that starts in the Gulf of Mexico, passes off the eastern seaboard of the USA, and then moves across the Atlantic in a north-easterly direction to wash against the shores of Iceland, the Faroes, northern Norway, the British Isles, western France and Spain. It is with this current that the larval eel makes its way to European rivers and against which the adult eel migrates back to the Sargasso Sea. If we consider each of the currents of the North Atlantic as a series of branching roadways, with side-roads based on particularly weaker or strong bands of current, then, provided that the salmon has an in-built detailed map of these currents and a compass, it can orienteer its way throughout the ocean. But there are other possible signposts that the salmon might use when orienteering.

Though vast, the North Atlantic is bounded by an intricate coastline, with scattered islands and submarine ridges. As we saw in the last chapter, all the marine feeding grounds of the salmon are close to such land features. Perhaps they, too, are integral features on the map used by the orienteering salmon. One piece of evidence that the complex of land and islands are important features comes from New Zealand, where the salmon was introduced but failed to produce a sea-going migratory population. It has been suggested that those salmon smolts that ran to sea from New Zealand rivers were unable to orienteer in the South Pacific because there were not enough landmarks for them to use (they may, of course, not have had a map!).

Another series of seamarks used by the orienteering salmon is likely to be variations in the salinity of the ocean. To us the ocean is simply salty water. But its degree of saltiness varies widely and with a degree of geographical constancy. Pacific salmon (and almost certainly our Atlantic salmon, though I have been unable to discover similar tests on this species) can detect changes of salinity of 0.0005 molar concentrations, equivalent to 0.006oz of salt in a pint of water. Full-strength sea water contains about 0.7oz of salt in a pint, but salinity falls sharply close to the coastline where rivers are disgorging fresh water. By tasting the saltiness of the sea water the salmon may be able to locate itself quite precisely on the map of the North Atlantic.

Sea temperatures also vary in a fairly regular seasonal pattern across the Atlantic, albeit with some variation from year to year. We do know that salmon will move to feeding grounds off Greenland only when the sea temperature has reached 40°F (p. 72). Are variations of sea temperature also signposts used by orienteering salmon?

So salmon are capable of detecting the sort of oceanic features that we can map. The salmon may, indeed, have such a map, although it is not, of course, a map as we know it, for it is inside the sensory cells of the salmon's brain. Each salmon inherits its map in the genes that came from its parents in the fertilized egg. Such an in-built map is not unique in the animal world. A young cuckoo can find its way from Europe to Africa and then back again the following spring without being shown the way by its parents. Using its in-built map it follows a precise track that has been used by generations of cuckoos. So, too, does the salmon. But to orienteer the salmon also needs a compass.

We use our compass and the earth's magnetic field to work out compass directions. The north end of the magnetized iron compass needle points to the earth's magnetic North Pole, and the south end of the compass needle points in the opposite direction, to the magnetic South Pole. We can now take a quite precise bearing using this information. It was in the 1980s that T.P. Quinn discovered that salmon can respond to the earth's magnetic field as though they had a compass. He shifted the magnetic field around by 90° and found that salmon shifted their swimming direction by 90°. He used sockeye salmon, but more recently this ability has also been demonstrated with Atlantic salmon. It was then necessary to locate the compass within the salmon. As K.P. Able commented in *Animal Migration, Orientation & Navigation* (1980), 'for magnetic-compass orientation the animal must have some sort of paramagnetic material which responds to the earth's magnetic field or deposits of permanently magnetised material in its tissue.'

As early as 1978 it had been shown that the honeybee has a magnetite (magnetized iron) compass in its abdomen, and that the bee uses this to orienteer when it is away from the close vicinity of the hive. In 1982 similar deposits of magnetite were found in yellowfin tuna, a fish that can orienteer with great precision over vast distances through the ocean. Then in 1990 three British scientists, A. Moore, S.M. Freak and I.M. Thomas, reported the presence of magnetic particles in the lateral line and head of the Atlantic salmon. These magnetic particles in the parts of the salmon body most sensitive to its surroundings suggest that the sensory system is linked to the earth's magnetic field and that the magnetic compass is automatically connected, via the brain with its in-built map, to the engine – the skeleton, muscles and fins. So when it is on its long journeys the salmon is constantly being fed information that tells it precisely where it is on the Atlantic map.

Besides orienteering, many migrating animals can also navigate. Many species of small birds migrate at night, using the major constellations as their guide. Should thick cloud suddenly obliterate the sky when they are in mid-flight then they may be caused to drift far off course by the wind and make landfall far from their intended destination. On the next clear night, however, they can use the stars to navigate back on course. The navigational aid used by the salmon is the sun. Salmon have been shown to be able to detect the azimuth or altitude of the sun. This piece of information can be used by sailors, together with compass, calendar and watch, to pinpoint a precise position. To do this the sun must be seen, and in the thick cloud that prevails so often over the North Atlantic this is no easy matter. The cloud scatters what light gets through so that the exact position of the sun cannot be discerned. However, the salmon can also detect polarized light: light that penetrates the cloud directly from the sun without being scattered. So even on cloudy days the salmon can detect precisely the position of the sun.

We have already seen that the salmon has a form of compass and an in-built chart of the North Atlantic. All that remains is the need for a calendar and accurate watch. A calendar is based on day length: virtually all animals and many plants living in temperate and arctic latitudes have a precise calendar based on day length as discerned by the eye and analysed in the brain. A similar system can also compute the time of the day, based on the changing altitude of the sun in the sky.

So the salmon has all it needs to navigate as well as orienteer its way through the high seas. The two systems work side by side. Earlier I noted T.P. Quinn's work on the sockeye salmon's ability to detect the earth's magnetic field and alter direction if that should be changed experimentally. Quinn also found that if the sun can be seen by a salmon (when the sun is above the horizon) the salmon's solar navigation will override its orienteering system. This is advantageous for precise route finding, for the position of magnetic North Pole is constantly shifting, by about half a degree every three years – not much in figures but a considerable distance over a period of a few generations of salmon. It seems therefore that the salmon uses all the methods of orienteering and navigation at its disposal, that some override others, and that if one cannot be used then the salmon can use another. So a one-sea-winter salmon is compelled, by its internal control system, to move from Faroese to Greenland feeding areas, or a two-sea-winter salmon that has been feeding off Greenland must return to its native river. The migration is quite automatic. The brain of the fish knows exactly where it is and will instruct the body of the fish, using its in-built orienteering and navigation ability, to move on. Thus, from a loose shoal of salmon feeding in the Davies Straits, those that were born in the Miramichi or Restigouche will automatically separate and head southwards, while those that were bred in Tay or Tweed or Namsen will head eastwards. And back they go towards their natal rivers.

When the salmon reaches shallow, offshore waters other clues guide it finally home. Observations suggest that most salmon reach the coast at certain 'landfalls' and then follow the coast to the immediate vicinity of their own river. For instance most of the salmon destined for the rivers of northern Ireland make landfalls in large shoals close to Malin Head. From here they move along the coast, each river receiving its run of fish as the shoal passes by. Many fish destined for the rivers of eastern Scotland make a landfall off the coast of north-east England and move northwards to their natal rivers. Great shoals of salmon have been seen lying off St Bees Head and off the Blackpool coast in north-west England: fish destined for the Solway rivers and north-west English rivers respectively. Hebridean fish appear to make landfall at the Butt of Lewis, the shoals moving along the chain of islands. Alas, all too many of these 'coasting' salmon are intercepted by nets set at right angles to the coastline, for many of these ancient routes are well known.

The taste and smell of home

The salmon is almost there. Having made its way back through the deep ocean and then along the coastline our salmon is nearly home. But now it must identify its own river. This it does entirely by the smell or taste of its natal river; the smell or taste that was implanted in it during those last few days before it set out to sea. That each river has its own particular scent and that this scent is used by homecoming salmon are not new ideas, for they were proposed by Frank Buckland as long ago as 1873 in *British Fishes*:

> Doubtless, to the fish each river has got its own smell . . . When the salmon is coming in from the sea he smells about till he scents the water of his own river. This guides him in the right direction, and he has only to follow up the scent, in other words 'to follow his nose', to get up into freshwater, i.e., if he is in a travelling humour. Thus a salmon coming up from the sea into the Bristol Channel would get a smell of water, meeting him; 'I am a Wye salmon,' he would say to himself. 'This is not the Wye water; it's the wrong tap, it's the Usk. I must go a few miles further on,' and he gets up steam again. When I see an old gentleman sniffing at the tops of port wine decanters at dessert, I always think of *Salmo salar* looking for his own river.

But we now know a little more about this ability of salmon to home on to the scent of their rivers. Experiments have demonstrated that salmon in which the olfactory lobes have been destroyed or separated from the brain are incapable of homing to their natal river. In another experiment (with Pacific coho salmon) some smolts were imprinted, just before migration, to water containing a synthetic chemical called morpholine. These imprinted salmon homed in to water containing morpholine, but fish that had not been imprinted with morpholine as smolts moved away from the chemical. So it is not necessarily a natural chemical to which the smolts and salmon respond.

In recent years many rivers have been messed about with by man. One bit of fiddling involves the transfer of water from one river to another and this can affect the homing salmon. For instance, in the late 1960s and early 1970s the River Lune had a big run of salmon whilst the River Wyre (which shares an outer estuary with the Lune) had a small and declining run. In the 1970s a system was developed to use the Wyre as a route for diverted Lune water. Water was pumped from the Lune to the Wyre, and allowed to flow down the Wyre before being abstracted again several miles downstream. Many salmon destined for the Lune, having detected the scent of Lune in the Wyre, ran the Wyre instead.

We do not know exactly what the 'scent' of a river actually is. One suggestion is that the scent consists of chemicals – perhaps a 'pheromone', a chemical message – released by parr into the river to attract homing salmon. One observation on the Apple River, Nova Scotia, seemed to confirm this. In 1932 a dam that prevented salmon moving into the headwaters was removed. However, salmon failed to colonize these headwaters. Then salmon fry were put into the headwaters and salmon immediately colonized them. It was argued that those fry produced the chemical necessary to attract salmon. However, salmon might well have colonized that year without the presence of introduced fry: it is an erroneous example of 'cause-and-effect'. There are far more examples of salmon recolonizing a river or part of a river quickly despite the absence of fry or parr. Further, despite detailed investigation, no chemical has been found to be produced by parr that is specific, in type or concentration, to one particular river.

The scent is likely to be a complex one, and perhaps a combination of chemicals from the plants and animals living in the river system together with chemicals leached into the river water from the surrounding land. Evidence of this comes from a study carried out on Nova Scotia's Moser River by A.G. Huntsman. Huntsman tagged large numbers of smolts leaving two branches of the Moser. The majority (80 per cent of returning adults) eventually returned to their natal streams, but after making landfall on the Nova Scotia coast many were found in the estuaries of other rivers – except one. That one was St Mary River, a river whose catchment is completely different, both geologically and agriculturally, from the others. The scent of St Mary River was so clearly different from the one implanted in the smolts (Moser) that they could distinguish and dismiss that one immediately. But it took time for them finally to decide that the Moser was home, and 20 per cent came to the wrong decision.

Return to the river and the first upstream run

Having reached the mouth of their natal river salmon may move quickly from salt water to fresh or they may tarry in the estuary. Observations have shown that, in many estuaries, salmon will move upstream with each tide, but if conditions are not suitable for moving further upstream, they will fall back as the tide ebbs. They may do this for several days, even weeks. But then, when river conditions are right, they swim up the estuary with the flowing tide and, instead of falling back on the ebb, continue on into the fresh water.

What are the right conditions for salmon to run from estuary into the river?

Spate rivers

Many rivers are spate streams and, following prolonged droughts, much of their length may be shallow trickles through which the salmon cannot pass. Salmon usually run into such rivers when the river is in spate, when the water is clearing, falling, but still high. This behaviour has been known for over 150 years, for in 1843 D.S. Williamson noted that:

It is well known that salmon do not travel in dry weather. Before they ascend a river they require 'a leading water'. They persist in hovering about the estuary, ascending with the tide but, unless there be a fresh in the river, returning with it and, what is very strange, however low the river may have sunk, no sooner does it become quietened by a heavy fall of rain, than they rush up in shoals, run up with great veracity, and are taken many miles from the sea in the course of a few hours.

This effect can most clearly be seen in the tiny spate streams of the west coast of Scotland and the Hebrides, and some tiny rivers in the west of Ireland. I was once fishing a small Donegal stream. Fishing! The first eight days of my visit had been fishless, as a summer drought had virtually eliminated the river below the lough, which was so low that the outflow was a trickle. Then, throughout the night, it poured down. At dawn the river was a raging flood but by midday was falling and clearing quickly. Suddenly small summer salmon and sea trout began to run in their hundreds: everywhere I looked, fish were breaking the surface as they forged their way upstream. I fished 400 yards of river and had

16 salmon and 29 sea trout between 1.30 and 10.45 p.m. Two days later the river was back at summer level and not one fish ran through.

An understanding of the importance of a sudden spate on salmon waiting in the estuary to run the river resulted in the record catch of salmon on the Grimersta River in the Outer Hebrides on 23 August 1888 when, in nine hours, A.M. Naylor caught 54 fish. Grimersta is only a very short river, just over a mile long, draining a chain of lochs, Faoghail an Tuim, Faoghail Charrasan, Faoghail Kirrival, Airigh na h-Airde and, at the top of the system, Langavat, the biggest Hebridean loch. Water can be held back in these lochs behind artificial weirs and then, when salmon are congregating in the sea loch Ceann Hulavig and waiting to run the river, released to create an artificial spate. It was following such an artificial spate that Mr Naylor took his record catch, and during the six-day fishing week three rods took 333 salmon. Yet had it not been possible to manufacture a spate not one fish might have been taken, for the fish would still have been waiting in the sea loch!

In many rivers salmon do not need a spate, for they can pass from estuary into fresh water every day of the year. This is generally true of big rivers, such as the Spey, Dee, Tay and Tweed in Scotland, the Wye and Severn of Wales, the Namsen, Tana and Alta of Norway, and the Miramichi and Restigouche in Canada. Salmon can often pass into the deeper lower reaches of much smaller rivers until they come to an obstacle. On the lowest of summer water conditions I have seen grilse passing upstream from Ireland's Foyle estuary into the Mourne and from the Mourne into the Strule. On the River Bush they will creep in with the tide and pass upstream to Bushmills town. And on the Ribble they will pass the town of Preston in a spring tide and creep upstream to the Hodder, Calder and Ribble confluences no matter how low the river. The later in the season, the more determined are the fish to run, no matter how low the flow. On the Spey I saw several silver fresh-run salmon caught 56 miles above the tide in July 1982 and 1983 when, following prolonged droughts, the river was 'showing its bones'. Over several evenings in September 1994 on the River Nith, with the river height 18in below the gauge at Thornhill, Dave Evans and I watched large numbers of salmon swimming up the shrunken flow. Larger fish, which might have scaled 25lb or more, turned back at one shallow run, but others kept on going, splashing their way through the thin water. Many times I have caught salmon that are running the river in low water, these fish having bruised bellies where they have grazed themselves when passing through rocky shallows. So whilst salmon seem to prefer to run on high water, they will run when the river is low until they reach water that is too shallow to pass through.

Wind, tide and temperature

Analysis in 1953 by F.R. Hayes demonstrated that high tides backed by strong onshore winds encourage salmon to run from salt to fresh water. Spring tides are those that occur on full and new moon. They rise much higher up the estuary than neap tides (which occur at half moon). They also tend to hold up the downstream flow so that on the ebb there is a short downstream surge of fresh water. This effect is greatly increased with onshore gales that push the spring tides higher. On several clear water rivers in north-west England I have watched salmon in freshwater pools at the head of the tide after the ebb where there were none before the flood, and noted more salmon (even when the river is at summer level) on a spring tide backed by strong winds:

NUMBER OF TIDES		NUMBERS OF SALMON COUNTED	
		before the tide	after the tide
Neaps	47	29	31
Spring	62	72	194

Extreme water temperatures can also inhibit salmon from entering the river from the sea. When the temperature is very low (less than about 40°F) or very high (greater than 68°F) salmon seem to prefer to remain in the sea rather than run the river.

There is one other feature that affects the timing of salmon runs from sea to fresh water: genetically controlled behaviour. In most rivers salmon have one, sometimes two, and occasionally three quite distinct running periods (though these do overlap). For example, some rivers have a small spring run, a very large summer run and a moderately sized autumn run, whilst others may have no spring run, a tiny summer run and a big autumn run. In the latter no salmon will enter the river in spring, no matter how conducive the river conditions are for running.

If the salmon are ready to run into a small spate stream in July they will not run unless there is enough water for them to do so. They may move into and out of the estuary with every tide but be unable to penetrate the fresh water. Eventually heavy rain falls and there is a spate. Yet anglers might be quite disappointed that the run appears not so prolific as they expected. 'There is water . . . where are the fish?' It seems that the longer salmon have to wait out in the estuary or just offshore in the sea before they can run, the higher their mortality and the fewer of them survive to run. Of course, if there are commercial nets they will take a higher proportion of the fish than they would have, had the salmon been able to run as soon as they reached the estuary. But also it seems that if the fish cannot run when they are physiologically prepared to do so, many die and become food for the crabs. (We will describe the timing of salmon runs in the next chapter.)

The length of run

How far do salmon travel on their run from the sea into the river? The answer to this depends on the river, and also varies from salmon to salmon and upon the timing of the run. For instance, the tiny Cumbrian Esk is a clear water spate stream that flows into the Irish Sea through a complex estuary at Ravenglass. In autumn, salmon will move from the estuary into the river in low water conditions, but be unable to pass further than the first two pools above the tide, Corner and Donald's pools. Thus the initial upstream movement is only a few hundred yards. However, in a clearing spate I have spotted fresh-run fish that have come in from the estuary and moved upstream about four miles.

By contrast the Spey, Tay and Dee are huge rivers and there is no barrier just above the estuary to their initial run. Using radio-tagged salmon on the Tay, John Webb found that, 'Of the 22 [tagged] fish that entered the main Tay, 18 moved upstream without significant delay except in the area of the Perth bridges, where delays of *ca* 3–25 minutes were observed. Most fish passed the Almondmouth area within 8 hours of release' (1987 data in 1989 *SFRRept*), and that fish usually 'moved through the lower reaches without any evidence of significant delay at potential obstacles such as Stanley weir or Campsie Linn' (1988 data in 1990 *SFRRept*). John Webb found that fish that entered the river earlier in the season moved further upstream on their initial run, before settling in one pool, than salmon that entered the river later in the year.

A similar study on the Spey by Robert Laughton showed a similar pattern, fish running quickly upriver from the estuary before stopping and making further advances. Again, salmon that enter the river early in the season make longer initial runs than those entering the river later in the year (Fig. 10). This initial migration (of about 50 miles) takes 10–14 days for early-season salmon and (in a journey of up to about 12 miles) up to five days for late-season fish.

It is clear from such timings that the fish are not swimming continuously upstream in this initial run, for tagging has shown that salmon can swim upstream at maximum speeds of up to 10 m.p.h. with an average of 4.5–6 m.p.h. Size of fish and flow of river seem to have no significant effect on this speed provided that the depth of the water is not a barrier to the fish, i.e. the fish can swim through. If, however, the fish kept those speeds up for many hours they would all find themselves jammed together in the headstreams of

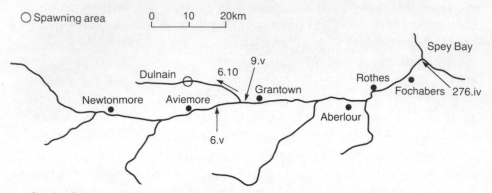

A spring fish, tagged 27 April; ran 80km (50 miles) in about 10 days, remained in resident lie to 6 October before running R. Dulnain to spawn.

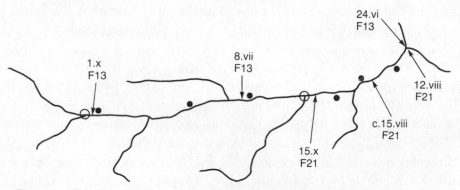

Two grilse: F13 tagged 24 June, ran 80km (50 miles) in about 14 days, remained in resident lies to late September when ran a further 40km (25 miles) before spawning. F21 tagged 12 August, ran 15km (9 miles) in about 3 days and remained there to mid-October when it ran 40km (25 miles) to its spawning site.

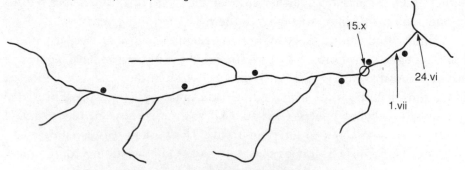

A summer salmon, tagged 24 June, ran 10km (6 miles) in 7 days, remained in resident lies to early October when ran 15km (9 miles) to spawning grounds.

Fig. 10 – The upstream migration of a spring salmon, summer salmon and two grilse through the River Spey (data after R. Laughton, 1989)

the river! If the early-run Spey salmon kept up those speeds they would reach 50 miles upstream in about 10 hours, not the 10–14 days shown by tagging, and the late-run would cover their initial run of 12 miles in less than three hours, not the five days shown by tagging. This suggests that, in even big rivers where salmon can pass with relative ease, they travel for an average of no more than one or two hours each day, resting in between running and also breaking the time spent running with rest periods.

Such rates of upstream movement are much slower than many anglers have imagined. In the 1970s and early 1980s, when the Spey estuary was still heavily netted, we anglers on the upper-middle Spey around Grantown always looked to Tuesday, Wednesday and Thursday as being potentially the best period of the week, for we reckoned that by then fish that had run through the estuary the previous weekend (when the nets were off) would arrive. The following catch records, from 15 weeks' fishing, seem to confirm this:

	Monday	Tuesday	Wednesday	Thursday	Friday	Saturday
Salmon	1	3	11	14	9	2
Sea trout	26	39	84	72	49	16

In fact, if we anglers 50 miles up the Spey were benefiting from the weekend removal of the estuary nets, then it was not the previous weekend's fish that we were catching, but those from the weekend before that!

John Bettaney told me of a similar observation on the Aberdeenshire Dee in spring. If he heard that a large number of salmon had arrived in beats 5–6 miles downstream of where he was fishing, just below Banchory, then he expected them to arrive with him the next or next-but-one day. They did, invariably!

When salmon are making their initial run they will bypass obstacles such as waterfalls, weirs, dams with fish passes and stretches of extremely fast, rough 'white water' with relative ease provided that the water temperature is not too low: generally 40–41°F is considered critical (see p. 86).

One fascinating example of the importance of water temperature on slowing down the initial upstream run of salmon is the River Cassley, where there are three falls or cataracts in succession, separated by slower pools (see Fig. 11). Salmon will run the lower stretches of the river in late winter but are unable to ascend from Round Pool to Cemetery and Crow's Nest Pools until the water temperature reaches 45°F. They are unable to go further, to the Falls Pool, through the cataract around Fir Tree Island, until the water temperature has reached 48°F, and they are unable to reach the upper stretches above

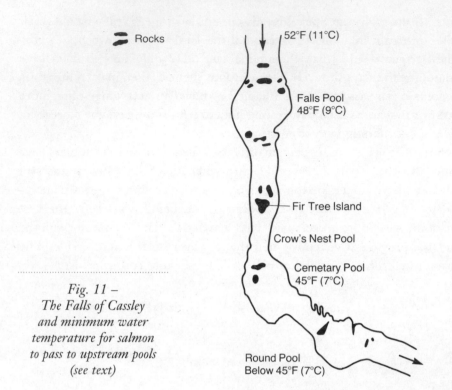

Fig. 11 –
The Falls of Cassley
and minimum water
temperature for salmon
to pass to upstream pools
(see text)

Falls Pool until the water temperature has reached 52°F. The effect of this can be seen from the average date of first salmon caught at various points on the river (from data in D. H. Mills and N. Graesser, *The Salmon Rivers of Scotland*, and other published reports):

Round Pool	6 February
Cemetery Pool	4 April
Falls Pool	28 April

Clearly anglers fishing the Cassley above the falls in spring must know that the water temperature is high enough for fish to reach them if they are to stand a chance of catching one! In summer this problem does not arise, for with a water temperature in excess of 52°F the fish can swim easily, on their run from the sea, through the falls.

So this initial run from the sea to the pool in which the salmon will rest before making their final move to their spawning areas is a continuous one, with breaks in between. Salmon anglers fishing every day on one beat on a small river might be able to observe this pattern. For instance, on

30 September 1991 there were reports of the arrival of a big run of large salmon in the Ribble above Preston and, three days later, of the arrival of a run of big fish, presumably the same ones, 12 miles upstream at the Hodder–Ribble confluence. On 3–4 October there was no sign of these fish three miles upstream from the confluence in the beat that I was fishing. They arrived on the 5th: every pool was well stocked with these pristine silver, two-sea-winter salmon weighing from 14 to 26lb. At least some of them remained in the lower Hodder pools for four days, and then they were gone. Save for resident fish (see below) that would spawn in this part of the river, the lower Hodder was fishless. That run had gone through.

I believe that the vast majority of salmon caught by anglers are on their initial run: usually not running fish, fish that are actively swimming up the river, but fish that have pulled in on their initial run. When swimming upstream salmon may pause for a few seconds or minutes and they are likely to take a fly. When halting for longer periods, from a matter of only hours to a few days (as in the Hodder example given above), salmon are likely to take the fly, but they are most likely to take immediately after and just before continuing on their run. Once they have reached the end of their initial run and are waiting to move to their spawning area, the fish seem to 'go off the take', and the longer they have been settled in their resident lies – where they might wait for several months in the case of spring-run or summer-run fish – the less likely are they to be caught by legitimate means.

The reason for this is almost certainly hormonal. M. Fontaine discovered that secretion of hormones from the thyroid gland fluctuates, being higher in running salmon and lower in resting or resident salmon. These hormones affect the metabolism of the salmon: its alertness and energy production. The more thyroid hormones, the more alert the salmon (a migrating salmon needs to be alert) and the more likely is it to respond to the angler's fly. Once in its resident lie the thyroid secretion falls and the salmon is in a state of torpor and unlikely to respond to the angler's fly (see Fig. 12). We will return to this thyroid hypothesis and consider its further implications in Chapter 5.

The salmon has now completed its first run. In a small spate stream this run might have taken a few hours or even less: for salmon running the Barvas River in the Outer Hebrides the run is barely 200 yards into Loch Mor Barvas. In a big river this run might last for several days or weeks and be broken by resting periods lasting up to a day or more. The fish now take up a resident lie, usually in a big deep pool or, if there is a lake on the river system, in the lake usually close to the inflowing spawning streams (p. 164). Here the salmon will remain until it is time for that last movement to the spawning grounds. Salmon that

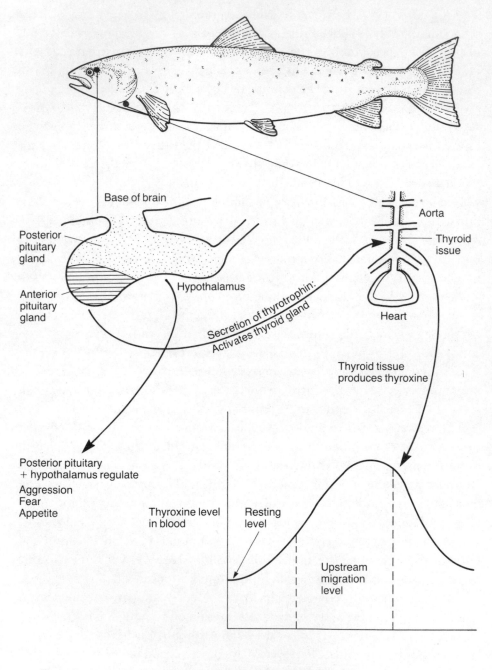

Base of brain

Posterior
pituitary
gland

Anterior
pituitary
gland

Hypothalamus

Aorta

Thyroid
issue

Secretion of thyrotrophin:
Activates thyroid gland

Heart

Thyroid tissue
produces thyroxine

Posterior pituitary
+ hypothalamus regulate

Aggression
Fear
Appetite

Thyroxine level
in blood

Resting
level

Upstream
migration
level

Thyroxine increases alertness and energy levels in salmon. When thyroxine rises to above
resting level, either side of a spell of migration, salmon are more likely to take the fly.

Fig. 12 – The thyroid hypothesis

have been resident in lakes will move into their own natal streams feeding the lake. Salmon that have been resident in deep river pools may spawn in the main river close to that pool or travel, often some distance, into small, shallow side streams, again usually the ones in which they were born. Their journey is now over.

Preparing for spawning

Associated with this final movement to the spawning ground is a great increase in hormones produced by the thyroid gland and reproductive organs. For not only is the salmon on the move again, requiring an increase of energy production and alertness, but it is preparing for spawning. Already its eggs or milt will be developed and it might be possible (if such a fish is caught) to express milt or eggs by gently massaging the belly of the fish. Such 'ripe' salmon are readily caught. But they should gently be returned to the river to contribute to the production of smolts.

Moving by night or day

There are two main patterns of salmon movement through a river. If the river is not high, following heavy rain or snow-melt, but there is no barrier to prevent them passing upstream, movement is mainly crepuscular or nocturnal, from about sunset to dawn. In rivers north of the Arctic Circle, where there may be 24 hours of light in summer, the salmon appear to run from late evening to early morning (about 10 p.m. to 8 a.m.) when the midnight sun is lowest in the sky. It is interesting to note that on the Alta River angling is prohibited between the hours of 12 noon and 6 p.m., the period when few salmon are moving upstream. It is also the period of the day when anglers are least likely to catch a salmon!

Earlier I described how, in low water conditions, Dave Evans and I watched salmon, some of them over 20lb in weight, moving in the late evening through very shallow water on the Nith. On many rivers, salmon that have spent the day resting in a deep pool will move into the neck of the pool in the late afternoon and then run upstream at last light. On three small rivers that I know well I have often watched salmon leave the neck of a deep pool, move upstream into the shallow run and then, finding that they cannot pass through to the next pool, splash their way back downstream. Because these salmon are often such good takers of the fly, this evening run into the pool necks is perhaps the most bountiful for the salmon angler when the river is low. Similarly, but less frequently, at dawn. At dawn on 31 October 1982, the last day of the fishing season, I saw a big salmon move in the neck of a pool and then splash its way upstream through extremely shallow water (we had had no rain for three weeks). I ran 300yd to the top of the run and dangled my fly across the narrow tail of the small pool above the run. Eleven minutes later what was almost certainly that same salmon took my fly. It weighed 15lb, and its belly was red raw from being scraped on the sharp boulders. It was a bright silver fish and had presumably made its entire run from tide to where I caught it (over 19 miles) in low water, creeping upstream for a few miles each night.

The only things that prevent salmon running at night are major obstacles: dams and waterfalls. These they will leap only in good light, for they need to focus clearly on the lip of the obstacle they are going to leap before they can make a successful attempt (see p. 22).

If a river is high, following heavy rain or snow-melt, salmon may move upstream throughout the day, but the timing depends on the quality of the water and that depends on the stage of the spate. It rains heavily and the river begins to rise. Initially this rise may be of clear water. In small rivers this clear water rise may be for less than 6in, on some big rivers it may be for 1ft or more (once, on the Namsen, I witnessed a clear water rise of 4ft). Salmon will run in this clear water rise no matter what the time of day. However, with continuing rain the rise continues but usually becomes more coloured and dirty. The spate washes clay and silt, leaves, logs, weed, dead sheep and cattle and a host of other rubbish downstream – everything that has accumulated on the bed and banks of the river and its tributaries since the last flood. From my observations, salmon tend not to move upstream in this stage of the spate and, instead, shelter in slacker pieces of water away from the main flow. This is to be expected, for if salmon tried to weather a dirty water rise in the main flow they would risk damage to their gills from the gritty particles being washed downstream. Once the river begins to fall then salmon will start to move.

It has been said that salmon will not run in dirty water and, from the salmon angling point of view, that dirty or peaty water sickens them and they will not take the fly. This is absolute rubbish! Just before they start or just after they complete a run, or as they pull in for a break in their journey, they readily take the fly. Salmon will continue to run the river through the day until the river runs clear and low. Then they will revert to crepuscular and nocturnal running.

There is one qualification to this pattern of high water through the day, and low water through the night upstream migration. And that is in late-run fish that enter the river late in the year and run quickly through to the spawning grounds. They appear to run no matter what the state of the river by day and by night. Frequently, in my home rivers (which have mostly an autumn run of fish), when watching salmon spawning in December, I have seen late-arrival fish hurtling through, and watched sea-liced salmon, which had obviously not been in the river very long, being chased away by fish that had been in the river for several weeks.

Thus the salmon orienteers and navigates and finally homes in precisely to its spawning stream, and almost always the one in which it was born three or more years earlier. How does the salmon, with its tiny brain, achieve so much? For it has not been taught as would a sailor or aircraft pilot, or been shown how to use map, watch and compass as would a boy or girl scout going for their orienteering badge. It is solely in its genes: the ability to migrate accurately at quite precise times is an inherited behavioural character of the salmon, just as redd-cutting and quivering are essential inherited behavioural characters in mating salmon. The salmon does not have to think, or reason, or calculate. It is an automatic behaviour. The salmon brain decided that it must guide the feeding salmon, way out in the ocean, back to breed in its own river – and back it goes.

CHAPTER 4

GRILSE OR SALMON?

The grilse is a much less fish in general, it is much smaller at the tail
in proportion and it has a much more swallow tail, much more forked;
it is smaller at the head, sharper at the point of the nose, and
generally a grilse is more bright in the scale than a salmon.

A note written in 1884 by Mr Johnstone, in
F. DAY, *British & Irish Salmonidae*, 1887

L ast night I was demonstrating the tying of some new salmon flies to members
of a fishing club. During the mid-evening break I overheard one angler
detailing his catches when on holiday in Ireland last summer: 'Just a
few sea trout and grilse. No salmon.'

It is quite incredible that, while so many anglers consider salmon to be a
greater prize than grilse, they do not know the difference between a salmon
and a grilse, neither can they distinguish a grilse from a salmon! We see this
most strikingly when it comes to recording their catches. I fish the
Aberdeenshire Dee every August; a time when the river is usually full of grilse
and with a few silver, fresh-run salmon that are not grilse. As do all anglers, on
arrival I rush straight into the fishing hut and scrutinize the fishing return
sheets for the previous weeks. Several small salmon, weighing between four
and six pounds, will have been taken. They are recorded under the heading
GRILSE. The next column is headed SALMON, and under this are listed a
few fish weighing between six and a half and nine pounds. The inference, or
belief, held by anglers is, therefore, that a fish weighing up to six pounds is a
grilse, and anything larger is a salmon.

But what is a grilse and how does it differ from a salmon? How big and how
small do grilse and salmon grow? Why such a wide variation in weight? There
are patterns of salmon and grilse runs into rivers, from river to river and from
year to year; what are these and why? This chapter attempts to answer these
questions, questions that I am often asked when I visit fishing clubs or am talking to other anglers at the waterside.

What is a grilse?

First, all grilse are salmon, but all salmon are not grilse! Let us immediately and quickly dispel any thoughts of snobbery or meaningful evaluation of worth based on size. The capture of a grilse is as meritorious as the capture of a non-grilse salmon. Perhaps more so, for there is some evidence that the easiest fish to catch are spring-run, non-grilse salmon, and that the most difficult fish to catch are summer grilse. And as far as the table is concerned, a grilled piece of grilse is as delicious as a piece of non-grilse salmon.

When one year's smolt production goes to sea in spring, some will spend just one winter at sea and return home the following summer or autumn, having spent about one year to 18 months away. They are grilse or 1+SW salmon (SW = sea-winter, 1SW = one-sea-winter, + = a few extra months after that one winter). Some of the smolts may remain out at sea for two winters and return home as 2SW salmon or, if they have remained in the sea for some months beyond their second sea winter, 2+SW salmon. Others may remain out at sea for three winters and return home as 3SW or 3+SW salmon. A very few fish remain out at sea for longer than this and return home as 4SW or 5SW salmon. The only way to judge how many years a salmon has spent feeding in the sea is through either scale or otolith reading. So, despite Mr Johnstone's description, quoted at the head of this chapter, J.A. Hutton's advice, given in his book *Wye Salmon & Other Fish* (1949), is still valid: 'I have often been asked how to distinguish a Grilse from its older cousins [salmon], which latter may sometimes be even lighter than some of the Grilse. My reply was "Examine its scales".'

Scale reading

Scale reading is not particularly difficult, and it will teach you a lot about the salmon that you catch. Remove several scales from midway down the side of the salmon: several, because the salmon may have lost a few scales during its life, and replacement scales will give a falsely low reading. If you are away from home and need to store them, put the scales into a small envelope and label the envelope with name of river and pool, date, weight, length and sex of the fish. Examine at least two or three scales carefully. A x15 hand lens will do. Alternatively you can use a slide projector: put the damp, slimy scale on a clear 35mm transparency and allow it to dry (it will glue itself to the surface of the transparency) before projecting the image of the scale on a white screen. If you have access to a low-power microscope then so much the better.

In this section I refer to the five scales that are illustrated in the photograph section (nos. 29–33) of this book. You will notice that the scale is built up of concentric rings called 'circuli'. The number of scales does not increase as a salmon grows. Instead each scale grows larger as newer circuli are deposited around the older ones. In some ways these circuli are like the annual rings laid down by a tree as it grows. The difference is that in a tree just one ring is laid down each year, whereas the salmon scale gains several circuli each year. Nevertheless we can use the way these circuli are arranged to tell us a lot about our salmon's life. Notice also that the clearest part of the scale to read is the front or anterior part that was hidden away under the scale in front.

First of all we can tell how old our fish is. In winter the circuli are closer together than those formed in summer. These winter clumpings of the circuli are called annuli and used to age the fish. Start on the inside of the scale and work outwards. The first annulus marks the salmon's first birthday (salmon being born in winter), and so on. In the river the salmon grew slowly as a fry and then parr. Perhaps there are one, two or three years' slow river growth (shown by one, two or three narrow annuli from the centre) followed by perhaps one year where the annuli are much more widely spaced with a large amount of summer sea growth before the next annulus. So here, in Photograph 29, we clearly have a fish that spent three years as a parr. There was a growth spurt when the fish went to sea. Then there is an annulus, indicating its one and only sea winter. But then the circuli widen, indicating that the fish continued to feed after that one winter at sea before returning home in October when I caught it. Fishery biologists would describe this example as 2+1+SW, meaning that the salmon had lived in fresh water for two years, then spent one winter (1SW = sea winter) and a few extra months (+) at sea before it returned to the river. This was a grilse weighing 10^1/$_2$lb, caught on the Lune.

But beware. At least one of the scales you have chosen may have a large part in the centre that completely lacks circuli. This is a replacement scale. The original scale has been lost and the salmon has quickly grown a new one which, of course, lacks the early details of the original scale. An example of a replacement scale is shown in Photograph 30.

Photograph 31 shows a scale from a fish that again spent two years in the river as a parr before going to sea. But it remained at sea for two winters, with a full intervening summer, before returning home at the end of the winter. This is a 2+2SW fish. Because it had not fed after its second sea winter it is 2SW not 2+SW. This, then, was a salmon and not a grilse, though it weighed only 9lb and was caught on the Dee in March.

The scale shown in Photograph 32 is also from a fish that had spent three winters at sea, but there is extra growth in the scale outside that of the second winter. Note also three years of life in the river as a parr. This salmon is thus 2+3+SW. It weighed 35lb and was caught on the Namsen in August.

Your salmon may have spawned previously. This too can be seen from a scale. Spawning is a traumatic experience, for it coincides with a period of fasting and involves much loss of condition. During fasting the fish will have migrated upstream, developed her eggs, cut redds, and then migrated back to sea as a kelt. All the energy and biochemical materials necessary for these arduous tasks will have come from materials stored in the body. So not only will the scale not grow, but some of the scale may be broken down and the material absorbed by the fish. So at spawning no new circuli are laid down around the edge of the scale and instead the scale becomes worn or eroded. Then, as the kelt returns to sea and begins to feed once more, brand new circuli are laid down around the worn scale edge. This junction can be seen clearly on the scale and is known as a spawning mark.

In Photograph 33 the fish was a 2+3+ salmon when it made its first spawning run. The spawning mark is quite clear. The fish had then fed in the sea through the following summer before returning to the River Namsen in August. It weighed 34lb.

You may catch a salmon with worn or twisted fins and a blunted, worn snout. These are the tell-tale signs of a fish-farm escapee. Unfortunately, farmed salmon are escaping all too often and many are caught, especially in rivers in the west and north of Scotland and Norway (see p. 200). Scale reading can often confirm the fish-farm origin. When they are in the farm, food is usually superabundant and, save for the coldest winter conditions, the salmon will continue to feed and grow throughout the year. Thus the winter annuli tend not to be as tightly packed in a farmed salmon as in a wild salmon, and the growth circuli are very wide. In the confines of the fish farm, where the fish are kept at very high density, the rate of scale loss can be very high. Thus the incidence of replacement scales is very high.

Scale reading is a fascinating by-product of salmon angling. In most instances it is quite a straightforward procedure. Only in very old salmon, which may have spawned and the scales suffered great erosion, is the record difficult to assess, and then even the experts may disagree. Fishery departments and laboratories are invariably pleased to receive scale samples for reading, and they will usually send a copy of the details back to you. You must supply the following information: Fish species, Date caught, Location, Weight of fish, Length of fish from fork of tail to tip of snout (in cm). Enclose at least 10 scales taken from the side of the fish, about half-way along the body.

For the British specimens, send your sample to: Freshwater Fisheries Laboratory, Faskally, Pitlochry, Tayside, Scotland.

For Irish specimens, send your sample to: The Salmon Research Trust, Newport, Co. Mayo, Ireland.

Growth

Generally the longer a salmon remains feeding out in the Atlantic the larger it will grow. I must, however, qualify this: as in humans, growth in salmon is a function of genetics and food availability. Some of us, on the same diet, grow more quickly and larger than others: that is a consequence of genetics. But if two of us have the same genetic tendency for growth but one of us eats very little, then the one who eats more may grow much larger than the one on the starvation diet. So, too, with salmon. There is a great variation in weight between salmon of precisely the same age. This variation may be due to genetics, but it may also be due to the heavier fish having fed more ravenously or in richer oceanic feeding areas than the lighter fish.

The genetic effect on growth is an interesting one. Firstly, males tend to be larger than females of the same age: for example, of a sample of 108 rod-caught Ribble grilse, males averaged 8lb 2oz, females 7lb 6oz. But also there is wide variation within each age group in each river population: the range for male grilse from the Ribble was 5lb to 12lb 4oz and for females 4lb 4oz to 10lb 8oz. Furthermore each river seems to have its own genetic 'strain' as far as growth is concerned. On p. 18 I mentioned how salmon from different tributaries of the same river system can sometimes be identified 'by eye'. So, too, the weight of salmon of the same age may vary from river to river.

On the Wye, Hutton gave average weight of male grilse as 6^1/4lb, female grilse as 5^1/2lb, with a range from 2lb to 13lb. On the Aberdeenshire Dee in August the grilse average 6lb, with range 3^1/2lb to 9lb. On the Mourne system, also in August, the average is 4^1/2lb with a range from 3lb to 7lb. And on the Grimersta in August the average is 5^3/4lb with a range of 4lb to 7lb. Similarly with 2SW salmon caught at the beginning of the fishing season in February: on the Aberdeenshire Dee these fish average 8–9lb, on the Tweed 7–8lb and on the Eden 10–12lb. So the fact that one salmon is heavier than another does not mean that the larger fish is older or has been out feeding in the Atlantic longer than the lighter fish. There is an average (or mean) weight for a batch of salmon all of the same age and there is variation either side of this average. Thus a big 1+SW grilse may be larger than a small 2+SW salmon. For instance, I have scale read September salmon, weighing from 9 to 12^3/4lb, from Spey, Dee, Nith, Annan, Ribble and Lune that were all 1+SW grilse, and September salmon from the same rivers weighing 9^1/2, 10^1/2, 10^3/4, 12 and

$12^{1}/_{2}$lb (all in the grilse range) that were 2+SW salmon. The two can only be identified by scale reading.

Salmon runs and sea ages

We must consider first the rivers in the milder southern part of the range of the Atlantic salmon; those that are not iced up from autumn to spring. These would include the rivers of the British Isles and mainland Europe east and north to Jutland. The runs of salmon into these rivers may be divided up into three fairly distinct categories: a spring run, a summer run and an autumn run. The general pattern of weights of fish in these runs is shown in Fig. 13.

The spring run may commence very early. In fact the name 'spring run' is something of a misnomer, for it includes all fish that run the river after the last fish that spawned the previous autumn. On the Tweed there are fish running in November that have undeveloped ovaries and testes, which will wait over one year in the river before they spawn. They are 'springers' despite the fact that they may be caught in November, along with fish that will spawn within a few weeks. Similarly on the Tay and Dee, big rivers into which, it has often been said, fish may run from the sea on every day of the year: on the opening

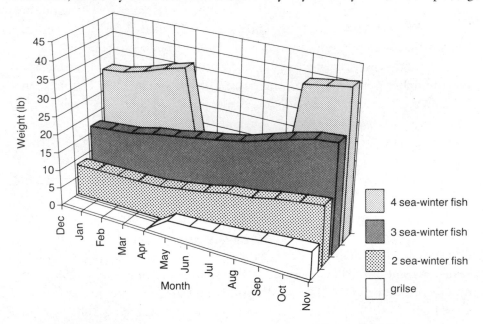

Note that these are averages; there is a wide variation within each group.

Fig. 13 – Average weights of four salmon age groups throughout the year

101

day of the fishing season there will almost certainly be, in the Tay, spring salmon upstream to Loch Tay and in the Tummel to the dam at Pitlochry and, in the Dee, fish as far upstream as Aboyne. These 'spring' salmon, which might be angled for in a blizzard in February, may have run into the river from the sea from the beginning of December.

The spring run continues until the end of May, depending upon the river. The spring run may consist of three age classes of salmon: small 2SW springers averaging 8–9lb in February; large 3SW springers averaging 16–20lb; and very large 4SW or 5SW springers weighing about 24lb and upwards.

The summer run is really a continuation of the spring run (hence the slight difference of opinion at to when the spring run ends and the summer run commences), but it also sees the appearance of another age category of salmon. Generally the summer run can be considered to begin in June and continues to late August. The summer run usually consists of just two categories of salmon: 1+SW grilse averaging about 5lb when the run commences, and 2+SW summer salmon that usually fall into the 10–14lb class. Exceptionally, 3+SW salmon are caught, usually averaging 21–26lb.

The autumn run usually coincides with the arrival of the seasonal 'back-end' rains and cooler weather in late August or September. Spring and summer salmon will spend some months in the river before it is time to spawn and thus their ovaries and testes are fairly undeveloped when they are fresh run. By contrast the autumn-run fish have usually begun to develop their ovaries and testes when they start their upstream migration from the sea, and the later the run the more developed are the reproductive organs. In October and November on several rivers – Nith, Annan, Lune, Ribble – I have caught salmon with sea lice, on a falling spate, that were straight from the sea but which were almost ready to spawn, so advanced were their reproductive systems. Such fish will head upstream through into December, when some earlier-run fish have completed spawning, and be ready to spawn as soon as they reach the redds.

The autumn run may consist of four categories of salmon. Grilse often feature, but because they have been feeding at sea for almost 18 months, they are much heavier than the little grilse that ran in early summer, with an average weight of 6–8lb and are often confused with salmon by anglers. Fish from the smolt run as the 2SW small spring- and summer-run salmon will now be averaging 14–18lb. Large 3+SW salmon may be averaging 30lb or more, and there may be some 4+SW very large autumn salmon weighing 40lb or more.

Two points need to be made about this general pattern. Firstly, a fish may run early in the year but be caught later. So fish that run in spring may be caught in spring and summer. Statistics from catch returns will not indicate this and thus the summer and autumn runs may be exaggerated and earlier runs underestimated. Most confusing is where 'spring'-running fish (which will stay in the river for a full year before spawning) and autumn-running fish (which will spawn almost immediately they have entered the river) arrive at the same time, in November, and are both recorded as the same. This is a problem on rivers such as the Tay and Tweed.

The second point is that I have referred to average weights. Average weights vary from river to river, but within each class of salmon there is a wide variation that results in an overlap with fish of other categories that might be running the river at the same time. For instance I have scales from autumn-run salmon, taken from the Spey, Dee, Nith, Annan, Lune and Ribble systems, where the 1+SW grilse weighed between 6^1/$_2$ and 12^3/$_4$lb and 2+SW salmon weighed between 9^1/$_2$ and 21lb.

Very few rivers have all these categories of salmon run. Some have just one or two. For instance, many Irish rivers and tiny short streams draining the west of Scotland and the Hebrides are dominated by a grilse run that commences in June and continues well into the autumn, with a smaller run of 2+SW fish mostly in autumn. It would be a waste of time, money and effort to arrange a week's salmon fishing on such rivers in March or April! Other, often larger, rivers have at least four categories of run. For instance the Ribble, Lune and Tyne have a small spring run of 2+SW fish, a grilse run through summer and autumn, an autumn run of large 2+SW salmon and the occasional autumn 3+SW salmon weighing between 25 and 30lb or more. The most complex series of runs occur generally on the largest rivers. In the Spey, Tay and Tweed the spring run is dominated by small 2+SW fish, although occasionally a 3+SW springer may be caught. The summer run, though dominated by grilse, also includes 2+SW summer salmon weighing in the teens of pounds and the occasional larger fish (in 1983 I saw two of these in August on the Spey, both of them 3+SW fish, weighing 24 and 32lb). The autumn run on these large rivers is dominated by the 2+SW class of salmon, though with some grilse and a few larger 3+SW fish.

These brief notes give the general pattern of salmon runs in the western European range of the salmon. However, as in all population ecology, no pattern is set in stone and immovable. In recent decades we have seen a change in the populations of the four age groups (1+, 2+, 3+ and 4+SW) running our major rivers and the timing of these runs. Such changes are not new. From the earliest of records, in the eighteenth century, the sizes and timings of runs have changed. We will examine these changes in a moment, but first we will describe the runs that may occur on more northerly salmon rivers.

In the rivers of Norway, Finland, arctic Russia, Iceland, Greenland's only river the Kapisigdlit, eastern Canada and the north-eastern USA and rivers draining into the Baltic Sea one finds that the spring, summer and autumn runs are compressed. These rivers are iced over for a quite considerable period, many of them becoming ice-free sometime in May so the fish cannot run freely until then (though in some Russian rivers it has been said that the first arrivals run under the ice). After that the rivers freeze over again sometime between October and December (depending on the year and also on altitude) so that the last runs and spawning must be completed before the freeze-up. Thus, whereas in a big British salmon river such as the Tay fish may run in from the sea 365 days of the year, on these rivers the run may occur on a maximum of only 150 days, often less.

Like the smaller, more southerly rivers, the tinier streams may be dominated by a grilse and 2+SW salmon run, rather like the summer- and autumn-run rivers. Many of the Icelandic and Canadian rivers are of this type. By contrast some of the larger rivers of Russia, Norway and Canada have complex runs including 2+SW, large 3+SW and very large 4+SW salmon as well as 1+SW grilse. For instance, on the mighty Alta and Namsen, the first fish to run (the 'spring run') after the thaw are big multi-sea-winter fish. August sees the arrival of vast shoals of grilse and some smaller 2+SW salmon – the 'summer run'. And from late August and through September there is an 'autumn' run, again of multi-sea-winter salmon and the last grilse. The problem here is distinguishing these runs, for they follow each other so closely and an angler catching a brace of 25–35lb 3+SW salmon in August (during the 'summer run') may have caught fish that ran in late June (and are really part of the 'spring run') and are still pristine silver.

Fluctuations in the runs of grilse and salmon

Before we examine the changes that have taken place, over the years, in the timings and sizes of the runs of grilse and salmon we must first consider how the size of salmon runs is estimated.

Assessing the size of runs

There are two main ways of estimating the size of a run of salmon. The first is by counting the numbers of fish passing upstream. For this an automatic electric counter is most often used. This is positioned in a fish pass in a weir or dam. Unfortunately automatic counters are modern tools, the earliest dating from the 1950s, though it was not until the 1960s and 1970s that they became fairly reliable. But even today there are failures. In September 1983 three of us caught, in one river, more salmon than the counter some way downstream had recorded passing all year! Another counter recorded a huge run of fish; but a log swirling round the salmon pass was the culprit! And often records declare that the counter was 'out of action from 6 June to 14 August'. They are now fine pieces of equipment, but it is too early to use their records to examine long-term trends. A method used on the River Bush is to trap all salmon passing upstream of Bushmills town, the salmon being transferred by net, from the trap, over an impassable weir. From the angling point of view this is an undesirable way of counting the salmon run, for it seems that after fish have been trapped and handled in this way they are virtually impossible to catch: the beats downstream of the Bushmills dam have magnificent catches, but upstream of the dam relatively few are caught. On the weir on the Mourne, at Sion Mills, a man sits in a little hut and counts any salmon leaping over the weir rather than swimming through the fish pass and automatic counter.

The traditional way of assessing the sizes of salmon runs, and the data that we must use for determining long-term trends, is from records of catches by both commercial net fisheries and by rod-and-line anglers. There are problems here in that many commercial netsmen and anglers fail to give the true total of the number of salmon that they have taken. We can assume, however, that the tendency to lie has been constant through the ages and that, the error being a constant one, the data are comparable from one year to the next. We must also assume that the numbers of salmon taken illegally by poachers have been constant through the years, for poachers take without giving any catch returns.

A greater problem, when it comes to using very many years of catch records, is that fishing seasons have been altered, sometimes several times, over the past 100–150 years. It may seem, therefore, that a spring or autumn run has collapsed, suddenly, though the decline of catches was due really to the start of the netting season in spring being put back or the end of the netting season being brought forward by a month or more.

Another problem, if we are using rod catches, is that for some regions (Scotland) there was no legal obligation to give catch returns prior to 1950. Also, when it comes to comparing grilse and multi-sea-winter salmon, size is used as the criterion for distinguishing them. Most small fish classified as grilse will be just that, though there may be a few smaller 2+SW fish misclassified. However, the multi-sea-winter salmon will also include bigger grilse. The error will tend to be constant, however, and not greatly interfere with the identification and assessment of the runs of 'grilse' and 'salmon'. Despite these errors in catch statistics we must use them, for they are our main means of analysing the changes of the runs of salmon in our rivers.

The age of returning

What makes a salmon run as a 1+SW grilse or as a 2+ or 3+ or 4+SW salmon? Why is it that, when one year's smolts head out to sea in spring, some of them may return after only one winter at sea, some after two winters, and some after three or four winters? It is easy to argue that this is simply another example of nature's insurance policy: if they all returned to spawn in the same year then some catastrophe could wipe out the entire year's smolts production and one year's spawning. This is a very satisfactory reason, but it doesn't answer the questions 'why?' and 'how?' Such questions are, perhaps more than any other, at the forefront of the mind of the salmon angler, especially in recent years when very large multi-sea-winter salmon have become so scarce and, in so many rivers, small grilse seem to have become more abundant than the larger salmon.

No one knows the answers to these questions with any certainty. However, there are theories that have some degree of support from observation. The first theory is that the age of return is genetically determined. Support for this comes from rivers that have distinct runs of spring salmon, summer grilse and autumn salmon. As we saw in Chapter 3, salmon that run in spring tend to run and spawn farther upstream than grilse, which in turn tend to spawn farther upstream than autumn-run salmon. So, on the Aberdeenshire Dee, the river above Aboyne and the tributaries Badoch and Girnoch Burn are traditionally spawning grounds for spring salmon, the middle Dee and its tributaries spawning grounds for grilse and summer salmon, and the lower Dee and its tributaries, below Banchory, spawning grounds for grilse and autumn salmon. That being the case, then spring salmon would tend to spawn with spring salmon and produce smolts that would run back to the upper Dee as spring salmon, not grilse. This separation of the populations of spring salmon, grilse and autumn salmon is borne out by studies using genetic finger-printing on the Dee (p. 18).

Further evidence of some genetic mechanism determining whether a smolt returns as a grilse after one winter at sea or as a salmon after two or more sea winters was produced by D.J. Piggins in Ireland's Burrishoole Fishery. Here about 90 per cent of fish have returned, since records were first kept, as grilse and about 10 per cent as 2+SW salmon. Dr Piggins found that if grilse eggs are fertilized by grilse sperm, 99 per cent of the progeny will be grilse and 1 per cent 2+SW salmon. If eggs from 2SW salmon are fertilized by sperm from 2SW salmon, then 86 per cent of the progeny will be grilse and 14 per cent

2SW salmon. And if grilse and 2SW salmon are interbred, the progeny will be 96 per cent grilse and 4 per cent 2SW salmon. There appears thus to be a genetic equilibrium (known to population geneticists as the Hardy–Weinberg equilibrium) on the basis of which the proportion of grilse and salmon running the Burishoole fishery would be maintained. Such a genetic control of sea age is quite feasible. After all, are not most behavioural characters genetically controlled?

However, in recent years we have seen, especially in larger rivers, changes in the proportions of grilse and salmon. Surely, if one stream has a genetic strain of salmon that produces 2+SW spring salmon and not grilse, then the spring run of salmon will be maintained unless the salmon stocks in that stream become extinct.

The second theory that has been used to explain why smolts may return as either grilse or salmon is that the duration of their marine feeding life and timing of their return to the river are dependent on environmental factors, and have little or nothing to do with genetics. There is one famous experiment that gives this theory strong support. The Restigouche River had, in the early 1930s, an early-season run consisting of 2+SW and 3+SW salmon. H.C. White took fertilized eggs from these salmon, raised them in a hatchery, and liberated the fry in a branch of the Apple River that had no salmon run. The Apple River flows into the Bay of Fundy, a region where all the rivers were dominated by a grilse run. The fry grew quickly, as was to be expected in a river lacking native parr but an abundance of food. In 1934 White trapped smolts from these fry, clipped off their adipose fin, and let them swim off to sea. The following year White recaptured 98 1+SW grilse with clipped adipose fin in the Apple River, and in 1936 trapped 62 2+SW salmon. White concluded that:

> Except in the rate of growth in the river, for which obvious reasons have been given (i.e. less crowded conditions), the Restigouche salmon introduced into Apple River could not be distinguished by their behaviour from the indigenous salmon [those of other Bay of Fundy rivers close to the Apple River], and hence failed to show any evidence of a 'Restigouche' inheritance. Although the failure is definite as to any racial distinction between Restigouche and Apple River salmon, the possibility of there being such distinctions in other places is not excluded. The significant point is that, in this instance, there has been a demonstration that environmental conditions, acting on the individual from the fry stage on, make the full observed difference in behaviour between Restigouche and Apple River salmon almost as great as is to be found in the salmon in Canadian waters.

Of course the parr growing in the Apple river were not in the Restigouche! It is important here to remember one major principle of genetics: phenotype (what you see) = genotype (what genes the salmon has) + environment (environmental effects on the genetics of the salmon). In other words, the Apple River environment may have overridden the genes in all the introduced fry for producing 2+SW and 3+SW salmon. More recent experiments in Ireland, Scotland and Sweden have suggested a strong genetic influence on the age of return (whether as grilse or as multi-sea-winter salmon) and also the timing of that return (whether as spring or summer or autumn fish), but that there may be environmental triggers also involved.

Both W.L. Calderwood and J.A. Hutton noticed that there seems to be a relationship between time spent as a parr in the river and time spent at sea or, as Hutton put it, 'If Parr remain for three years in the river there is a tendency for them to spend a shorter time in the sea, and to return as Grilse or as Small Salmon. On the other hand, Smolts, which migrate when only one year old, are more likely to remain in the sea for a longer period. The following are the actual figures.'

	RETURNED AS SMOLTS			
	1 year	2 years	3 years	Total
		Percentages		
Grilse or small fish	36.2	60.8	76.3	60.5
Large or very large fish	62.8	39.2	23.7	39.5

These figures speak for themselves. It must be noted that both Calderwood and Hutton based their conclusion on scale reading on salmon that had returned from the sea: they did not know the parentage of the smolts.

W.M. Shearer has also shown, on one river at least (the North Esk), that the longer a fish has spent in the river as a parr, the later in the year will that fish return to the river. In other words, taking one year's run of 2+SW salmon in the North Esk, those that spent just one year in the river as a parr will tend to return before those that spent two years as a parr, whilst those that spent three years in the river as a parr will return last.

So the number of years the juvenile salmon spent in the river has some influence on whether it will return as a grilse or as a multi-sea-winter fish, and also the time of the year that it will run into the river. However, it seems unlikely that variations in river conditions could change so significantly as to affect the time juveniles spend in the river. Or is it so unlikely?

The effect of river conditions

If we consider a small salmon river where there are very few deep pools and the fish must lie in shallow water with little protective cover, small grilse may have an advantage over larger multi-sea-winter salmon. Grilse are far more capable of moving through shallow trickles. They are less likely to be predated. They are more likely to spawn. So it is logical that natural selection would produce, in small rivers, fish of small size. In other words, a grilse-dominated run. And so it does, for most small salmon rivers are predominantly grilse rivers: in Ireland (save for the bigger Shannon, Blackwater and Erne), Iceland, the west coast and islands of Scotland, the tinier Norwegian and Canadian spate streams. In big rivers, with deep holding pools and where fish can pass upstream easily on most (if not all) heights of water, the salmon run includes fish of a variety of ages and sizes. There are, however, clear instances of rivers being altered, by man, with a consequent change in the salmon run. For instance the Shannon, Erne and Awe produced many multi-sea-winter salmon, including some very big specimens (see pp. 119–22). Damming of these rivers (but with fish passes) for hydroelectric schemes was followed by a decline of multi-sea-winter salmon and an increase of grilse runs. Cumbria's River Eden was famous for its good run of big multi-sea-winter salmon, most of which spawned in the major tributary the Eamont and in the Lowther, a tributary of the Eamont. The Lowther flows from Haweswater Lake and, in 1938, Manchester Corporation dammed the lake outflow and raised the lake level by 100 ft, retaining water that should have flowed down the Lowther, through the Eamont and into the Eden. Through summer and autumn the Lowther is now a tiny stream, its pre-1938 banks left high and dry. It could not hold the former big salmon: they are gone and the run now consists of a grilse run and a very late run of smaller 2+SW salmon. On many other rivers the changes in the river are less obvious. But damming the headwaters for reservoirs, land drainage and water abstraction have resulted in a reduction in flow and loss of depth, especially during a prolonged drought. This too may have contributed to a recent decline of large multi-sea-winter fish, an increase of grilse, and a tendency for the fish to run late so that they spend less time waiting to spawn in the river. But this is not the entire story, for the decline of the spring run of multi-sea-winter salmon and the increase of grilse from 1960 has occurred on all rivers (see Figs 14–17).

During the 1980s Tony George analysed historic fluctuations of salmon

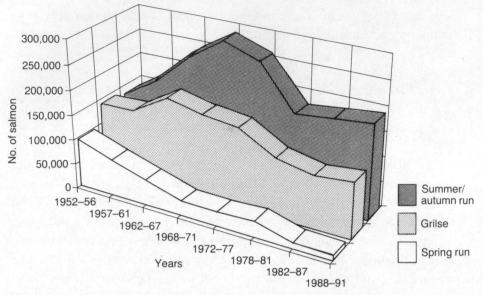

Note that the slight decline of the commercial grilse catch from 1978 is probably largely due to a decline in commercial fishing in these years; this will also have affected the catches of salmon.

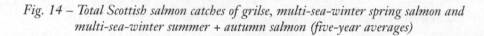

Fig. 14 – Total Scottish salmon catches of grilse, multi-sea-winter spring salmon and multi-sea-winter summer + autumn salmon (five-year averages)

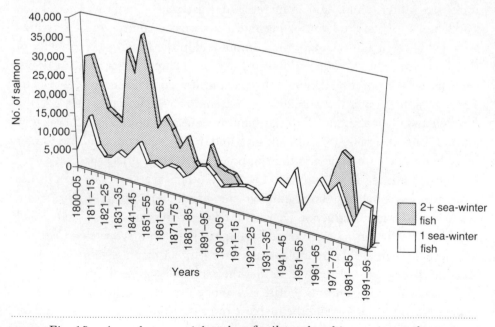

Fig. 15 – Annual commercial catches of grilse and multi-sea-winter salmon on the Tweed (five-year averages)

110

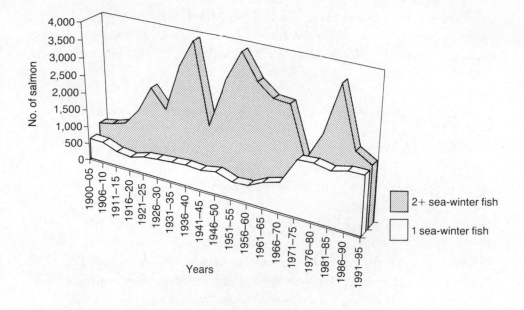

Fig. 16 – Annual commercial catches of grilse and multi-sea-winter salmon on the Dee (five-year averages)

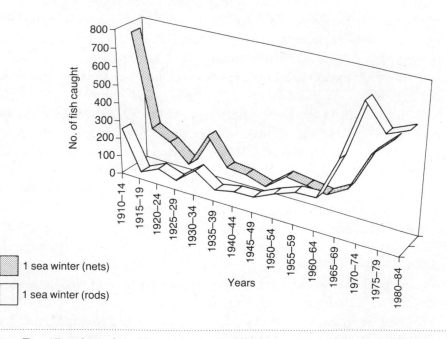

Fig. 17 – Annual catches of grilse and multi-sea-winter salmon on the Wye (five-year averages)

runs (in *Trout & Salmon* magazine and his M.Phil. thesis, 1982). He proposed a theory of grilse: multi-sea-winter salmon fluctuations based on climatic variations over the North Atlantic. The following table summarizes his findings (I have extended it with data from 1982):

1792–1812	Warm period	*Multi-sea-winter salmon predominant*
1812–50	Cooler period	*Grilse predominant*
1850–85	Warm period	*Multi-sea-winter salmon predominant*
1885–96	Cooler period	*Grilse predominant*
1896–1921	Warming	*Grilse slowly decreasing, multi-sea-winter salmon increasing*
1921–62	Warm period	*Multi-sea-winter salmon predominant*
1957–79	Cooling, then cold period	*Grilse predominant*
1979–82	Warming	*Grilse decrease, multi-sea-winter salmon increase*
1982–90	Cooling	*Grilse increase, multi-sea-winter salmon decrease*
1990–4	Warming	*Grilse decrease, multi-sea-winter salmon increase*

There is some evidence to support George's theory. It has been shown that grilse tend not to move into sea water with a temperature of less than 40°F. When the sea temperature in the Davies Straits is less than 40°F very few go there to feed. In the Faroes Bank feeding grounds 2SW salmon may be found where the water temperature is less than 40°F but not grilse. And J.H.A. Martin and K.A. Mitchell demonstrated that the proportions of grilse and multi-sea-winter salmon caught in the Aberdeenshire Dee were directly related to average annual sea temperatures off Grimsey Island (on the Arctic Circle off northern Iceland). When sea temperatures are low grilse dominate the Dee catch. When sea temperatures are rising the proportions of grilse decrease and multi-sea-winter salmon increase. When sea temperatures are high multi-sea-winter salmon dominate the Dee catch. When sea temperatures are falling the proportions of multi-sea-winter salmon decline and grilse increase. The conclusion is that, when sea temperatures are low the salmon feeding at sea head back home after one year at sea, as grilse; when sea temperatures are high then the salmon remain at sea feeding and return after two or more years, as multi-sea-winter fish. In theory, if it were possible to predict sea temperature fluctuations, then it would seem possible to predict the proportions of grilse and multi-sea-winter salmon running our rivers.

However, it is not quite as clear as that! Martin and Mitchell* (and Tony George in most of his analyses) talk of proportions or percentages of grilse and multi-sea-winter salmon that make up the catches, not actual numbers of fish.

In fact, during the period of Martin and Mitchell's study, the number of multi-sea-winter salmon remained relatively constant despite sea temperature fluctuations. But the numbers of grilse increased (and formed a greater percentage of the catch) when sea temperatures were low and decreased (and formed a smaller percentage of the catch) when sea temperatures were high. In numerical terms it was the grilse population that was fluctuating widely. We see this if we compare the 1952–6 with the 1982–6 Scottish rod catches:

	GRILSE		MULTI-SEA-WINTER SALMON	
	Number	% of total catch	Number	% of total catch
1952–6	6,800	13	36,500	87
1982–6	19,200	26	50,800	74

Note the problem when using percentages. The multi-sea-winter fish appear to have decreased, but in fact their numbers increased!

If we look at the figures, not percentages, of grilse and multi-sea-winter salmon caught on the Tweed (see Fig. 15) we see that from 1800 to the present day, catches of the latter have fluctuated between about 5000 and 15,000 fish, with frequent peaks and troughs: a three-fold fluctuation. Such fluctuations are quite common in many wild animal populations over the long term. Grilse were exceedingly abundant in the first half of the nineteenth century, declined through the third quarter of the nineteenth century but increased at the end of the nineteenth century. Thereafter the grilse population remained low (with some fluctuation) up to the early 1960s when there was a big increase in numbers. The grilse population fluctuated by a factor of 15, and the fluctuations of grilse, not multi-sea-winter salmon, appear to match George's theory. So the greatest contribution to variations in the Tweed salmon populations, as measured by catches, appears to be fluctuations of the grilse component, and the grilse and multi-sea-winter populations appear to fluctuate independently. Certainly when grilse numbers increase multi-sea-winter salmon numbers do not decrease and vice versa.

If the production of grilse and of multi-sea-winter salmon has an underlying genetic cause we would expect the populations of these to fluctuate independently. If production can be modified by river and marine environments then we would expect fluctuations to depend one on the other. To go back to the George Theory, we would expect a decline of grilse to coincide with an increase of multi-sea-winter salmon and vice versa. But we don't.

On the Aberdeenshire Dee (see Fig. 16), a river not previously associated with a big run of grilse, the number of grilse remained fairly low but constant from 1900 to the late 1960s, when the grilse population then increased markedly. By contrast the multi-sea-winter population fluctuated widely, with peaks in the early 1920s, late 1930s and early 1980s, with troughs in the 1900s, late 1920s, early 1940s, early 1970s and, currently, in the 1990s. There are no correlations between the two sets of data.

Similarly, on the Wye (see Fig. 17) there was a grilse peak in the early 1910s followed by a small grilse run to a small peak in the early 1930s, followed by a slow decline to the early 1950s, since when the grilse population has slowly increased to a peak from the late 1960s. It is true that, in the midst of the period of low grilse population, the multi-sea-winter salmon population peaked on the Wye in the late 1920s (which accords with George's climate theory), but subsequently there has been no correlation between the two populations. In fact, the multi-sea-winter population troughed in the early 1940s when the Wye grilse stocks were also low – and at a time, in the Second World War, when extra efforts were being made to harvest more fish as part of the war effort.

It may be true that in periods of cooler climate and seas more grilse are produced. These automatically result in a fall of average weight of fish running the rivers (see Fig. 18) and an increase of the numbers of grilse in the overall catch. However, it seems that there is little evidence that a cooler climate and seas results in a decrease of multi-sea-winter stocks. I would suggest that several factors are responsible for the fluctuations of multi-sea-winter salmon. We have already seen that the damming of and reduction of flow in rivers is probably responsible for the loss of big salmon in some rivers, such as the Awe and Shannon. I would also suggest that food availability in the sea is another major cause: this is discussed later in this chapter (p. 129).

Average weights of salmon from the Dee and Lune have shown a steady decline due to the decrease of big 3+SW salmon and the recent increase of 1+SW grilse. But the decline has been a steady one. According to Tony George's climate theory we would have expected an increase in average weights after 1921, when the seas were warm and multi-sea-winter salmon predominated. We don't. And we would have expected a sudden rapid decline in average weight from about 1957 when the seas were cooler and the grilse stocks increased greatly. The decline is quite small, and really a continuation of a general trend throughout all the years for which we have records. The decline of big salmon from both rivers is almost certainly due to a reduction of average flow rates through increasing water abstraction and land drainage, and

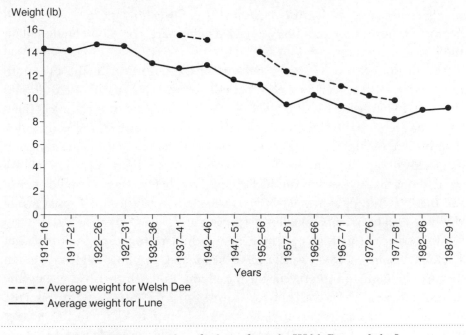

Fig. 18 – Average weights of salmon from the Welsh Dee and the Lune

probably the loss of the spawning grounds of large multi-sea-winter salmon in the highest feeder streams (especially in the case on the Dee).

The timing of runs

One phenomenon that we have seen in recent years is a decline of the spring salmon run and an increase of the summer and, especially, autumn runs of multi-sea-winter fish. Through much of the era of modern salmon angling, most major British salmon rivers were spring rivers (some were hardly fished after late May) or had a big run of spring fish – rivers like the Wye, Welsh and Aberdeenshire Dees, Eden, Tay and Tweed. Many others had an important spring run. For instance in the 1950s and 1960s up to 25 per cent of the Nith total catch was caught in spring; by the early 1990s this had fallen to barely 1 per cent. This spring run was highly prized for it afforded sport during January and February, at a time of the year when the economy of the river valleys was at its lowest. It provided employment for gillies, an income for hotels and shops, and provided the estates owning the river with an income to support their other country businesses. The decline of the spring run has thus been greeted almost hysterically by anglers, hotel proprietors and fishery owners alike. For instance, on the Aberdeenshire Dee, fewer anglers are going to fish for the few remaining springers, estate incomes are correspondingly falling and hotels are closing.

Yet the spring run has never been a constant feature. In the twentieth century there have been two peak periods for the spring run, 1920–40 and 1950–70. In the very early 1900s and 1940s the spring run was relatively small and it has recently declined since the 1970s. I remember sitting with Sandy Penny, gillie on the Lower Redgorton beat of the Tay, and bemoaning the demise of the spring run. Sandy's experience of the Tay is vast. He quickly pointed out that the spring run had disappeared before, that it would return, and that it would disappear again. And when the spring run collapsed in the 1940s he could remember anglers despairing at the loss.

Also associated with this phenomenon is the late running of autumn fish. Angling seasons evolved, usually many years ago, to allow anglers to catch fresh-run salmon and to prevent them catching ripe fish that had been some time in the river and were ready to spawn. But since the 1970s at least, the autumn runs on some rivers have been getting later and later so that a large proportion of the run (over 50 per cent on rivers like the Hodder and Esk) are running in from the sea after the close of the angling season.

Why do timings of runs of multi-sea-winter salmon change from spring to summer/autumn and then revert to spring? One theory, which is widely believed by anglers, relates to the increasingly late run of autumn fish. Eventually, so the argument goes, these autumn salmon run so late that they become spring salmon; the run spills over from autumn to spring. This is unlikely for one main reason. Springers arrive back with relatively undeveloped ovaries and testes (even those that arrive back in November and December; see p. 101) whereas autumn-run fish arrive with well-developed ovaries and testes. For a very late autumn-run fish (in December) to become a springer, it would have to have some mechanism to switch off ovary or testis development until it returned to the river.

A second theory is that fishing, by rod and net, selects out the spring run. Spring-run salmon are the easiest of all salmon to catch, for these will most readily take a well-presented fly. They are also more likely to be caught because they are in the river for so long. Such pressure, so this argument goes, will result in the spring run being fished out and the grilse and autumn-run fish increasing. Bernard Aldridge, the late Earl Mountbatten's river keeper on the Test, described to me how the collapse of the Test spring salmon run in the early 1970s had coincided with the development of the Greenland net fishery. Others also have blamed overfishing off Greenland for the demise of the spring runs. Alas, this theory does not take into account that the spring run has increased and decreased in the past, despite intensive angling and inshore commercial fishing pressures and the lack of the high seas fisheries.

Two more reasonable theories are related to river conditions and sea conditions.

I have already noted W.M. Shearer's discovery on the North Esk that the more years a fish remains in the river as a parr before going to sea the earlier in the year will that fish return to the river. It may be that, in periods when the spring run is abundant, river conditions encourage the parr to remain longer in the river so that they return as springers, whereas as river conditions change more go to sea after one or two (instead of two or more) years as parr and return later in the year as a summer or autumn run. But that theory does not hold water when we look at a wide range of rivers, for instance the Test and Avon, two productive chalk streams in southern England. Here most parr become smolts at the end of their first year and return in spring: or did, for in these rivers the spring run has collapsed in recent years. Similarly, in the rivers of north-western Scotland most parr become smolts after three years in the river, yet they return in summer or autumn.

The best theory is that of Tony George, which relates Atlantic climate to the timing of salmon runs. We have used George's theory to explain fluctuations of grilse populations. It also explains the changes in the timings of the runs of multi-sea-winter salmon:

1600–1780: climate cold, 34–35°F, cooler than at present, and known as the 'little ice age'. There were no spring runs, the fish running in summer and autumn.
1780–1800: temperature rising; a spring run becomes established on the Aberdeenshire Dee in 1790.
1817–50: temperature falls. The spring run declines and a summer–autumn run develops.
1860–78: temperature rises. The spring run becomes dominant and the summer–autumn run declines.
1885–97: temperature falls. The spring run declines and the summer–autumn run slowly becomes dominant.
1898–1930: temperature slowly rises. The spring run becomes dominant.
1920–60: climate very warm. An outstanding spring run dominates.
1960–70: temperature falling. The spring run begins to decline.
1970 to present day: Atlantic climate fluctuates, but cool. The spring run

continues to decline and an increasingly late autumn run becomes dominant.

How cool? How warm? We are not talking in terms of large temperature fluctuations but very small ones. In a cool period, the Atlantic temperature will be only 3–4°F colder than the temperature in a warm period. Can that make such a difference? It probably can. But far more research is needed on the fluctuations of the North Atlantic food chains, at the top of which sits the salmon, and the long-term effects of temperature variations on the productivity of food chains, before we can link changes in the timing of salmon runs and variations in the ocean environment.

However, we are not just talking of fluctuations in the spring and summer–autumn runs of salmon. There has also been, associated with these fluctuations, a decline in recent years of big 3+SW and 4+SW salmon. In fact, their numbers have not so much fluctuated: they have crashed! This is especially so in the British and Irish fisheries, less so perhaps in the Norwegian and Russian fisheries, whilst in the Baltic Sea fishery there seems to have been an increase in numbers of these huge salmon.

Big salmon and big bags of big salmon

The following is a list of big salmon that weighed 50lb or more. It is based entirely on published records. For that reason it is certainly far from complete, though it is sufficient to illustrate the points I want to make about the demise of big salmon. Ideally I would have liked to include in this list fish weighing over 35lb. However, although fish weighing more than 35lb are today worthy of reporting in magazine river reports, fifty years ago they were so common that most were not published unless several were caught on the same day or in the same week.

Fish of that size were far from rare not all that long ago, judging from asides made in many publications. For instance, Arthur Oglesby commented, in *Salmon*, that the Aaro 'was said to yield more fifty-pounders than any other Atlantic salmon river in the world'. In 1991 I was taken to a house in the Gaula valley to see the outline, on an unpainted wall, of a 50lb fish caught, in the late nineteenth century, by Mrs Blackburne's party. That record has not been published.

Because of this problem the list is in two parts. The first consists of records from the British Isles. The British have always been record-mad and this part of the list is probably fairly complete. The second is from the rest of the Atlantic salmon world: that list is far from complete but it again illustrates points that I want to make. Unless stated, all the fish were caught on rod and line. Peruse this list and the notes that follow of some big catches of big salmon. Then we will consider the pattern of big salmon records.

WEIGHT	DATE	RIVER	CAPTOR	NOTES
84lb	1869	Tay	–	Netted
69³/₄lb	1743	Tweed	Lord Home	Doubts as to precise weight prevent it being the British rod record
67lb	autumn 1812	Nith	Jock Wallace	It took 10 hours to land this fish; not officially accepted
64lb	Oct 1922	Tay	Miss Ballantyne	Accepted British record
63½lb	1905	Wye	–	Netted
61½lb	Oct 1907	Tay	Mr Stewart	
61½lb	Mar 1924	Exe	–	Netted
61lb	late 18th century	Tweed	Earl of Home	
61lb	1924	Deveron	Mrs Morrison	Mrs Morrison also caught one of 48½lb here in 1923
61lb	Mar 1870	Tay	J. Taggart	
60lb	1907	Tweed	–	Found dead
60lb	1888	Eden	L. Bridges	
60lb	1924	Usk	–	Netted; record for the Usk 48lb in 1913
59½lb	Mar 1923	Wye	Miss Davey	A 4SW fish
57½lb	Oct 1886	Dee (Aberdeen)	J. Gordon	
57½lb	Oct 1886	Tweed	Mr Pryor	
57lb	1874	Suir	Mr Maher	This Irish river produced fish of 44lb in 1922, 45lb in 1926, 46lb in 1927 and 48lb in 1928

WEIGHT	DATE	RIVER	CAPTOR	NOTES
57lb	1888	Annan	–	Netted
57lb	Oct 1909	Awe	–	
57lb	Jul 1921	Awe	Major Huntingdon	The major also had a 51lb fish
56½lb	1944	Tay	–	Netted
56lb	c.1880	Eden	Mr Francis	
56lb	Nov 1892	Eden	G. McKenzie	
56lb	1913	Usk	–	Netted
56lb	1923	Awe	H.T. Thornton	Mr Thornton also had a 51lb fish
55½lb	Sep 1898	Tay	Capt A.G. Goodwin	
55½lb	Oct 1903	Tay	P.M. Coats	
55lb	Oct 1883	Tay	Marquis of Zetland	
55lb	Sep 1887	Garry	A. Grant	
55lb	1889	Tweed	Mr Brereton	
55lb	Nov 1913	Tweed	Mr Kidson	
55lb	autumn 1927	Awe	Mrs Huntingdon	Major Huntingdon's wife (see above)
54½lb	1809	Tay	Mr MacIntosh	
54lb	1880	Awe	Schoolmaster at Taynuilt	
54lb	1877	Awe	J.B. Lawes	
54lb	1884	Tay	Lord Ruthven	
54lb	Feb 1903	Shannon	Mr Milburn	
54lb	Oct 1942	Tay	J.T. Ness	
54lb	1969	Tay	V. Ianetta	
53½lb	1873	Tweed	–	
53lb	1897	Spey	W.G. Craven	
53lb	Oct 1899	Tay	Lord Blythwood	
53lb	1901 or 1902	North Esk	J.M. Oldham	
53lb	1914?	Shannon	W. Ivis	
53lb	1915 or 1916	Tay	Mr Dow	
53lb	1913	Awe	A. McCall	
53lb	Oct 1923	Tay	Sir S. Coats	
53lb	Oct 1924	Tay	P.M. Pritchard	

WEIGHT	DATE	RIVER	CAPTOR	NOTES
52½lb	Apr 1928	Wye	R. Devereaux	
52lb	1883	Erne	E.P. Bates	
52lb	autumn 1885	Derwent	L. Ferguson	This river produced a 42lb fish in 1903
52lb	1917	Tay	Mr Macbeth	
52lb	Oct 1918	Dee (Aberdeen)	M. Ewen	
52lb	Mar 1920	Wye	Col Tilney	5SW fish
52lb	autumn 1924	Don	Mr McGowan	
52lb	Mar 1930	Blackwater	E.C. Walthall	This river produced fish of 45lb in 1902, 43¾lb in 1906 and 49lb in 1913
51½lb	Jul 1875	Tay	J. Gellatly	
51½lb	Oct 1922	Tweed	Dr Fison	
51½lb	Nov 1929	Annan	J.J. Varrie	4SW fish
51½lb	1929	Blackwater	Mr O'Mahony	
51lb	1902	Tweed	Lord Home	
51lb	Oct 1903	Tay	Mr Fletcher	
51lb	1903	Blackwater	Mr Bowle's gillie	
51lb	1903	Tay	M. Coats	
51lb	1905	Tay	Mr Fieldhouse	
51lb	Sep 1907	Awe	C. Child	
51lb	1913	Awe	L. Milne	In 1913 Mr Milne also had fish of 40, 45 and 48lb from the Awe
51lb	Oct 1913	Tay	S. Coats	The 4th 50+lb fish for the Coats family on the Tay!
51lb	Mar 1914	Wye	J.W. Smith	4SW; 15 minutes after landing this Mr Smith hooked a 43lb-er
51lb	Spring 1921	Tweed	H. St George	

WEIGHT	DATE	RIVER	CAPTOR	NOTES
51lb	about 1925	Awe	Major Huntingdon	
51lb	1929	Shannon	W. McDonnell	
51lb	1934	Awe	Mr Thornton	
50lb 10oz	1929	Shannon	R. Slattery	
50½lb	autumn 1885	Annan	P. Loudoun	
50½lb	Nov 1925	Tweed	Mr Rudd	
50½lb	Feb 1930	Wye	Col Heywood's keeper	4SW
50½lb	1933	Shannon	Lliam Ford	
50lb	1874	Tay	–	Caught in Loch Tay
50lb	1880	Tay	–	Caught in Loch Tay
50lb	Sep 1883	Tay	H. Clarke-Jerwoise	
50lb	1909	Shannon	G.C. Williams	4SW
50lb	1925	Wye	–	Netted
50lb	1928	Shannon	M. Tuohy	
50lb	Jul 1928	Tay	Major F. Pullar	
50lb	Oct 1928	Tay	Miss L. Ward	
50lb	Feb 1930	Blackwater	J. Latham	
50lb	Apr 1930	Wye	T.R. Merton	4SW
50lb	Mar 1935	Wye	Capt Yates	4SW

The first point is that these big fish are a thing of the past, though one day they may reappear. Oh that they would . . . and soon, for none of us is getting any younger!

Of the dated records there is a single peak, in the decade 1921–30, with many records before 1920 and very few (in fact only six) after 1930, and none in the last quarter of a century:

pre-1860	1861–70	1871–80	1881–90	1891–1900	1901–10
4	2	8	12	6	12

1911–20	1921–30	1931–40	1941–50	1951–60	1961–70
16	27	3	2	0	1

1971–1994
0

It will be noted in George's climatic theory of salmon run fluctuations that the period 1885–96 was dominated by grilse, but there were in fact several records of big salmon. It is true that grilse numbers increase greatly in cool Atlantic conditions, but in numerical terms multi-sea-winter stocks do not significantly decline. The peak of big salmon between 1911 and 1930 concurs with George's theory, but if we follow that theory we would have expected similar numbers of big salmon to continue to run into the 1960s. We don't. It is worth noting also that, whilst in the twentieth century probably most of the 50lb salmon records were published, before then fewer such records were published and the nineteenth century records of big fish are thus probably well below the true total.

It is also worth considering the relative numbers of dated spring, summer and autumn big fish records:

	SPRING	SUMMER	AUTUMN
	(to end May)	(all July)	(from late August)
pre-1930	3	1	20
1930–60	10	2	10
Total	13	3	30

The pre-1930 predominance of autumn-run big salmon accords well with George's theory of climatic factors controlling the timing of multi-sea-winter salmon runs into British rivers. However, in the 1930–60 period, when the spring run was so dominant, the spring run of big salmon appears to have increased, though big salmon were still running in autumn. There is no doubt that in the period 1930–60 the spring run of salmon was dominant, but these figures perhaps suggest that the dominant spring run may have consisted mainly of 2+SW salmon, together with some 3+ and 4+SW fish and that there was still a back-end run that included these older, bigger fish.

When one peruses the literature one finds that the end of the nineteenth century and the first four decades of the twentieth century produced some very big bags of big fish of which these 50+lb salmon were just the pinnacle. The following is a selection of these. Notice especially the years involved, and drool over some of the bags. What would we not give for these today!

Percy Leeming, who fished mainly on the Spey and Earn from 1897 to 1923, took 2203 salmon in a total of 760 days' fishing, an average of three salmon per day. His best days were 21 fish on the Spey and 19 on the Earn. He had several in the 30-pound category, his best being 40½lb on the Spey. G.F. McCorquodale was another great Spey angler. In 34 years (1891–1935) he caught 8924 salmon from that river, an average of 263 fish per year. His best year was 1920 when he had 492, and his best 12 consecutive days' fishing (excluding Sunday) was in October 1911 when he had 90 salmon averaging 17½lb. Mr McCorquodale's daughter was also no mean angler: her best bag was 13 salmon in six hours.

On the Tay Mrs Radcliffe took a brace of springers weighing 42 and 41lb in one day in 1924. However, the Tay spring record belongs to Major Baker Carr who, on 9 March 1922, had 17 fish with an average weight of 16¼lb, the best scaling 30lb. The autumn day-bag record is of 20 salmon, averaging 18¼lb, by C.A. Murray in the 1920s. J. Watson Lyall's record (undated, but certainly also in the 1920s) for Loch Tay came on five consecutive February days, when he had 26 salmon for 551lb (an average of 21lb 3oz). On his best day Mr Watson Lyall had eight fish weighing 16, 18, 19, 20, 21, 23, 23 and 28lb.

Tweed is still a great salmon river, but it does not produce the big bags of big fish that it did earlier this century. Lady Joan Joyce probably holds the spring record of 26 salmon and two sea trout caught on 15 February 1935, while G. McGilloch holds the autumn record with 19 salmon on 20 November 1930. They averaged 20½lb, the biggest scaling 39lb.

The Aberdeenshire Dee has always been a prolific river and, in recent years, considered almost exclusively a prime spring river. In 1918 one would have expected a record spring catch from this river, for the Atlantic was warming and the spring run predominating (p. 117). But it was in October 1918 that Ernest Crossfield took 11 salmon, averaging 23lb, in one day.

Loch Lomond is not famed as a big salmon water, though its record fish are 42lb (taken in 1912) and 44lb (taken on 15 April 1930). But it has another remarkable record: one day in June 1919 A. Frisken had five salmon, averaging 12lb, in two hours' fishing. This gives an average of 24 minutes per fish, about half of this time being spent in playing the fish. The loch must have been stuffed with 2SW salmon!

The Thurso is not regarded as a big-fish river; but its record salmon scaled 47lb. And the year . . . 1923!

On the Usk Colonel R.P. Sandeman took 18 salmon on 10 October 1889, at an average weight of 14lb 5oz, the heaviest scaling 33lb. Three years later Colonel Sandeman was back on the Usk during the first fortnight of October. In 11 days' fishing he took 108 salmon. That the Usk was not just an autumn river at this time is borne out by five days in May 1896 when Colonel Sandeman had 20 fish, the biggest 36½lb. Another Usk angler, A. Crayshaw, fished the river from about 1873 to 1930. His best catch was 26 in one day (in 1873), his best season 1888 when he had 264 fish. Altogether Mr Crayshaw caught 13 salmon weighing over the 40lb mark from the Usk, ten of them in the decade 1921–30.

The Wye has long been famous for its big 'portmanteau' salmon. It also produced big bags of big fish. On 19 May 1913 Major Walter de Winter had 17 fish, averaging 18lb 7oz, the biggest exactly 30lb. In six days from 4–9 April 1916 J.A. Hutton caught 31 salmon averaging 21½lb, the biggest 32lb. However, the most famous angler on this water was Robert Pashley, the 'Wizard of the Wye'. In some years he took over 10 per cent of the total Wye catch on his own rod (in 1926 13½ per cent)! Between 1908 and 1947 he caught 9122 salmon at an average weight of 15½lb. Taking weight as the criterion, his record day was on 28 April 1928 when he had seven fish for 170½lb: an average of 24¼lb. He once had 18 fish in a day, on 30 September 1932, averaging 11¼lb. During his career he also had 29 portmanteau salmon weighing from 40 to 48½lb.

The Welsh Dee salmon run was dominated in the 1920s and 1930s by 2+SW salmon averaging 14–16lb. But these years also produced many fish in the 30–40lb class and the Dee record of 42lb.

On the Eden F. Milburn's record bag is never likely to be surpassed, at least not in the foreseeable future. In one day in March 1922 he took 13 salmon totalling 315lb and averaging 24¼lb.

The English chalk streams were once famous for their bags of large spring fish, running into the thirties of pounds. The record comes from the Frome, 48½lb, and the year . . . 1929!

On the Shannon Lliam Ford had a magnificent bag in 1933 of six fish weighing between 21 and 50½lb. Colonel Maunsell's bag in one day in 1928 also takes some beating: eight fish, four of them over 30lb and the best pulled the scales down to 37lb.

A survey of the angling press for the 10 years 1985–94 makes an interesting, though sad, contrast with these records from the end of the last and the first half of this century. Whilst the Tay is still a big-fish river, with records in the 30lb class each year, a 42lb fish taken in October 1992 was the largest reported. In 1993 a 46lb salmon was reported from the Nith. It was noted as being 'the biggest salmon to be reported to *Trout & Salmon* [magazine] for years'. Unfortunately the man who claimed to have caught this big fish was later interviewed by the police and the body taken away for analysis! A 32lb 2oz salmon taken on the Wye on 16 March 1990 was referred to in *Trout & Salmon* magazine as 'an enormous fish'; I wonder if Pashley would have agreed? It is thus clear that the big salmon have greatly declined in the last 50 years. Today the capture of a 40lb salmon is rarer than the capture of a 50lb salmon used to be, while fish in the 30lb class are keenly reported for they are as scarce as 40 pounders were in bygone days, perhaps even scarcer.

It is certain that the overall annual runs of 2+SW salmon have not declined, though the timings of these runs have altered with time. What we have lost is the runs, always fairly small though still significant (especially to anglers), of the bigger 3+SW and 4+SW fish. And big bags of fish, with one or two of these big fish in the bag, gave an average weight in the high teens or twenties of pounds. Why? Where have they gone?

Before considering the demise of the big salmon we will look at some records in other parts of the salmon's range.

WEIGHT	DATE	RIVER	CAPTOR	NOTES
79.38lb	Jul 1928	Tana	H. Hendrickson	World rod-caught record
76lb	Jul 1921	Aaro	–	*
74.97lb	Jul 1925	Dramens	–	Netted
73.867lb	1878 or 1879	Tana	A magistrate from Utsjok	
73.86lb	Jun 1923	Sulen	–	Netted
72½lb	1927	Vosso	Herr Denissoff	
69½lb	1921	Aaro	J. Aarven	
69½lb	Jun 1924	Namsen	S. Kjolstad	4SW
68.56lb	Nov 1919	Vosso	–	Netted
68½lb	1921	Aaro	Herr Denissoff	
68.2lb	?	Bjora	–	
68lb	1923	Vosso	Herr Denissoff	
65lb	Jun 1920	Vosso	F. Isdahl	Mr Isdahl caught a 47lb fish the same day
64lb	1929	Aaro	–	
64lb	Jun 1961	Vosso	–	
63lb	?	Sand	–	
61lb	1924	Bolstad	H. Charrington	
60½lb	1965	Vosso	O. Haraldsen	
60lb	1929	Alta	–	
60lb	1929	Vefsen	–	

WEIGHT	DATE	RIVER	CAPTOR	NOTES
60lb	1951	Alta	Lord Dudley	
58½lb	1911	Evanger	Lady Haworth	
58½lb	1931	Eira	–	
57½lb	1923	Evanger	Mrs Barlow	
55lb	?	Sand	–	
55lb	June 1961	Vosso	–	
54lb	1886	Cascapedia	Mr Dunn	North American record
54lb	1920	Cascapedia	Mr Nadean	
54lb	1973	Laerdal	–	
53lb	1892	Cascapedia	Mr Stanley	
52lb	1928	Vefsen	–	
52lb	1934	Tana (Finnish bank)	–	
52lb	1935	Tana (Finnish side)	–	
52.038lb	1928	Sundal	–	3SW then spawned twice in 3 years, with visits to sea in between spawnings
50lb	1928	Bjora	–	
50lb	1929	Sundal	–	

*This specimen is on display in Bergen Museum.

Again note that of the 33 dated records, 18 (or 55 per cent) are from the 1920s.

The Alta is famed for its big salmon and also some very big bags. In eight hours, one day in 1925, General Trotter had 29 fish for 600lb (and the general was handicapped by having only one arm!). In 1845 E. Brettle had 65 fish in two days' fishing. In 1866 the Duke of Roxburgh had 39 salmon in one day and in 1895 30 in one day. In 1864 Mr Honeywood had 41 in a day (17 were grilse) while in 1867 he had 26 in one day. The Duke of Westminster, Duke of Roxburgh and Viscount Coke fished Alta every summer from 1913 to 1928 – the period of big bags of big fish. Through the night of 7 July 1926, Westminster caught 33 salmon with an average weight of 24¼lb, the bag including four fish in the 30lb class and specimens of 42lb and 45lb. Other

127

notable Alta bags include Roar Joraholmen's 44 salmon in one day and Sam Field's 17 in one night in 1958.

The abundance of multi-sea-winter salmon in the 1920s is further borne out by the catches, in 1924, by W. Radcliffe and H.C. Wilson, on an unnamed river in southern Norway. Mr Radcliffe fished for 34 1/2 days and caught 581 salmon, Mr Wilson 51 1/2 days for 771 salmon. The combined effort of 86 rod-days therefore produced 1352 salmon, an average of over 16 fish each day. Their best combined day was 58 fish, and each of them had a best day of 31 salmon.

Of the Aaro, Charles Ritz recorded that, 'I found on a table a pile of more than twenty drawings of fish over fifty pounds.' None of those, which dated from the 1930s, 1940s and 1950s, feature in the list.

It is clear that in Norway big salmon continued to run after their decline in the British Isles. In the obituary of C.M. Wells in *Salmon & Trout* magazine it is recorded that Wells fished the Bolstad between 1920 and 1939 and between 1946 and 1950. In these years Wells caught 68 fish of between 40 and 49lb, and 12 fish of between 50 and 58lb. One year, one of his guests, Murray Sowerby, had fish weighing 52 and 65lb as well as several 'smaller' fish. Wells also hooked and lost three fish that he considered weighed in excess of 70lb. Again these fish are not listed.

Arthur Oglesby notes that, between 24 May and 20 June 1966, the Bolstad–Vosso had eight salmon in excess of 50lb, and one over 60lb! Alas, Arthur failed to catch a 50 pounder himself, but had one of 49lb and in 1981 had four fish with an average weight of 37.86lb.

Big fish still continue to run these Scandinavian (and recently opened Russian) rivers, though not in the numbers that they once did. Each year several rivers in this region produce fish in excess of 40lb: Alta (which produced one of 49lb in 1993), Tana, Ommedal, Namsen, Gaulfoss, Drammen. One *Trout & Salmon* correspondent from the Stjordal in 1994 noted that 'I have had a report of a fish in excess of 40lb being caught, one of the largest for many years.' And there is still the chance of a mammoth fish for the person who visits the Kola rivers, for in 1993 the same magazine reported that 'The nearby Varzina produced . . . the largest Atlantic salmon ever caught on the fly. This was a huge fish measuring 57.5 inches, caught and released by Sir Seton Wills . . . 70lb-plus seems to be the general opinion.'

Why have the big salmon still survived, albeit in smaller numbers than formerly, in Norwegian and arctic Russian rivers but not in the British rivers? High seas netting cannot be to blame, for the decline occurred before the feeding grounds of the salmon were discovered and then exploited. Certainly damage to rivers is responsible in some rivers: earlier I described how damming,

1 left *The author with grilse; River Alta, Norway*

2 below *River Alta, Norway*

3 above *The Alta produces some very big multi-sea-winter salmon, but not as many, nor as big, as it once did* (see page 127)

4 above *Geoff Haslam with a 2-sea-winter Namsen salmon*

5 left *A trio of salmon from the Namsen, weighing 27, 17 and 14lb. The bigger fish was a 3SW specimen, the smaller ones 2SW*

6 bottom left *Namsen grilse. Note the sea louse near the tail, indicating that it is fresh from the sea*

7 right *17lb of fresh Namsen salmon*

8 below *The River Namsen, one of the world's greatest big-salmon rivers*

9 *Geoff Haslam preparing to tail a salmon from the Norwegian Bjora river*

10 *An Irish summer grilse*

11 left *Northern Ireland's little River Bush. On one beat, the annual catch averages one fish per metre of river bank!*

12 above *The River Mourne, part of the Foyle system. This is probably the world's most prolific salmon river (see page 207)*

13 top left *Fishing the River Mourne*

14 left *The Strule, part of the Foyle system*

15 above *Iceland's River Grimsa*

16 right *The prolific Icelandic river, Laxa i Kjoss*

17 above *A salmon leaps on Canada's Miramichi*

18 right *A typical Canadian Atlantic salmon river, the Margee*

19 bottom left *Scotland's mighty Spey*

20 below *The Tweed in autumn. The best fishing here is now in the autumn, the spring run having declined in the recent years*

24 *Lough Conn, Northern Ireland*

21 above *A fish nearly played out on the Spey*

22 right *Aberdeenshire's Dee, where decline of the spring salmon stocks has prompted drastic conservation measures (see page 211)*

23 left *Lough Melvin, Northern Ireland*

25 above *Loch Maree, Scotland*

26 below *The Ribble, one of Britain's lesser, though still important, salmon rivers (see page 205)*

27 left *Fishing the River Ribble*

28 below *That great salmon angler Hugh Falkus, of 'the river is a smolt factory . . .' fame*

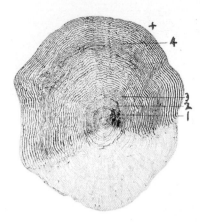

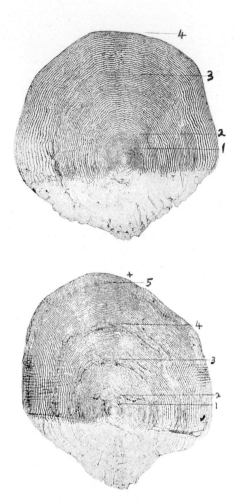

♀
Dee
April
1989

spawning
mark

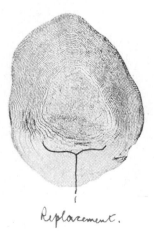

Replacement.

29 top left *Scale taken from 2+1+SW grilse weighing 10½lb, caught on the Lune in October (see page 98)*

30 top right *An example of a replacement scale (see page 98)*

31 above left *Scale from a 2+2SW salmon weighing 9lb, caught on the Dee in March (see page 98)*

32 above right *Scale from a 2+3+SW salmon weighing 35lb, caught on the Namsen in August (see page 98)*

33 left *Scale from a fish that had spawned as a 2+3+ salmon, then fed one summer in the sea before returning to the Namsen where it was caught, weighing 34lb in August (see page 99)*

34 and 35 *A bag of 35 fish caught over two nights by two rods, averaging 28lb. The date is 7–8 July 1929 and the fisherman responsible were Mr N. D. Hamilton and Viscount Coke*

36 right *Mr N. D. Hamilton
with one of the great catches
from this 1920s period for
salmon fishers: a remarkable
60lb fish*

37 and 38 below *Diary page
and summary for 1928 fishing
and results on the River Alta*

Summary. 1928.

Roxburghe 120 salmon = 2691 lbs
Corbet 100 " " = 2541 lbs
Coke 118 " " = 2923 lbs
Hamilton 123 " " = 3130 lbs
Chandler 1 " " . 19 lbs

Total 462 salmon . 11.304 lbs.

41 lbs in Vina Gora.

15 fish over 40 lbs including 2 fifty pounders in one night.
52 fish over 30 lbs

462 salmon averaging 24 lbs.

DATE	HEIGHT OF RIVER	RODS	BEAT	FISH	TOTAL	WEIGHT	DAYS TOTAL	DAYS WEIGHT
June 30th	1'5"	Li. Hamilton	U. Vina.	21.15.17.23.23.22.33.19.21.21.22.30.24.27. 1 Kelt	14	318 lbs		
		Ld. Coke	L. Vina.	22.42.24.29.15.20.25.24.12.31.31.30.22.23. 1 Kelt	14	350 lbs	50	1192 lbs
		Maj. B. Corbet	U. Jora.	29.28.24.27.28.28.29.25.24.16.25.24.17.	13	325 lbs		
		Duke of Roxburghe	L. Jora.	17.16.24.27.21.18.21.16.20.	9	199 lbs		
July 1st	1'2"	Coke	U. Vina.	23.31.30.32.20.16.29.20.25.	9	226 lbs		
		Hamilton	L. Vina.	25.21.32.36.29.30.33. 1 Kelt.	7	206 lbs	31	748 lbs
		Roxburghe	U. Jora.	28.20.26.27.21.39.26.18.14.23.	10	214 lbs		
		Corbet	L. Jora.	29.19.17.16.23. 2 Kelts	5	102 lbs		
2nd	1'1"	Hamilton	U. Vina.	25.13.38.29.	4	105 lbs		
		Coke	L. Vina.	13.15.29.34.26.33.21.24.	8	195 lbs	28	684 lbs
		Corbet	U. Jora.	30.28.25.31.28.24.24.	7	190 lbs		
		Roxburghe	L. Jora.	35.25.22.19.16.21.19.23.14.	9	194 lbs		
3rd	1'0"	Coke	U. Vina.	25.24.	2	49 lbs		
		Hamilton	L. Vina.	36.21.22.23.21.20.24.19.25.14.29.25.39.28	14	346 lbs	26	629 lbs
		Roxburghe	U. Jora.	20.18.20.23.20.26.16. 1 Kelt.	7	143 lbs		
		Corbet	L. Jora.	34.22.35. 1 Kelt	3	91 lbs		
4th	1'0"	Coke	U. Sandia.	15.31.27.25.19.29.28.31	8	206 lbs		
		Hamilton	L. Sandia.	34.24.26.34.25.37.25.25.20.21.	10	271 lbs	36	931 lbs
		Corbet	U. Jora.	28.41.48.17.19.22.27.23.	8	235 lbs		
		Roxburghe	L. Jora.	31.15.24.19.23.16.17.20.31.24.	10	220 lbs		
5th	-1"	Hamilton	U. Sandia.	39.24.20.26.34	5	143 lbs		
		Coke	L. Sandia.	44.29.34.20.24.23.25.25.	8	224 lbs	25	677 lbs
		Roxburghe	U. Vina.	20.19.34.26.24	5	123 lbs		
		Corbet	L. Vina.	23.24.23.34.29.31.23.	7	187 lbs		

YEAR 1928.

PAGE TOTAL ... 196 4862 lbs

BROUGHT FORWARD

CARRY FORWARD 196 4862 lbs

land drainage and water abstraction may have reduced a river from a big-fish river into a grilse and small 2+SW salmon river. But some rivers remain untouched, or relatively so, by human damage, yet they no longer produce big salmon. There is, however, one piece of circumstantial evidence that might give us a clue.

It had been observed, from the late 1920s to 1931, that huge tuna (tunny) were feeding in the North Sea and off the west coast of the British Isles on herrings, these big fish having been seen following the herring boats and even taking dead herrings from around the boats when the nets were being drawn aboard. In 1932 a few anglers tried fishing for these tuna with rod and line, and managed to catch 21 fish, the best scaling 789lb. In 1933 the British Tunny Club was founded in Scarborough and that season members caught 80 fish, 20 of them being certified by the club as scaling between 456 and 763lb, one, not certified, weighing a massive 851lb. The following year, 1934, the herring shoals and tuna were far offshore, owing to bad weather, but the club members still managed to catch 29 certifiable fish of between 419 and 812lb. Sport fishing for tuna continued up to about 1960, though in the 1950s numbers were declining rapidly. Why? Because of the over-exploitation and decline of the herring stocks from about 1955.

The tuna is a species of the warmer water of the North Atlantic and it used to head north to feed on herrings off the western coasts of the British Isles and in the North Sea in summer. But was it the only fish to decline when the herring stocks collapsed? Perhaps not. It is hard to believe that these same herrings were not also the food of the Atlantic salmon and that the demise of the big bags of big multi-sea-salmon was not due to the loss of this food source.

Some firm evidence for this comes from the 14th Annual Report of the Fishery Board for Scotland, published in 1894 at a time when big salmon were being reported regularly. The Report includes an analysis of the stomach contents of 1694 Tweed salmon, most of them caught in the estuary. Overall about 15^1/$_2$ per cent of these contained food (in spring the figure was as high as 43^1/$_2$ per cent) and herrings featured prominently. These salmon were clearly feeding, mostly on herring, almost up to the time that they began to run the river. Today they do not. W.M. Shearer also reported that, of 88 salmon caught in North Sea drift nets in 1964 (during the period when the herring stocks were declining), 48 per cent of fish in spring had fed on herrings. Similar corroborative evidence come from the Baltic. Here the herring stocks declined in the first half of this century, but since the late 1970s stocks have again grown. The consequence has been an increased size of salmon running some of the Swedish rivers (such as the Morrum, where in 1993 one angler caught two 40 pounders in one day).

The final thread of evidence linking big salmon with herring stocks is the sudden surge of big salmon records in the 1920s. Between 1914 and 1918 the herring fishing fleets were largely laid up because of the First World War. Herring stocks exploded so that through the 1920s and 1930s herring, tuna and big salmon flourished.

Why have Norwegian rivers and the salmon rivers draining into the Arctic Ocean from Russia kept a run of big fish? No one knows, but it is possibly because these have been feeding off northern Norway and in the Arctic Ocean where the food necessary for them to attain great size over three or four years' feeding at sea has not declined.

What seems so remarkable is that anglers in the nineteenth and first half of the twentieth century could catch such big fish with the relatively crude tackle that they were using. Back-breakingly heavy built cane or greenheart rods, dressed silk lines and gut leaders, heavy hooks and heavy brass reels. But perhaps it is not so remarkable after all! In fact, the tackle being used was ideal for the job. The old brass 4½in Hardy Perfect reel and heavy rod may seem cumbersome today compared with light carbon fibre rods and aluminium reels, but they were an efficient combination for playing big fish in fast, turbulent water. The modern plastic fly lines seem so easy for casting a fly, but the old silk lines, with their narrower diameter, had less water and air resistance, and so had the edge over the modern lines when it came to casting and fly control in the water.

In the old days the big flies that caught big salmon were often dressed on big, strong, single hooks, in sizes up to 4/0. Today most anglers in spring and autumn (when there is the best chance of coming across a sizeable salmon in the British Isles, or in Scandinavia and Russia) might well opt for a fly dressed on a tube or Waddington, armed with a small outpoint treble hook. They feel more confident in landing a big fish on a small treble hook than on a big single iron. In fact they are wrong! The big single is far better than any other hook for landing a big fish. I remember landing a spring salmon on the Eden on a tube fly and size 10 treble hook. The fish was not that big, a mere 27lb, but the two points of the hook that had penetrated the jaw of the fish had opened by the time I had landed the fish and I reckon that if the fish had fought for another few minutes I would have lost it owing to hook failure. In contrast I know several Norwegian and Finnish anglers who still use flies dressed on big singles rather than tubes and small trebles in their big-fish rivers. So if you ever go to fish for big salmon, let me urge you to try big, single hooks and leave your tube flies and Waddington shanks at home!

But unless there is a sudden revival of the populations of big salmon most of us will never have the chance of playing one, let alone landing it!

CHAPTER 5

SALMON BEHAVIOUR IN FRESH WATER

Our accumulated knowledge of the salmon and the methods of fishing
for it can be likened to a jigsaw puzzle. Some anglers would undoubtedly
say that many of the pieces are unavailable and will inevitably remain so:
that the picture cannot possibly be completed. I feel that
all the pieces are within reach . . . .

R.V. RIGHYNI, *Advanced Salmon Fishing*, 1977

It is vitally important that the salmon angler knows precisely what the
salmon is up to when it is in the river, for without that information the
angler becomes just a casting machine who hopes that eventually a fish will
co-operate by taking hold of the fly or bait. This is especially important when
there are few salmon in the river. If a pool is stuffed with fish, then the casting
machine will take some; when there are very few, the casting machine may well
fail to catch any at all. Indeed, some anglers, after several years of catching few
fish, admit defeat and shun rivers or times when there are few fish about,
preferring to pay vast sums to fish only when and where salmon are abundant.
Yet the capture of a single salmon in arduous conditions is far more of an act
of angling skill than catching a dozen on an overpriced beat that is full of fish.

It has been said, rightly, that 90 per cent of salmon are caught by 10 per cent
of anglers or, as my old pal Roy Brierley put it, 'When I hear of a salmon being
caught on this river, I know it will have been taken by one of four names!' Roy
was correct. One year five rods took from one beat, fishing one or two days
each week over six weeks, 24 salmon; many other rods managed only three
between them! Those five rods may have fished hard, known the water and
been able to handle their fishing tackle well. But their chief advantage was in
large part down to their understanding of what the fish were up to.

The most successful salmon anglers know their beat well (or they take a
short cut by paying for a gillie to give them the necessary information). They,
or good gillies (and there are many bad ones), know precisely where the
salmon will be at all heights of water. I know someone who is convinced that

131

one small pool under some trees is a salmon lie, yet in 16 years not a single fish has been seen or caught there! Yet that person does not know the precise location of salmon in that river beat. The successful anglers will know the best times to catch the fish, both in the year and in the day. I was once told of a London surgeon who bemoaned the fact that he hadn't caught a salmon on his Tweed beat in six years. He fished it in July and he was unaware that the beat had not produced a July fish for donkeys' years! The successful anglers know what fly to use and the best way of showing it to the salmon: they don't just go casting and hope that a fish will oblige. And of course they persevere and have sufficient confidence not to become disheartened. Fish hard and think like a salmon. That is the way to catch them!

Why a salmon takes a fly or bait

What is the salmon doing when it is lying in the river? The first thing that it is *not* doing is looking for food, for the salmon does not feed after it has left the sea and is waiting to spawn.

There are some who would disagree with this statement, just as there are those who still maintain that the earth is flat and the moon made of cheese. For instance, G.P.R. Balfour-Kinnear noted, in *Flying Salmon* (2nd ed., 1947), that 'Some . . . say that it takes the fly as food and actually does eat while in fresh water, though very sparingly. Personally I am inclined to agree with this last theory. I would also account for the suspended digestive process by suggesting that the salmon eats so little and so seldom, while in fresh water that it has very little to digest . . .'

However, the facts are these:

• The gut of the salmon is atrophied when it returns to the river; it is incapable of digesting food. The gut does not atrophy, as Balfour-Kinnear suggests, because it is eating 'so little and seldom, while in fresh water'.

• Rarely are any items found in the stomach of a salmon caught in a river or lake, and these items appear just as likely to be inanimate objects (tiny pebbles) or bits of leaf or twig, as tiny animals such as insects or crustaceans.

• In the sea the salmon selects foods of a fairly large size, such as lesser fish, large shrimps and prawns. If the salmon fed in the river or lake we would expect similar foods to be taken. Furthermore, in the sea the salmon is an opportunistic feeder; it will take whatever is available. Not so in the river or lake! I have watched salmon parr, small trout and shoals of small dace swimming close to salmon lying in the river and never seen a salmon respond to their presence. Indeed, as Hugh Falkus has said so many times, if salmon (or big sea trout) did feed in the river then the river stocks of small fish would quickly become depleted.

So salmon do not feed in rivers, but that is not to say that a salmon will not occasionally use its mouth to take hold of something that, to our eyes, may suggest food and that it is feeding.

Very occasionally a salmon will be seen taking into its mouth an insect from the water surface. Neil Graesser described vividly such an instance in his book *The Finer Points of Fly Fishing for Salmon* (1989). Graesser had spotted a salmon taking daddy-long-legs and the occasional grasshopper that was being blown on to the river. He then described how he collected some of these insects from the riverside herbage and dropped them into the flow. 'Nearly every time an insect floated over him, he sucked it in quietly, but whenever a grasshopper was released he made a far more vicious rush at it.' Was that salmon feeding?

Fly fishing

The whole art of fly dressing and fly fishing for salmon was originally based on imitative trout fly fishing, where the natural foods of trout are matched with artificial flies. Indeed, some early writers assumed that the only difference between fly fishing for trout and fly fishing for salmon was that the trout ate small flies whereas the salmon took larger natural flies. In 1651 Thomas Barker, in *Barker's Delight, or the Art of Angling*, explained that 'The Salmon swimmeth most commonly in the midst of the river . . . If you angle for him with a flie (which he will rise to like a Trout) the flie must be made of a large hook, which must carry six wings, or four at least.'

Richard Brookes took this a stage further in *The Art of Angling* in 1766 when he explained that 'There is a Fly called the Horse-leech fly, which he is very fond of; they are of various Colours, have great Heads, large Bodies, very long Tails, and two, some have three, Pair of Wings, placed behind each other.' The Horse-leech fly is one old name for dragonflies, and the long tail referred to is really the tapering abdomen.

In the later editions of Richard Bowkler's *The Art of Angling*, published by his son Charles through the second half of the eighteenth century, there are three dragonfly imitations specifically designed to catch salmon that were feeding on dragonflies. George C. Bainbridge continued the dragonfly theme in his *The Fly Fisher's Guide* of 1816, but also added two other salmon flies that imitated insects, the Quaker Fly, undoubtedly a drab moth or butterfly (e.g. meadow brown) imitation, and a Wasp Fly, which, as its name implies, imitates a wasp. It was during the nineteenth century that salmon flies began generally to become gaudy affairs. The reason for this was partly that gaudy feathers, tinsels and silks became readily available, but also that there was a widespread belief that salmon ate butterflies. One of the earliest of butterfly imitations using such exotically lurid materials was by Ireland's Pat McKay (c. 1810–70). His Golden Butterfly included silver and gold tinsels, bright yellow floss silk, golden pheasant, wood duck, cock-of-the-rock and kingfisher in its dressing. It was from this basis of imitating the larger insects that salmon might eat that the whole range of late nineteenth to early twentieth century 'classic' or 'fully dressed' salmon flies, and the shrimp–prawn flies (including some of the very latest), evolved.

But salmon do not feed in rivers on dragonflies, wasps and butterflies, any more than they feed on shrimps or prawns, or earthworms or tiny insects. They may take them into their mouths, but they are not feeding on them.

One very popular way of fly fishing for salmon (especially in the north-eastern USA and Canada and, to a lesser extent, in Scandinavia and some Scottish rivers such as the Dee) is with a dry fly, and many of the dry flies in use are insect imitations. I emphasize the words 'dry fly'; I am not talking of wake lures or Yellow Dollies or Bombers which may attract the salmon by their movement across the flow. I am talking of a dry fly that floats passively, without dragging, down the flow as does an insect that has just fallen on the water or hatched at the water's surface. In the course of a day the salmon must see many hundreds if not thousands of natural insects drifting downstream in this way. If salmon really did feed on insects, then these are what they would be eating (in the same way as Graesser watched them taking daddy-long-legs and grasshoppers).

The dry fly technique is to fish a known salmon lie or to cast where a salmon has been seen to move, usually in the middle of a warm, bright sunny day with the river on the low side. Cast after cast after cast is made and, eventually, up comes the salmon. It may take on the first cast. It may take on the hundredth cast. One on the Stjordal took on the 138th cast, one on the Miramichi on the 68th cast, one on the Dee on about the 200th cast. But never have I found a solitary insect in the stomach of any salmon taken on such dry insect imitations.

Only once have I seen a salmon definitely take an insect (a small sedge) from the water surface. That was on the Lune and I caught that salmon on a size 10 dry Brown Sedge. There was no sign of the natural sedge in its mouth, throat or stomach. That great angler Howard Croston told me of a similar experience he had with a 14lb salmon on the Lowther.

Big sea trout, which are anadromous fish like the salmon, also have an atrophied gut when they are in the river or lake. I stress 'big sea trout', fish of two pounds or more, and not small herling that will feed quite keenly at times on their first return from the sea. Big sea trout will rise to take insects from the water surface far more frequently than salmon and it is said that they are then feeding. On numerous occasions, on a total of 17 rivers, I have watched big sea trout that seemed to be feeding on (or at least rising to) blue-winged olives, autumn duns, pale wateries, small sedges, black gnats, once daddy-long-legs and, once, small metallic green beetles from the river surface. Many of these sea trout have then fallen to my dry fly, as shown in the following table.

	NUMBER CAUGHT	NUMBER WITH FOOD IN THEIR STOMACH
Nith	32	0
Annan	12	1 (one insect)
Spey	38	0
Border Esk	9	2 (three insects)
Aberdeen Dee	16	0
Lune	11	1 (one insect)
Misc	31	3 (seven insects)
TOTAL	149	7 (twelve insects)

Less than 5 per cent had something that could be considered a food item in the stomach, and there was an average of only 0.2 food items in these sea trout, in spite of the fact that they had been seen taking a potential food item from the water. I think that it is fair to say that these sea trout were not feeding, any more than I am feeding when I chew my pencil as I ponder the next sentence (and I am sure that the odd pencil fragment does find its way into my stomach and would be found if the contents of my stomach were analysed!). Yet big sea trout have a greater reputation for feeding than salmon!

The point is that, because salmon take our fly or bait into their mouth, we automatically associate this with feeding. After all, that is what we are doing, usually, when we pop something into our mouth. As T.C. Kingsmill Moore put it in his classic book *A Man May Fish* (1960):

Modern man uses his mouth only for eating (apart from talking and kissing which have no interest for fish) and he assumes that when a fish takes something into his mouth the reason is that he wants to eat. This overlooks the cardinal anatomical fact that a fish *has no hands*. Everything that a man does with his hands, or other animals do with their paws, a fish must do with its mouth if it does it at all.

Response to animate bait

Leaving aside for one moment inanimate baits, such as metallic spinners and fur and feather flies, consider the salmon's response to the animate baits, prawns and worms. It has been said that salmon may rush around or flee from a pool when a prawn is cast into the water. I have never seen this myself (because I have so rarely fished a prawn). But assuming that it is correct, why should they respond in this way? When a salmon takes an angler's prawn in a river it may just nip at the whiskers or head. It is a completely different reaction, but neither behaviour is a feeding action, for a salmon that is feeding on prawns simply engulfs them whole.

The use of the free-lined humble worm (with just enough Plasticine on the line to sink it) can teach us much about why the salmon takes any of our baits or flies in the river or lake. Of course, because earthworms are commonly used as baits for a variety of fish that do feed, it is easy to assume that salmon take our worm for the same reason. It has been said that a salmon mistakes a big bunch of lobworms for an octopus or squid: a feeding response? But when a salmon at sea takes a squid it doesn't chew it slowly. It swallows it in one gulp (or at least, that is what farmed salmon do when feeding in their sea cages). It has been said that a salmon take a worm and chews it to extract the juices. But explain the following as feeding behaviour: I was fishing in a hot sunny afternoon on the Spey and, as a change from the fly, I decided to give the worm a go. I was wading a clear, steady pool and saw everything clearly. I cast the worms up and across the flow and as they passed below me I saw a dark shape move to intercept them. I felt the typical pull and grating sensation as the salmon picked up the worms and manoeuvred them in the front of its mouth. Before striking I waited for the fish to take the worms into its mouth. But it didn't. After a few minutes the salmon slowly swam upstream, brushing the side of my waders as it went past, with the worms right at the front of its mouth. Then, about five yards upstream of me it dropped the worms and slowly swam back, downstream. I have since witnessed this behaviour twice more, both times on the Hodder. That was no feeding response!

Once, again on the Spey, I watched a salmon take my worm in the front of its mouth and hold it there for perhaps a minute. Then it dropped the worm, which then continued to drift downstream. Once, on the Avon near Tomintoul, I watched a salmon approach my single lobworm, prod at it with its snout, and then retire.

On five other occasions I have seen salmon react in quite different ways that have resulted in their being well hooked. One day I found three salmon lying in a clear, gravel-bottomed lie. I cast a bunch of worms upstream so that they came back downstream on the bottom of that lie. If the worms were to either side of the fish they ignored them, but if the worms came down in front of their noses they simply moved to one side to let them pass. This went on for over an hour. Then, on the umpteenth cast with the worms coming down in line with one of the fish, instead of moving aside the salmon picked up the worms, held them in the front of its mouth for perhaps thirty seconds, and then slowly took them down. When I landed that salmon I found the hook had taken hold in the sphincter muscle at the entrance to the oesophagus.

On an almost identical occasion, but this time with just one salmon in a small lie, I fished the worm for almost half an hour before the salmon responded (other than by moving aside if the worms came too close). The worms were moving gently downstream on at least the sixtieth cast when the salmon surged forward and, in a split second, engulfed them. Again the fish was hooked at the back of its throat. Now if those salmon were hungry, or wanted to feed, would they have waited for so long before taking hold? No! Had I not been able to see the fish, nor known that they were there, I might have imagined that the fish took immediately they first saw the worms and, because the worms finished off in the back of the mouth, I might have been led to believe that they had taken them as food.

Consider other responses to the worm that I have observed. Three times I have seen salmon swim forcefully at the worms and hit them with their tail (twice) and head (once), but then leave them and return to their lie. I felt a hard knock on the line as they did so. Thereafter those salmon ignored the worm. Once I hooked a salmon on worm after such a hard knock and found that the fish was foul-hooked under the chin.

I do not believe that salmon that have been feeding on swift-moving prey for a year or so in the sea would be so incompetent at catching slow-moving worms in their mouth if they were trying to eat them. Several times I have watched salmon pursuing my worms both slowly (as the worms drifted down-stream in the flow) and quickly (as I reeled them in). In September 1993, on the River Nith, one salmon chased my bunch of worms three times in four casts. If they were chasing them because they wanted to eat them they would have taken a firm hold, for they could easily have caught them.

On no occasion when I have been able to watch the response of the salmon to worms has the response been a typical feeding response. In his book *Salmon Fishing* (1984) Hugh Falkus described 13 possible responses of salmon to the prawn. I have not witnessed all these responses, but it seems from my observations plus the summary by Falkus that it is possible to give a scale of 1–10 for the salmon's response to a prawn:

1. Ignores it: there may or may not be some visible sign that the fish has sensed the prawn's presence, for sometimes the fins can be seen to quiver and, instead of lying motionless in its lie, it may move a little from side to side or up from the riverbed.
2. Examines it but then ignores it.
3. Follows the prawn but does not attempt to take it.
4. Hits the prawn with its head or tail or, if the prawn is lying still on the bottom, rolls on it.
5. Nips the head or whiskers, or sucks at the eggs (in a berried prawn).
6. Sucks the prawn into the mouth but then blows it out undamaged.
7. Sucks the prawn into the mouth, crushes it, but then blows it out.
8. Grabs a firm hold when the prawn enters its lie.
9. Leaves its lie and rushes to grab the prawn.
10. Leaves its lie and flees from the prawn, returning to its lie later.

Only two of these responses could possibly be construed as feeding responses, for a salmon that intended to eat a prawn would just swallow it, not play around with it or swim away from it. But the fact that the salmon grabs the prawn firmly in its mouth does not mean that the salmon intended to eat it. Observations of caged fish indicate that the feeding salmon would hardly just take the prawn in its mouth, but would be more likely to swallow it right down in one gulp.

Response to inanimate bait, or fly

Observations suggest a similar range of responses of salmon to the angler's flies:

1. Alas, more often than not the salmon completely ignores the fly.
2. Fin movement increases as the fly passes in front of the salmon. On subsequent casts the fish may either ignore the fly or make a stronger response.
3. The salmon rises a very short distance towards the fly as it passes over its head or moves forward towards it as it crosses in front – moving a very short distance, its body length at most, and without breaking the water surface. I have seen salmon making this response the first time a fly has passed over them but subsequently ignored the fly (even with changes of size and pattern). Twice I have witnessed a salmon making this response the

first time the fly passed, then ignoring the fly (again, despite changes of size and pattern), but then taking boldly after about 20 minutes and 2¹/₂ hours.

4. The salmon moves more strongly to the fly. With a dry fly or a fly fished just below the surface the angler sees this happen (the salmon swirls at the surface) and assumes that the salmon has missed the fly or 'come short'. Sometimes a change of fly pattern or size will result in the fish taking hold on the next cast, although often the fish will ignore the fly on the next cast.

5. The salmon chases the fly. Several times, when working a fly across a slow pool, I have had a salmon follow the fly in, almost to the rod tip. Twice I have induced a salmon that was following the fly to take hold by accelerating the rate of retrieve. Once the same salmon, presumably, followed my fly in three times without taking. More often a salmon will follow the fly in but ignore it on subsequent casts.

6. The salmon 'hits' at the fly. I have seen this only once when I think the salmon was not trying to take the fly into its mouth but bump the fly hard with its snout (a similar response comes when fishing worm and prawn). In his book *A Line on Salmon* (1983) John Ashely-Cooper described how he watched a salmon in the Vatnsdalsa River, Iceland, rise to his fly and then turn, hitting the fly with its tail. Anthony Crossley described a similar incident in *The Floating Line for Salmon & Sea-Trout* (1939) in which the salmon rose to the fly but then 'drowned' it by barging the fly with its body. I suspect that the occasional salmon that are foul-hooked in the gill cover or chin, the side or base of the dorsal fin or the tail just in front of the caudal fin are fish that have not intended to take the fly in their mouth (if they wanted to do this they would have done so) but have been belligerently barging into the fly.

7. The salmon takes the fly in its mouth and may or may not be hooked. The salmon's response to the fly is more difficult to watch precisely than its response to worm or prawn because the latter can be fished so much more slowly. But I think that the salmon might take the fly into its mouth in one of three ways:

a) the fly is tweaked; it never is fully in the fish's mouth. This perhaps explains those offers to the fly where the line is pulled out for a short distance and then nothing. If fishing from the reel, there is a short 'zzzzzz' and nothing more. It might also explain the sudden hard 'knock' that we sometimes get, especially when fishing a deep fly on a sinking line.

b) the fly is sucked in and immediately blown out. I think that I have seen this once from a bridge over the Lune. I was watching an angler casting over five fresh-run grilse. One of them rose and took the fly. I saw the fly line stop momentarily but then the fish swam back down to its lie without the fly. The angler felt and saw nothing.

c) the salmon takes hold firmly and ought to be well hooked.

Again, a range of responses from a predatory fish that, if it was intending to take and swallow the fly as food, could intercept a fly perfectly with great precision. The fact that in only one of these is the fly firmly taken into the salmon's mouth indicates that most responses are not feeding responses. Furthermore, even on the rare occasions when the salmon does take our fly into its mouth properly (response 7c) it does not mean that the salmon takes it as a food item.

One has to ask again, why does the salmon take our fly or bait? Apart from when they are feeding, T.C. Kingsmill Moore suggested that there are three other reasons why any fish may take something into its mouth: fear of the object, anger at the object's presence, and curiosity. Hugh Falkus then takes this a stage further by suggesting six reasons why a salmon might take our fly or bait. Gary Anderson agrees with Falkus's reasons for Atlantic salmon on the western side of the Atlantic in his book *Atlantic Salmon: Fact & Fantasy* (1990). These six reasons or motives, given by Falkus and then by Anderson, are:

1. the sudden reawakening of the feeding habit,
2. aggression (the fly invades the territory of the salmon),
3. irritation (the often repeated appearance of the fly irritates the fish),
4. inducement (the fish is induced to chase and grab a fleeing fly),
5. curiosity (what is it?),
6. playfulness.

Falkus considered that the typical take that results in the fish being hooked is indicative of the feeding habit response, and that the aggressive response is indicated by a violent positive 'crunch' take. In both of these the salmon is usually well hooked. It is also usually well hooked if it takes by inducement (though, as I have just described, the fish may follow the fly and turn away without taking). Curiosity, irritation and playfulness may result in a variety of 'takes' – from one that the angler may not be aware of to a gentle tweak, a knock or pull; but these rarely result in a well-hooked fish.

Salmon taking times

It is a remarkable fact that salmon will not take our fly consistently well throughout the day. There are times when they take with gusto, times when the occasional fish may take, and periods when the fish seem completely uninterested in our fly.

A few years ago I returned to the fishing inn by the River Nith with a salmon and discovered that two other anglers had also been successful. During our conversation we discovered that all three fish had been caught between 11 and 11.15 in the morning. Not another fish had been hooked that day, despite there being a lot of fish in the river. That is quite a common phenomenon, so much so that we can often expect to catch salmon at certain times on rivers that we know well. For instance on the Dee, in August, when the river is on the low side and the weather warm and sunny, I expect to catch from 9.30 a.m. to 12 noon and from 6.30 to 8.30 p.m. because experience has taught me that, in those conditions, few fish will look at my fly outside those periods.

Sometimes we can even sense a taking time. One morning in October 1982 Geoff Haslam and I went down to the Hodder. Geoff went upstream to fish a tiny pot near our fishing hut whilst I fished the neck of the big pool. After about half an hour Geoff returned to change his rod and just as he set off back upstream I hooked a fish. Geoff stopped and came back to tail the fish for me, but immediately the fish was on the bank he set off hurriedly upstream to the little pot. Less than 10 minutes later he returned with a silver salmon. 'I knew that it was there and that I had only a few minutes in which to catch it!' he told me. 'So I had to rush off quickly.' We admired the two fish, caught within a quarter of an hour of each other, and then fished hard through the rest of the day without a single offer.

I have had, on a few occasions, a similar sixth sense that it was time for a salmon to take. One was when I took a student, Nick Abbot, down to the river to witness the last day of the 1983 season: it is usually the kiss of death to invite someone to watch you salmon fishing! Several of us arrived at dawn for the end-of-season party, but by 10 a.m. not a fish had been seen, never mind caught. 'Come on, Nick,' I said, 'let's catch a salmon!'; for I suddenly felt in my water that there was a taking fish resting in one small lie.

That fish took and was tailed out by Roy: it weighed 12lb. We celebrated with a large Scotch and my angling pals fished hard for nothing. By 11 a.m. they were sitting on the bank, nattering.

At 11.15 I had a second certain feeling that there was another taking fish in that small lie. Nick and I waded in, on the third cast hooked the fish and, Roy refusing to tail it for me, beached it. It was a grilse of about 6lb.

Everyone then fished hard through until about 4 p.m. when we gathered for a last Scotch. Just then Tony Hindle strolled down to the river, passed a bottle of Sheep Dip to the gathered assembly and said that he had popped down to catch the last fish of the season. He made one cast, and hooked and landed a silver 14 pounder!

It would be quite useful if there were hard and fast rules about salmon taking times. But while there are no really 100 per cent rock solid rules, there are pointers that might be useful:

- Salmon take well when the river begins to rise during or immediately after heavy rain. They do not take well when the river has become coloured and is in flood, but when the river begins to fall and clear the salmon take well again right through to the river reaching summer level (see Fig. 19).
- When the river is not in a raging flood, between late spring and autumn, between dawn and mid- to late morning and in the late afternoon through to dark are always great salmon taking times. Actual timing seems to vary from river to river. I have yet to catch a fish on the Dee in summer between the first glimmer of dawn and 8.30 a.m., though from 9.30 a.m. to noon is a great taking time. By contrast, on the Spey dawn to 8 a.m. is as good a time as any. In spring (mid-January to late April) and late autumn (mid-October to the end of November) late morning and the afternoon through until dark is a good taking period (Fig. 20).

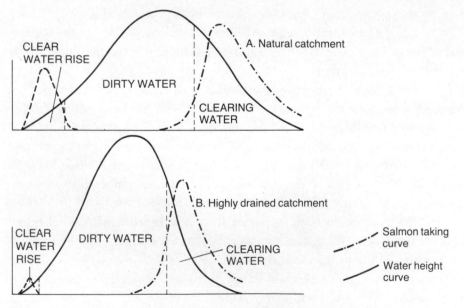

Note how, in a well-drained catchment, spates are of shorter duration, and peak taking periods of salmon correspondingly shorter.

Fig. 19 – River height changes through a spate and best salmon taking times

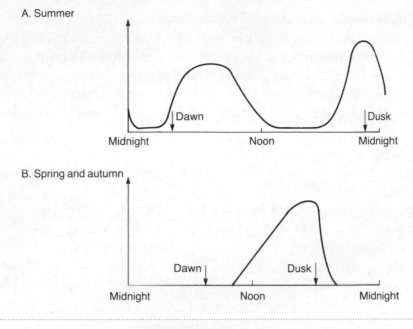

Fig. 20 – Salmon taking times through the day

These pointers should not be considered rules, for I have taken salmon when the river was in a roaring flood, and at all hours of the day and night when it was not in a raging flood.

These good taking times relate quite closely to the times of day when salmon are preparing to run, are resting in between bouts of running, or have just completed a run (see p. 91). And I am sure that it is these salmon that make up the majority of our catch, not salmon that have completed their initial run and are lying doggo until the spawning season. However, salmon that may have been in the river for some considerable time and are making their final movement to the spawning grounds are again taking even though they are often coloured, ripe and not fit to be taken from the river. I will suggest later why salmon that are on some stage of upstream migration are the ones that we are most likely to catch.

Reasons and excuses for not catching fish

Many earlier angling writers have suggested other pointers for good taking times – or, more often, bad taking times. When the river is rising. When the river is more acid. When air temperature is colder than water temperature.

When the air temperature suddenly falls. When a cold wind is whipping up the water surface. When there is no wind. When . . . whenever we can think of a good excuse (not reason) for not catching fish! Through the kindness of Lord Home of the Hirsel I present you now with the 'Reasons to account for want of sport' produced by General Sir Percy Feilding KCB which include times and reasons for salmon not taking the fly. I have appended notes as appropriate:

1. *'The river is waxing.'*
A rising river results in poor fishing. Generally true.
2. *'The water is too black.'*
Salmon do not take well in filthy water that is carrying a lot of flotsam. But coloured water is another matter: on a falling spate the fish take well despite colour in the water. It has also been written that peat puts salmon off the fly. Yet some of my best bags in Ireland have been in water the colour of Theakston's bitter!
3. *'The wind is no' in the right qurt.'*
4. *'There's a fog on the river.'*
5. *'There's mist on the hills.'*
These three reasons relate to the adage that salmon will not take a fly when air temperature is colder than water temperature. A cold northerly or north-easterly wind, especially in spring and autumn, is said to put the fish off taking the fly. I have no evidence for this. I think that the angler is more affected than the fish. I have caught too many salmon when the rod rings have been freezing up (including one icy, misty dawn in July on the Spey) to believe it myself. However, this adage has been put forward by so many writers that many anglers have come to believe that it is true.
6. *'There's thunder about.'*
7. *'The glass is falling.'*
I am sure that salmon can detect changes in the weather, especially barometric changes through their sensitive lateral lines (see p. 24). The arrival of thundery conditions or a low pressure system is usually associated with impending rain, and rain is often associated with a rising river level. The salmon must prepare to shift its lie and perhaps run upstream, in which case it is more likely, not less likely, to take. I have caught too many summer and autumn salmon on a 'falling glass' (i.e. when a deep low has been sweeping in from the Atlantic) to worry about it.

Warning: Should a thunderstorm suddenly develop, if you are fishing a carbon fibre rod lay it aside until the storm has passed, for a carbon fibre rod is a very efficient lightning conductor and if you are holding it when lightning strikes you are likely to be killed.

8. *'The weather is too warm.'*

It is certain that from late morning to early evening in high summer, when the river is low, the weather is very hot and the sun streaming down from a cloudless sky, is a difficult time to catch salmon. But wait until evening, or go out in the early morning: if fresh fish are running you will catch them then.

9. *'The fish have been too long in the water.'*

We are, in the main, trying to catch running salmon. Those salmon that have been resident in a pool for weeks or months are virtually uncatchable. But who wants to catch stale, red, potted fish?

10. *'It is too stormy.'*

This relates to low pressure conditions (see 7, above).

11. *'There are too many white clouds about.'*

White clouds are associated with sunny days and often warm days (see 8, above). Certainly sun glaring directly into the eyes of the salmon means that the fish may not be able to see your fly properly. But when the sun is covered by white or grey cloud salmon may respond well.

12. *'She is too big.'*

A river in flood can be tricky. One fining down and falling is always the best because this is when the biggest runs of fish may occur (especially in small spate streams).

13. *'She is too sma'.'*

On big rivers fish can run in all heights of water, but in tiny spate streams we need water for the fish to run (see p. 84).

14. *'She is too dirty.'*

Fish tend not to run when the spate is at its peak and carrying a load of filth. But when it starts to clear . . .

15. *'She is too clear.'*

It doesn't matter how clear the water. If salmon are running they can be caught.

16. *'There's too much sun.'*

See 8 and 11, above.

17. *'There's too little wind.'*

The angler's fault: if there are fresh salmon in the pool or lake, fish finer and cast so that the line does not splash on the water.

18. *'The wind is too gusty.'*

This relates to low pressure conditions (see 7 and 10, above). Perhaps the angler's fault, an inability to cast in strong winds.

19. *'There's going to be a change in the weather.'*

This relates to weather conditions mentioned earlier (see 6, 7 and 10 above).

20. *'The fish are not settled after the flood.'*
It is a fallacy that fish need to be settled before they take the fly. After a flood the fish will run. Find a resting lie used during the run and you will catch fish.

21. *'The man at the thick end of the rod is a duffer.'*
There is a feeling amongst some old gillies that the quality of salmon anglers has declined since the 1960s. In the old days, so the argument goes, many salmon anglers would have four or more weeks' fishing holiday and fish for two or three days each week on their home rivers. Today many are so busy that they have only one or perhaps two weeks' salmon fishing each year. As well as fishing more often than you really ought, take a rod in your spare time and have some casting practice every week on your local lake, canal or river. If you are new to salmon fishing, go and have some lessons before you start thrashing the river.

22. *'The thistles on the bank get in the way of the fly.'*
A salmon cannot take if the fly is not in the water. Learn to spey cast.

23. *'The fisher is in love and not minding his business.'*
We should not be mechanical casting machines, thinking of irrelevancies such as the office, bank balance and love when we are fishing. We need to concentrate! (See Volume Two, *Salmon on the Fly*.)

24. *'The flies are too big or too sma'.'*
Salmon fly size is important. (Again, see Volume Two, *Salmon on the Fly*.)

25. *'There's too many leaves falling.'*
Leaves floating down the river in autumn snag on the fly and the salmon will not take it. This problem can be reduced greatly by using single hooked flies. (See Volume Two, *Salmon on the Fly*.)

26. *'There's too much grue on the river.'*
Grue is ice formed in the river in subzero temperatures. Salmon tend not to run in very cold conditions. If there are no fresh-run salmon there is little chance of catching a fish.

27. *'There are no fish.'*
The first rule of fishing for salmon is to make sure that there are fish in the river. If there are no fish don't go fishing for them! However, do not believe that, because you don't see any fish, there are none there. Salmon are notorious in some rivers in that they rarely show themselves at the surface. On innumerable occasions my friends and I have caught salmon and yet never saw one all day.

28. *'There has been no spate to clear the rocks.'*
Prolonged low water conditions in summer are always difficult, because salmon may not be running (especially in small spate rivers). But even where

fish are running, angling can be hindered by growths of blanketweed, that slimy alga that clogs the fly on every cast. A spate will wash away the blanketweed.

29. *'There have been too many waxes and the fish are no' settled.'*
One famous adage is that a hopping river, or a river that rises and falls several times in a few days, prevents the fish from taking. This is just not true. Fish when the river is falling and, if salmon are running, you will catch them provided you know their resting lies. In 1983 the river had five rises and falls in three days: I had a salmon on each fall from one known lie used by running salmon.

30. *'There's a bad light on the water.'*
Glaring afternoon summer sun can be difficult, and some writers have argued against light that gives the river a milky appearance. But if the fish are running . . .

31. *'There's too much snaw brae in the river.'*
Snow broth is a feature of very cold water in 'spring' rivers. This impedes the salmon run.

32. *'It's o'er gurly.'*
Always a useful excuse for not catching a fish! It's one that I use a lot.

No matter what the weather or river conditions, go salmon fishing whenever you can – you may find a fish that has not read the lists of reasons why you will not catch it!

Why some times are better than others

There are several theories why salmon take better at some times than others.

The solunar theory

The solunar theory of salmon taking times (and it is used also by some of my European friends to explain why some days and times are better than others for catching trout) is based on the lunar cycle and the effects of sun and moon on tides.

It is said that fish feed keenly at night when there is a full moon, less so at night when there is half moon and hardly at all when there is no moon: thus fishing for them by day in full moon periods is less effective than at other times of the month, when the fish feed (or, in the case of salmon, have taking times) during the day. When there is a full moon, fishing during the day will be far more successful if the moon is obscured by thick cloud.

Tides are affected by the state of the moon and by its and the sun's positions relative to the earth. When earth, sun and moon are in line (at full moon and new moon) so that sun and moon's gravitational forces are not working against each other on the oceans, the tides are fast-flowing, high spring tides ('spring', not from the season, but from the old English *springere* meaning to rise or leap). When sun, moon and earth are at right angles to each other, so that the gravitational forces of moon and sun are acting against each other, the tides are more sluggish, low neap tides. According to the solunar theory, when they are feeding in the sea, salmon develop a feeding intensity based on the timing of tides and on the speed and height that the flowing tide attains. When they return to the river they retain this behaviour and are more likely to take an angler's fly or bait around high water and more keenly around spring tide periods.

There is no statistical evidence to support this theory. If there are fresh fish in the river, salmon can be caught no matter what the state of the moon or tide.

The oxygen theory

In 1959 Richard Waddington, in his book *Salmon Fishing*, proposed the oxygen theory of salmon taking times which was later expanded by Reg V. Righyni in two books, *Salmon Taking Times* (1965) and *Advanced Salmon Fishing* (1973). This theory seeks to explain how the times when salmon are more likely to take a fly or bait are affected by changes in the oxygen levels in the river or lake, which are themselves affected by climatic variation. Basically the theory is that the amount of oxygen that can dissolve in the water depends on water temperature, being at maximum when water temperature is 40°F and declining as temperature rises. Any factor that causes a sudden rise in temperature in the day will reduce the volume of oxygen that the water can hold, whereas any factor that causes a sudden drop in water temperature will increase the amount of oxygen that the water can hold.

All of the climatic factors that are contained in General Sir Percy Feilding's list of problems that we have just looked at can, so the theory goes, cause these sudden changes in oxygen level, either individually or by two or more acting together. For instance, as the sun rises over the trees on a late spring morning it may warm the water which will, if fully saturated with oxygen, become supersaturated with oxygen and some oxygen will be released from the water. By contrast, if the relative humidity of the atmosphere is low, or atmospheric pressure is high, or there is a cool wind with northerly aspect, evaporation of water from the river surface will counteract the warming influence of the sun, and keep water temperature, and therefore oxygen concentration, constant.

It is these sudden changes of oxygen level in the water, the oxygen theory states, that trigger the salmon into a taking mood. As the oxygen level changes, whether by increasing a little or decreasing a little, so the salmon become alert and more likely to take the fly.

There is no real need to carry a meteorological station to the riverside to monitor the subtle changes of climatic factors through the day, for Reg Righyni worked out a simple rule of thumb: if it is a good drying day for washing on the line, it is not a very favourable day for catching salmon; if it is what gardeners would 'recognise as a *good growing day*' (Reg's italics), it is a promising day for salmon fishing.

It is a great theory and I would recommend salmon anglers to read the three books that describe it. However, the theory simply does not work!

In all clean salmon rivers and lakes there is ample oxygen dissolved in the water for respiration by salmon, though when the water temperature rises above about 68°F the amount of oxygen that the water can hold becomes dangerously low. Provided that the water temperature is within the normal range of 35 68°F and the water is clean, the sensory system of the salmon is not likely to notice the small and sudden change of oxygen level produced by changes in the intensity of sunlight, atmospheric pressure, relative humidity and so on, any more than we might notice a slight rise or fall in the oxygen level in the air we breathe.

There are two reasons for this. Firstly, it is the amount of oxygen carried by the blood around the body that is important to the salmon, not the amount in clean, cool river or lake water. This oxygen is carried from gills to body tissues by haemoglobin in the red blood corpuscles, and haemoglobin can become fully saturated with oxygen at the gills over a quite wide range of oxygen levels in the water flowing through the gills. So a slight change in the oxygen content of the water will have virtually no effect on the oxygen carried in the blood and the salmon will not notice the change in its body. Secondly, the part of the brain that monitors the need for us to breathe harder or the salmon to pump water through its gills more actively does not monitor the oxygen level in the blood but the carbon dioxide level. Even if oxygen was falling significantly in the water, the salmon would not monitor it. When we pant following physical exertion we do not do so to increase our oxygen intake: we do so to rid our blood of the extra amount of carbon dioxide that our tissues have made when working hard. If we are put in a sealed room we start to pant, not because the amount of oxygen in the room is declining rapidly, but because of the build-up of carbon dioxide. So, too, with the salmon. It will breathe harder if for some reason (perhaps leaping a high obstacle, fighting its way up white water or mating) the carbon dioxide level in the blood increases. It has nothing to do with oxygen levels.

If, therefore, the salmon can obtain the maximum amount of oxygen from the water at all normal water temperatures, and a slight rise or fall of oxygen in the water has no effect on the salmon and is not monitored by the salmon, rises or falls of oxygen in the water will not affect whether or not a salmon is prepared to take our fly.

The hormonal hypothesis

Dr David Goldsborough proposed a theory that was first described by Hugh Falkus in his book *Salmon Fishing* under the title 'The Goldsborough Hypothesis'. This hypothesis states that when it returns to fresh water the feeding drive of the salmon is suppressed and the sex drive increases. Two tiny organs are responsible for these changes of behaviour: the anterior portion of the pituitary gland, a small gland attached to the rear of the base of the brain, and the hypothalamus, the part of the brain to which the pituitary is attached. The two together are known as the pituitary–hypothalamus axis.

The pituitary–hypothalamus axis produces hormones, chemical messengers that flow to all parts of the body through the bloodstream. Amongst the effects of these hormones are the development of the reproductive organs, secondary sexual characteristics such as skin colour changes and the kype of the male, and sexual behaviour. The pituitary–hypothalamus axis also causes a suppression of appetite, so that salmon do not feel hungry and are reluctant to swallow food (they become anorexic) in the river or lake. Hormones produced by the axis also result in the development of aggressive traits. Or, as Falkus put it, 'The hypothesis, therefore, is that variation in salmon taking-behaviour is initiated by the pituitary–hypothalamus axis in increasing sex-drive via the gonadotrophins and associated steroid hormones, and behavioural changes – significantly appetite suppression, controlled by the hypothalamus.'

I would extend the Goldsborough Hypothesis a little further. The pituitary gland also regulates the production of the hormone thyroxine by the thyroid gland. Increased thyroxine causes increased energy production (or metabolic rate) in muscles and alertness in nerve cells, brain and sensory organs. It causes increased heart rate. It causes an increase in restlessness. It is a vital hormone in migrating salmon, and studies have shown a great increase of thyroxine in the blood of salmon that are migrating upstream and very low levels in salmon that are not migrating (those salmon that are settled, for long periods, in pools and that ignore our fly).

We can now link the fluctuations of pituitary–hypothalamus axis and thyroid secretions to the question of why and when salmon take our fly.

There are, I believe, only two reasons why salmon take the fly:

- a temporary return of the feeding habit,
- from aggression.

I believe that aggression is a far more important response than the feeding habit in terms of the proportion of takes by salmon of fly or bait. Both responses are under hormonal control and, because the amount of controlling hormone can vary, both the feeding response and the aggressive response can vary in their intensity. However, alertness is an essential ingredient in both the temporary return of the feeding habit and the arousing of aggression.

We will deal with alertness first. Salmon that are starting to move upstream, or are resting (perhaps for a few seconds or a few hours) in a bout of running, or have just finished running, have a high thyroxine level. They are alert. They are prone to taking the fly. When they stop for a day or more on their initial run, the longer they stop the lower their thyroxine level and state of alertness. They become increasingly less likely to take the fly. When they have become settled in one lie after their initial run, their thyroxine level becomes minimal and they are at their least alert and almost impossible to catch.

Evidence for this comes from a series of observations:

- The general pattern of taking times matches running times and also matches variations in thyroxine levels. Earlier we noted that the first rise of water in a spate, before the water colours, is a potentially good taking time. Fish caught then are not, I think, fish that have started to run. They are probably fish that have been in the pool but are dour, with low thyroxine levels. The initial rise in water, which will later encourage them to run, may result in an increase of thyroxine, which increases alertness, and this turns them into taking fish.

- The fact that, if you fish a known resting lie when fish are running, you can catch fish after fish after fish. That if a big shoal of fish arrives in a beat, with none following behind, fishing success declines the longer the fish have been in the beat. It is well known that stale fish are difficult to catch, and Neil Graesser, in his *The Finer Points of Fly Fishing for Salmon* (1989), describes a remedy:

I also knew one famous angler who would get his gillie to go up and down the pool with a lead weight attached to a length of blind cord, casting it in and pulling it out every two or three yards, before the angler would fish the pool. His theory was, 'What is the point of fishing a pool if all the fish in it are asleep? I want them to be awake so that they will see my fly', and in my experience there was a lot in what he said.

Others have sent their dogs for a swim, or thrown in a few flat stones. Twice

I have caught dour fish that had been turned on by a flotilla of canoes. The disturbance has, through the pituitary–hypothalamus axis, increased the alertness of the fish.

• Many anglers have noticed that a quite high proportion of the fish that we catch have some sort of injury: net damage, seal damage, sometimes damage from otters, cormorants and herons. I have carefully examined salmon that I have caught, or fish that have been caught by others over the past 10 years, for injury or damage no matter how slight and the figures are as follows:

	TOTAL EXAMINED	NUMBER WITH INJURY	% INJURED
Britain	119	21	18
Ireland	220	59	27
Scandinavia	118	33	28
TOTAL	457	113	25

It may be that this proportion of fish with some injury, no matter how slight, is the overall proportion of injured fish running our rivers. But I suspect not. I think that an injured salmon is far more likely to be one that will take our fly or bait than a salmon with no injury. Receiving an injury is traumatic and will result in raised hormone levels, including thyroxine level. The healing process also requires the secretion of hormones. It is likely, therefore, that an injured salmon has a much higher state of alertness than an uninjured fish and this makes it more likely to take our fly.

So salmon will take only when they are at their most alert, when thyroxine levels are high, during or either side of movements upstream.

The hypothalamus suppresses the feeding habit of salmon once they are back in fresh water. However, as Falkus pointed out, there may be a wide variation in the level of suppression so that, in a tiny proportion of salmon, the feeding habit is not fully suppressed, though they show a reluctance to swallow food (which is why salmon that are seen to take insects from the water so rarely have them in their stomachs; see p. 135). Because the level of suppression varies, so those salmon that still have some feeding habit will show a variation in that habit. Those that have it strongly will grab the fly or bait positively: this is what Falkus meant by 'feeding habit' (p. 140). But those salmon that have a very weak feeding habit may just play with it or not take it properly as a salmon with the fully developed feeding habit would do. They may chase the potential food, and perhaps grab it at the last moment (the Falkus 'inducement' category). They may prod it with their snouts, they may pick it up and carry it some distance, they may roll on it, they may take it into and out of their mouths (the Falkus categories of 'curiosity' and 'playfulness').

The pituitary–hypothalamus axis controls the sex drive, aggression and fear in the salmon and, on their return to the river, these are important behavioural traits. The salmon are preparing to spawn. Cock fish will soon be competing for mates. Hen fish will soon be competing for redds. Both cock and hen must develop their aggressive instincts to drive away competitors. Instead of being in the deep vastness of the ocean, where they have space to flee from potential predators, these big fish are now confined to a relatively small, shallow patch of water. Again, the level of these aggressive and fear traits will vary in the salmon population. Those with a high level of aggression will take the fly violently, with what Falkus called a 'crunch' take (his category of 'aggression'). But those salmon with a lesser level of aggression may simply nip or pull or 'come short' at the fly or bait (the Falkus category of 'irritation'). They may chase the fly or bait (the Falkus category of 'inducement'). And those salmon that have a high fear response caused by pituitary–hypothalamus axis secretions may actually flee from the fly or bait (as has been noted when fishing the prawn; see p. 138).

Yet in neither the hormone-controlled feeding habit nor sex-drive/aggression does the salmon react at a constant level. If feeding habit or aggression were constant in all of the salmon, then taking times would be all the time! They are not. The aggressive or feeding habit can be manifested only when the salmon are alert: in salmon straight from the sea that are on their initial run (which may take hours or days or weeks; see p. 87), at the start of the run, when the fish have pulled in to rest during a period of running, or just after completing a period of running. The longer the resting period, the less alert the salmon, and the less likely are the feeding habit or aggression to be manifested by the fish taking fly or bait. Waken the fish up, by chucking stones in the river, and they will be made alert for a short time and might respond.

When salmon settle down after their initial run, all their hormonal levels are minimal. They are unlikely to take anything. These we call stale or potted fish. But when a stale, potted salmon begins to move on to the redds the level of thyroxine rises and increases its alertness and the sex and aggression hormones peak. Once more the fish are likely to take.

One television film sadly showed this response. The anglers concerned failed to catch salmon in summer, despite the fact that the pools were full of stale, potted fish. They returned in September, just as those same fish were moving towards their redds: they had no difficulty in catching red, kipper-like ripe salmon. But to fish for such salmon is wrong. They are inedible and the trauma of being caught and released is likely to result in a less successful spawning, perhaps even death before spawning. Anglers should be exploiting the feeding habit and aggression of salmon that are on their initial run, fresh from the sea.

Where salmon lie

It is important to know not only that there are salmon in the river or lake, which may or may not be taking fish, but also where they are lying, for salmon are never uniformly scattered throughout a river or lake and to fish the entire water means that much time will be lost fishing where there are no fish. It is possible to pick the gillie's brain, if there is a gillie. Or someone who fishes the water frequently, if you can find one who tells the truth! But sooner or later you will visit a river or lake that you have never fished before and where there is no such help. Then *you* will have to work out where the fish are lying by 'reading the water'.

River lies

Let us deal with salmon lies in rivers first, for most salmon fishing occurs in rivers. In rivers there are two sorts of salmon lies, known as resting lies and resident lies, and the positions of each sort of lie may change as water height changes. Because both sorts can be found in pools and riffles, we must consider these river features first.

Except when fishing canalized lengths of river, or rivers with a fairly natural, uniform depth and flow (e.g. some chalk and limestone streams), the angler often looks to river pools as the best fish-holding locations. An understanding of river pools is thus an integral part of reading the water.

Many rivers, especially in their middle and lower reaches, meander across their floodplains to produce a pattern of pools separated by riffles (see Fig. 21). Riffles may vary from a few inches to several feet deep (anglers often call larger, deeper riffles 'streamy pools' or 'runs'); they usually have a cross-section with a fairly uniform depth (though usually deepest in the middle). The river bed in a riffle consists of big boulders together with shingle or coarse gravel, which results in a broken popply water surface. Deeper riffles often contain excellent salmon lies, especially in low water, although in high water they are often a raging torrent and the salmon will then have to move into more sheltered high-water lies (see below).

Water flows in at the 'neck' of the pool and passes out at the 'tail'. In meander

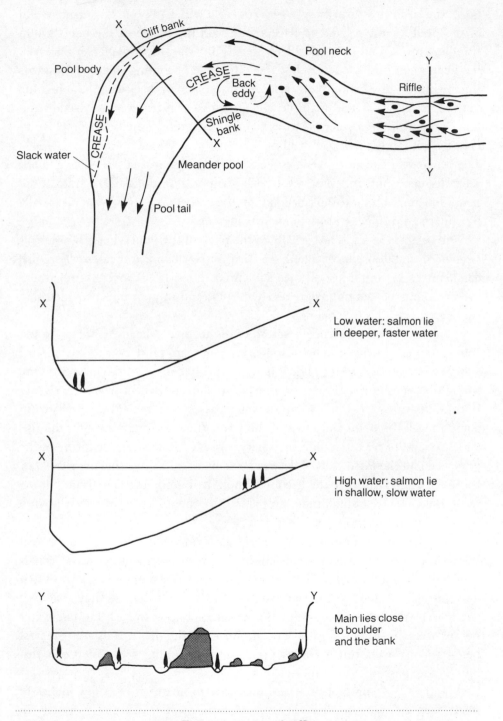

Fig. 21 – Pools and riffles

pools the main flow usually swings across to a cliff-bank on the outside curve of the pool leaving a band of slacker water on the inside of the bend where shingle, gravel, sand or mud is deposited. The cross-section characteristically has deep water immediately below the cliff-bank, becoming shallower towards the inside of the bend. Note also the presence of back-eddies. The line between slack water and main flow (sometimes also between back-eddy and downstream flow) is referred to as 'crease'. Salmon often lie in or close to creases, but rarely lie in back-eddies.

Some parts of salmon rivers, especially in the higher rocky reaches, are not meander pools but straighter, often rock-girt pools or 'dubs'. The route of the main flow through these dubs depends on the shape of the bed, which is usually irregular and produces a turbulent, swirling current.

The best lies in pools are usually in the neck of the pool where the water is deepening and flow concentrated in a fairly narrow band; at creases, where fish can lie in slacker water just off the main current; in slower-moving water where the bottom is becoming progressively deeper; and in pool tails provided that these are not glides (see below).

Weirs are often constructed across rivers to give a head of water for old water-mills, to provide a water abstraction point or to produce well-oxygenated water below sewage works. They may be a barrier for fish moving upstream, though on salmon rivers weirs often have a fish pass. Except when the river is in maximum flood, a fine curtain of water passes over the sill or the weir (in some the sill dries up) and most of the water flows strongly through the fish pass. Low weirs are often built by fishery owners to encourage scouring of the river bed and the formation of deeper pools in an otherwise shallow riffle. For those seeking to improve the lies for salmon, it should be understood that the most effective way of building a weir is to have the middle of the weir further upstream than the two ends.

Above a weir the flow is usually fairly uniform across the river (to protect the weir, the river is usually canalized for a short distance upstream). This part is not usually good fish-holding water. However, the salmon and sea trout that have just passed through the fish pass are often good 'takers' as they rest close to the weir sill. Immediately below a weir can be important fish-holding water on any river. The main flow is concentrated and the depth is usually greatest below the fish pass: this is always a good lie for running fish, which may rest here before passing upstream.

A waterfall is a natural weir, and may vary in height from a few inches to many feet. Salmon that have just passed over the fall often rest, usually in slacker water close to the banks if there is sufficient depth of water, just upstream of the fall. Salmon may rest for some time below the waterfall (in the plunge pool) before attempting to leap the fall unless the fall is very small, in which case they may pass through very quickly.

As has been pointed out earlier (on p. 22), salmon may not leap a waterfall or high weir unless the water temperature is above a minimum of about 40–41°F. If necessary, they will gather in the pool below the fall until the water temperature has risen to that minimum level.

Groynes are often built out from river banks, either to reduce erosion of the banks or, by fishery owners, to increase flow in a long shallow riffle so that the deflected current scours deeper lies. For maximum efficiency groynes should be constructed pointing at an angle upstream. Often groynes are built in a series, sometimes in pairs with a small gap in between. They are a very effective means of increasing the amount of deep, fish-holding water in a river beat. The water in the angles between groyne and bank will often be slack or with slow back-eddies; increased silt or gravel deposition is likely to occur there. The main fish-holding water develops along the crease between slack water and main flow, or (where the current is not too strong) in the deep fast-water channel immediately downstream of the groynes.

Bridge supports often act as groynes, speeding up flow and increasing scour. The cover provided by the bridge is often very attractive to fish. Unless the river is in flood, salmon often lie close to bridge supports where there is maximum depth and flow. Immediately downstream of a bridge there are often areas of deep, slack water close to the banks or behind midstream bridge piers: salmon rarely lie here. A great salmon lie is where the main stream has cut a deep pool immediately downstream of a bridge (the Old Bridge at Grantown-on-Spey is a classic example).

Hatches are a special type of bridge/weir where the amount of water flowing downstream can be regulated by opening or closing hatch gates. They are most commonly found on chalk streams. In summer most hatch gates are kept closed to conserve water in the river; in autumn when high rainfall may add much run-off water to a river, all hatches may be opened to allow flood water to escape quickly. Because of the concentrated, scouring flow, the pools below hatch gates are often very deep compared with the rest of the river. They are usually major lies for chalk stream salmon, with the fish lying in the main flow when water levels are low, or in creases between bands of slack and strong current when water levels are high and all the hatches open.

Rivers are canalized to encourage the river to discharge water more quickly and efficiently than a river in its natural state. Canalization is especially common in lower reaches, including low-water estuary channels, and also in middle and upland reaches where the river flows through towns and villages (canalization reduces risk of flooding). Canalized reaches are fairly uniform, with a shallow U-shaped cross-section maintained by river scour or by dredging. Canalized reaches are rarely good salmon-holding water.

It is worth looking for special or localized fish lies that can occur anywhere along a length of river. In even the shallowest of riffles, one feature may produce a lie of only a square yard in area that could hold a salmon. Find these lies and there will be the fish!

Large boulders tend to deflect the flow and increase scour around themselves; they make excellent salmon lies. Where the top of the boulder is submerged and not visible, the location of large boulders can be deduced from a bulge in the water surface just downstream of the boulder's position. Fish tend not to lie behind boulders where the water is very turbulent; they tend to lie just in front, to the side or (for very large submerged boulders) on top of the boulder. Putting very large boulders into a fairly featureless and moderately deep riffle is a very effective way of increasing the number of lies. When many Norwegian rivers are iced over in winter, boulders are transported on to the ice and, in spring, the boulders drop to the river bed and make the lies!

The roots of large waterside trees often act like tiny groynes, producing a narrow strip of deeper, fast water close to the bank. Salmon are often found there: one day I caught a salmon and three sea trout in such a lie, about eight yards long and three yards wide under a sycamore, on the River Wenning.

Salmon may lie in water only two or three feet in depth if there is cover where they can shelter. Where tree branches trail or hang low over the water is often an excellent lie. So, too, are floating 'rafts' (of twigs and branches, grass, weed, etc., washed downstream at high water) trapped amongst trailing branches or against reedstems. In low water salmon often hide away under the bank where the flow has made an undercut.

Sometimes the river bed may be solid bedrock with a shallow, rough flow and be inhospitable for fish. Erosion of a weak point in the bedrock might produce a deep pothole that holds fish. Such lies are often difficult to locate: examine the water thoroughly at low water, using polaroid glasses.

Following prolonged heavy rain or during snow-melt, river levels often rise to a point at which the fish must leave their usual lies and take up 'high-water lies'. These are usually positions off the main flow. For example:

• where normally dry or very shallow streams or ditches join the main river;
• in meander pools, close to the bank on the inside of the bend, over shingle that is normally exposed, often in less than two feet of water;

- in weir, groyne and bridge pools where the water is usually slack (close to the bank) but in flood has a gentle flow;
- close to the bank (literally under the rod tip) in gaps amongst trees over grass that is normally far above river level.

It is worth noting potential high-water lies for future reference during periods of low water: many anglers miss a splendid opportunity to catch a lot of fish because they fail to seek high-water lies.

Resting lies

These are places where a running fish may pull in for a very short rest of perhaps a few seconds or minutes. Fish that are actually on the move, swimming upstream, will rarely if ever take hold of a fly or bait as they swim past it. But find where they stop for even a brief moment and they are likely to take. In fact, if you can see fish running, and these can be identified by their smooth porpoise-like upstream progress rather than splashy leaps, fish just one resting lie and you may catch fish after fish after fish.

One such resting lie on the Alta River is half-way up a stretch of about 200yd of fast white-water rapids. Just off the main torrent there is an area, close to the bank, about 20yd long and 15yd wide, in the lee of a shingle spit, where the water is up to four feet deep and with a steady current. The fish rest at the edge of this quieter water, close to the shingle spit. The technique here is to wade down the top half of the shingle spit and cast a short line into the main flow so that the fly swings around over the resting fish. Every time I have fished that lie I have caught a fish. But some local anglers from the town of Alta will spend the entire day on that one lie and catch 15 or more salmon without moving.

Another two quite discrete lies are on my local river, the Hodder (see Fig. 22). In the neck of Papermill Pool is a big boulder and running salmon lie, when the river is high following a spate on the inside of that boulder and when the river is low on the outside of that boulder. In high water Hodder salmon tend not to show, so the high-water lie on the inside of the boulder must be fished with confidence that sooner or later a fish will stop there and, being a running fish, it will be a taking fish. In low water the salmon do show themselves and if a fish shows to the outside of the boulder there is a great chance of catching it. Immediately above the boulder is an area of deepish water with a nice broken surface. It is really an extension of the low water resting lie on the far side of the boulder. In low water fish rest here before facing about 100yd of very shallow water. In the evening salmon that have been in a resident lie (see below) in the body of Papermill Pool will move up into this area prior to

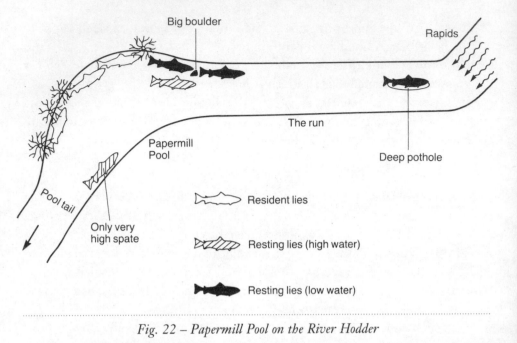

Fig. 22 – Papermill Pool on the River Hodder

running or attempting to run. Through the day they may have been virtually uncatchable, but now, having a raised hormone level and preparing to run, they are great takers.

Above Papermill Pool the river is shallow and flows down, largely over limestone bedrock, for about 150yd from a long, fast, boulder-strewn rapid. Just below the rapids, in midstream, there is a small, deep pothole in the river bed. In very high water the river thunders down through this pot and the resting lie used by running salmon is under the trees where the flow is more gentle. But when the river is only a fraction above summer level and fish are still running they rest momentarily in the pothole before attempting the shallow rapids. To fish carefully the entire length of river from rapids to the body of Papermill Pool will take a good hour. But only 10 minutes of this time will be spent fishing resting lies. Fifty minutes will be largely wasted, for very few salmon are ever caught outside these two lies.

Having described the resting lies that are used by running salmon in two particular pieces of river I need to broaden the approach and suggest pointers that may indicate resting lies in all rivers. But before I do this I must stress that what may appear to be a good lie might not be and only experience (either your own or borrowed from someone else) will show the best lies. For this reason it is worth keeping a record of precisely where salmon have been caught, at what time of year and at different water heights, on all the rivers that you fish. Each salmon may indicate a resting lie worthy of further investigation.

- *Pool necks*: these often include excellent resting lies, especially if there is a very fast, shallow run immediately upstream. In high water the fish will tend to rest out of the main flow but in deeper, slow water close to the bank. In low water the fish will rest in or at the edge of the popply-surfaced main flow. Take, for instance, the neck of Tarric Mor on the Spey – in low water in summer running salmon rest in the main flow, often in no more than three feet of water. When the river is high the fish rest in slower water over what, in low water, is a dry sandy beach.

- *Pool tails*: these are good resting lies especially if the fish have had to work hard running through fast water immediately downstream. In high water the fish will often pull in close to the bank (they will do this also on big rivers in low water if there is sufficient depth of water, say at least three feet). In low water, or in a shallow pool tails, the fish will often rest by big boulders in the pool tail. However, many salmon pools terminate in a glide, a smooth-bottomed tail where the water slides as one almost solid mass downstream. Glides are never good salmon lies. Look for a popply surface caused by an irregular river bed, for that signifies good resting water where the fish can lie in a small area of slacker water. A glide has a characteristic smooth surface because of the smooth bed, and lacks areas of slower flow in which the fish can rest.

- *Boulders*: some of the greatest resting lies on any river are by big boulders.

- *Under the bank*: all salmon anglers are tempted to fall into two traps. First is the belief that fish are always at or just beyond maximum casting range. Secondly, because they wear waders they feel it essential to wade as deep as possible: whether wearing wellingtons, thigh waders or chestwaders, to within an inch of the top. However, in the vast majority of rivers most of the running lies of salmon are closer to the bank than the middle of the river.

This fact was borne out most strongly the first time I fished the massive and mighty Namsen River from the bank. Around the town of Overhalla the Namsen is vast and generally fished by harling. I was on the bank and found that I could wade in a couple of yards at most (even with chestwaders). I stood on the bank, made the longest cast that I could, and watched the fly land seemingly only a pathetic distance out. 'What chance?' I asked myself. 'I am covering no more than a twentieth of the river!' But I buckled down to the job and decided that if any fish were pulling in for a rest within 10 yards of the bank I would catch them, and sod the other 200yd. On the sixth cast I took a running fish in a resting lie only two yards from the bank.

In high water or in a big, fast-flowing river, salmon cannot rest in midstream. The gentlest flows are close, very close, to the bank and that is where they will rest provided the water is deep enough, greater than about two feet. So in a fairly uniform stretch of water, when the river is high, do not wade but fish the band of water, perhaps only five or, at most, ten yards wide, next to the bank. Often fish will take tight in at the side, so let the fly hang there before making the next cast.

I must stress the point about not wading when angling for salmon that are resting tight up to the bank. Wade through the lies and you will disturb the fish. Robert McHaffie told me of a case in point. He had taken a fish from a known lie on the River Faughen. Later he returned to find another angler standing in the precise spot where he had hooked his fish. 'If buggers like that were forced to wear expensive leather shoes with lace holes when they went fishing they would not scare the fish and we would all catch more!' commented Robert. He was so right.

- *The inside of meanders*: in low water the inside of meander bend pools usually have a shingle beach, the water deepening to the other bank. These shingle beaches are often excellent resting lies when covered by a couple of feet of water when the river is falling after a spate. Again it is essential not to wade deeper than the ankles for if you are standing in knee-depth water you are wading through the lies.
- *Stream mouths and fords*: these may be dry or a mere trickle in low water, but when the river is in spate they become deep, slacker areas of water just off the main current. They may then be great resting lies for running fish.
- *Riffles and the bodies of pools*: see Resident lies, below.

Resident lies

These are lies that are used by salmon that have completed their initial run and are waiting for the breeding season. They are used also by salmon that are in the middle of their initial run but are resting for several hours or days before continuing. We are fishing for the latter and for fish that have only just completed their initial run. Let me illustrate this with a sketch of a meander pool and riffle on the Dee, in summer low water, when the water holds springers that completed their initial run some months earlier, some grilse and summer salmon that have completed their run within the last few weeks, and a few fish that are resting in the middle of their run (see Fig. 23).

The drawing shows spring fish (sp) that have completed their initial run and are residents in the pool; summer fish (su) that have recently completed their

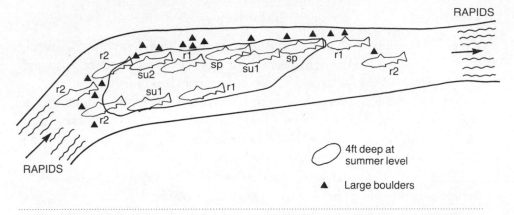

Fig. 23 – Salmon lying in a Dee pool in August (for explanation, see text)

initial run and are residents in the pool, some (su1) having been resident for one week and others (su2) for two weeks; fish shown as r1 are resting, having arrived in the pool that morning or the previous evening. Some may remain and become residents, others may move on in the evening; and fish shown as r2 that are running through and have stopped for just a few minutes.

Most resident lies are in deep, steady water where the fish have a good supply of oxygenated water and where they need do little work to maintain position. Those that have been in the pool for a long time (sp) are virtually impossible to catch. Those that have been residents for a relatively short time become more difficult to catch the longer they have been residents (su1 fish are more likely to take than su2 fish). Those that arrived in the pool some hours earlier may be resting before continuing their journey, or they may have completed their initial run and joined the residents. In either case these r1 salmon are likely to be better takers of the fly than the su1 fish. The best chance of catching those r1 salmon that will run further upstream that evening is to fish close to last light, when they move into the pool neck, occupying the lies used by the running fish (r2). The best takers in the pool and riffle are the r2 fish, but they will be in the lies for just a few minutes before making their way upstream to the next pool.

Should heavy rain fall and the river rise, then the resident fish (sp, su and some r1) will not be able to remain in their lies through the flood. They will move, as the water rises, into slacker water close to the bank that is, at low water, shallow water or dry gravel. As they move they may become, for a short period, 'taking' fish.

163

Lake lies

Lakes appear to be a uniform sheet of water to an angler sitting in a drifting boat. The salmon might be anywhere! Locating salmon in a wild loch or lough is especially difficult for anglers whose only experience of fishing big areas of water is lowland English rainbow trout reservoirs. I was fishing Lough Melvin with a friend who had never seen a wild lake and I was keeping the boat tight into the shore so that we were covering some great lies. 'I wouldn't fish here if this was Walthamstow Reservoir!' he exclaimed.

When salmon enter a lake via the outflowing river they may stop for a short period near the river. They are then good takers. More usually, however, they move into the lake and take up what are usually well-known traditional lies in shallows around islands or rocky skerries, extensive shallow bays (Victoria Bay on Lough Conn and Rossinver Bay on Melvin are classic examples) or the shallows off the mouths of feeder streams in which they will later spawn (see Fig. 24).

Shallows? How shallow? If the water is clear then you should be able to see the bottom and a reasonable estimate of depth range for lake salmon lies would be between four and eight feet, though on Melvin I have taken two fish from one lie close to a fence-end in exactly 2ft 9in of water and in Loch Maree in 3 1/2ft of water.

It is usual to have a gillie-cum-boatman who will guide an angler to the lake salmon lies, but on many Irish loughs it is possible to save money by hiring just a boat (or using your own). In the latter case it is essential to have a map showing the drifts that will cover the salmon lies or work out where they will be from a map showing underwater contours.

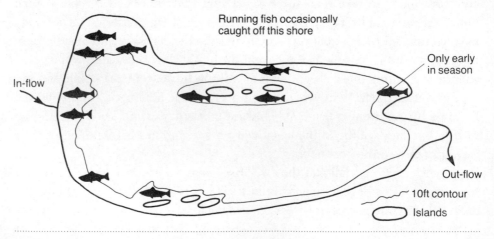

Fig. 24 – Salmon lies in lakes

CHAPTER 6

SALMON POPULATIONS AND THE BALANCE BETWEEN LIFE AND DEATH

There is only one thing certain in life: one day we will all die!

ANON., 1994

One trait of our late twentieth century, increasingly urbanized and industrialized civilization is the refusal to accept death as being a natural phenomenon. In human terms there are constant attempts to reduce the percentage of people who die from heart disease, from drug-, smoking- and alcohol-related diseases and from car accidents. Children are sent on adventure holidays where adventure is minimalized to remove all risks. Yet, no matter what, 100 per cent of us will die from one cause or other.

When it comes to animal deaths the North American and European civilizations are becoming even more neurotic. Butchers' shops, where carcasses are hung and cut up in front of the customers, are becoming endangered as those who are not vegetarians demand a block of protein that has been clinically dissected so that it does not resemble the animal whence it came. Even more popular are prepackaged cooked meats that just need warming in the microwave so that those eating the meal have no blood on their hands. And while people will think nothing of picking blackberries from the brambles on their excursions into the countryside, those of us who crop rabbits, wild duck, venison and salmon are being increasingly branded murderers.

Furry or feathered creatures especially are seen as humans in another guise and their deaths seen as a catastrophe. One butcher in southern urban England, who had a delightful sense of humour, put the following sign in his shop window:

WATERSHIP DOWN

You have read the book

You have seen the film

Now you can eat the cast!

FRESH RABBITS, £1 each!

I have been told that his shop was boycotted and he had to close down!

Allied to these attitudes is increasing publicity by so-called conservation organizations, supported by television, radio and the press, stating that many of our wild animals and plants are 'endangered' or 'on the verge of extinction'. News that a rural bird population, such as the partridge or skylark, is in decline is greeted hysterically, and blame put on the shoulders of farmers and shooters. But news that urban and suburban populations of song thrushes and finches are declining is played down, because the situation is caused by the ever-spreading roads and housing estates and the ever-increasing populations of household cats that belong to the supporters of these very conservation organizations. The last thing these so-called conservationists want is to criticize those who pour vast funds into their coffers!

When it comes to controlling the exploding populations of serious predators, all hell is let loose. Magpies and crows, grey seals, cormorants and goosanders are all known to damage populations of other animals to the extent that the control of their numbers would be beneficial. Yet conservation bodies, aided by a biased media, can whip up such vociferous, uninformed opposition that control is not carried out.

Salmon anglers are in danger of being carried along on the tide of emotion that says that the death of a fish, other than by an angler's hand, is close to a catastrophe. In fact, the salmon has been called 'an endangered species' (this term is the subtitle for one book on salmon) and 'close to extinction'. Neither of these descriptions is true: the salmon is neither endangered nor close to extinction. Panic sets in should there be a series of years when the number of salmon declines in a river. A fish found dead on the bank is immediately taken away for autopsy: something insidious, probably pollution, must have killed it. Death by natural causes, other than after spawning, is a rare verdict.

Yet death is essential. If every smolt that went to sea returned as a salmon we would be knee deep in the things and in no time the river would be a mass of rotting carcasses. A viable salmon population needs death just as much as it needs the river factory to work at 100 per cent efficiency in the production of smolts. The problem comes when death rate exceeds production, for then the salmon population will collapse.

In this chapter we will begin by examining the causes of death in salmon throughout its life cycle before looking at changes in salmon populations and prospects for the future.

Many researchers have investigated mortality rates in a variety of clean, productive rivers in Scandinavia, Britain and Ireland and eastern Canada. There is some variation between different estimates of mortality at different stages of the life cycle (especially between eggs and migrating smolts), but this is to be expected. Rivers are different: some might be a safer 'home' for parr than others (by having fewer predators); some might be able to support more parr than others (by having more food and feeding territories). Mortality rates will vary from year to year so that if a study was carried out in a poor year then the estimates of mortality would be higher than if it was carried out in a good year. Especially important is the fact that such studies include a high degree of statistical variation, or error, because of the sampling methods involved in calculating mortality. It is impossible to count precisely all the eggs and all the parr and all the smolts. Population studies use mean (or average) numbers to indicate what is happening in the total population. For this reason, in the life table below I have used rounded estimates based on those published in scientific reports of mortality.

LIFE TABLE

1.   200 SPAWNING ADULTS (= 100 pairs)
produce
500,000 EGGS
that eventually produce
2500 SMOLTS (99.5% mortality) or 5000 SMOLTS (99% mortality)
of which   of which
1250 SMOLTS   2500 SMOLTS
reach the feeding grounds (50% mortality)

2. From reaching oceanic feeding grounds to arriving back in the river we will assume 2% *natural* mortality per month. (This excludes netting on the high seas, in offshore waters and in estuaries.)

a.   All return as grilse after 10 months at sea:
1000 GRILSE   2000 GRILSE
For the spawning population to be maintained, the surplus available for

cropping by commercial fisheries and anglers is:

800 fish   1,800 fish

b. 60% return as grilse, 40% as 2+SW salmon:

600 Grilse   1200 Grilse

300 2+SW*   600 2+SW*
<hr>
900 total   1800 total

For the spawning population to be maintained, the surplus available for cropping by commercial fisheries and anglers is:

700 fish   1600 fish

c. 30% return as grilse, 50% as 2+SW and 20% as 3+SW salmon:

300 Grilse   600 Grilse

375 2+SW*   750 2+SW*

90 3+SW**   180 3+SW**
<hr>
765 total   1530 total

For the spawning population to be maintained, the surplus available for cropping by commercial fisheries and anglers is:

565 fish   1330 fish

d. All return as 3+SW salmon:

450 Salmon**   900 Salmon**

For the spawning population to be maintained, the surplus available for cropping by commercial fisheries and anglers is:

250 fish   700 fish

* Assuming an average of 20 months of sea mortality
** Assuming an average of 32 months of sea mortality

Most estimates for the egg to smolt mortality fall in the range of 99–99.5 per cent in clean rivers that are relatively unaffected by estuarine pollution, industrialization and the occasional pollution incident in the valley, excessive land drainage and water abstraction and other factors that can affect the river (see p. 172). In clean rivers the mortality is likely to be fairly constant for each river, mainly because each river is capable of supporting and producing a certain number of smolts, so that the optimal number of spawning salmon, producing a fairly constant number of eggs, will result in a fairly constant number of smolts through density-dependent mechanisms (see p. 173 and Natural mortality, below). However, mortality will vary slightly from one river to another primarily because different rivers are capable of supporting different densities of parr; the river of the same size that can produce fewer parr will have a slightly higher mortality than a river that can produce more.

There may be many rivers where mortality is far greater. If, for instance, a river producing all grilse had a 99.9 per cent river mortality, then only 500 smolts would migrate downstream, and the total production would be only 200 fish which would be just enough to replace their 200 parents. By contrast if a river that had a return of 60 per cent grilse and 40 per cent 2+SW salmon had a river mortality of 99.5 per cent, then the ensuing run of 120 grilse and 60 2+SW salmon would be less than that necessary to replace the parent stock.

Such a high mortality may well have occurred in rivers with industrialized estuaries earlier this century, where the smolts passing downstream had to run through often severely polluted water. Netting in inshore waters and estuaries and rod-and-line fisheries would further deplete these numbers and the salmon population of those rivers – such as Thames, Tyne and Tees in Britain, Rhine and Meuse in the Low Countries, and Connecticut in the USA – would crash.

It is of interest, however, that in rivers such as Thames, Tyne and Tees, where pollution exterminated the salmon, once the river is made clean the surplus of returning salmon are quickly capable of restocking the river. If we could clean up the rivers and blow up the dams that prevent salmon running, every traditional salmon river from Portugal and New York northwards would soon have a run of fish.

Studies have suggested that mortality from natural causes at sea is up to four times more varied than river mortality. Such variation of mortality affects the salmon from all rivers together for, as we saw in Chapter 2, salmon in the sea do not remain in river shoals but become mixed on their oceanic feeding grounds. A highly variable sea mortality, from one year to another or from one period to another, is probably the major cause of the wide fluctuations of salmon numbers returning to the rivers. We have already seen, for instance, in Chapter 4 (p. 112), how grilse populations fluctuate widely according to periodic fluctuations of climate and sea temperatures in the North Atlantic.

Nevertheless, as far as returning salmon stocks to clean salmon rivers is concerned, natural mortality is never so high as to prevent there being a great surplus of salmon, a surplus that should be harvested either commercially or with rod and line. The conservation of salmon stocks should have nothing to do with preventing this crop being taken, provided that the level of cropping is less than the surplus of returning salmon. It is about making that surplus as large as possible. And we do this by making the smolt factories – the rivers –

work at 100 per cent efficiency, and by ensuring that we do not damage the ocean environment by overfishing the marine foods of the salmon.

If a river is in perfect order (see Fig. 25), then as the number of females increases so too will the number of smolts produced until a maximum level of production is achieved. Production of more eggs by extra females will not result in a further increase of smolts if the river is working at this optimum level, and the extra adult salmon should be harvested. To increase the number of smolts beyond this optimum we need more factory space. This can be made available by opening up headwaters into which salmon could not previously pass (by having fish-passes on waterfalls) or by improving the nursery areas in the main river so that they can support higher densities of parr. An increased number of spawning females will then result in an increase of smolt production. The major problem on many rivers in recent years is that the smolt factory has been reduced, through damming of streams and land drainage that has greatly reduced the area of the river, and caused siltation in the nursery areas so that they cannot support the previous high densities of immature salmon.

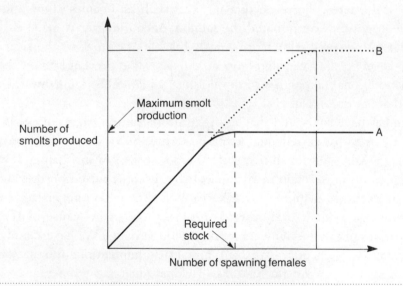

Fig. 25 – A hypothetical model graph for a river in perfect order

Natural mortality

Before we can analyse the current state of salmon stocks and suggest the ways we can increase the runs of fish to rivers that have lost their salmon or in which the stocks are pathetically low, we must consider causes of mortality. For at the end of the day we can increase salmon populations only by reducing mortality.

Egg mortality

It is often said that egg mortality in the redds is very low, for the extra sperm produced by precocious male parr guarantees virtually 100 per cent fertilization (p. 57) and the deep covering of gravel protects the eggs from predators, including carnivorous invertebrates that might burrow through shallow gravel. Where the density of spawning salmon is very high it is not unusual for later spawners to cut into the redds of earlier spawners and displace the eggs. However, where spawning density is that high the number of eggs that eventually hatch will be more than enough to produce the river's optimal parr density.

Dippers have been blamed for talking salmon eggs, but it is certain that they take only eggs displaced by later-spawning salmon cutting into earlier redds. In December 1977 I watched a hen salmon on the Eden cut into an earlier redd and the eggs being washed away in the current. As the eggs were washed down through a shallow riffle three dippers and at least two lean brown trout (which had completed spawning earlier) quickly feasted on them.

Only once have I seen eggs being taken as they were being laid – a rather disturbing experience with a moral for fishery managers. I had been invited to fish the Onny, a small tributary of the River Severn in Shropshire, for grayling in November. My host warned me that the river had been stocked with triploid female rainbow trout (a sexually sterile form that feeds keenly all year round), and requested that I return any of these to the river. 'They have been put in to give the trout anglers more variety!' he explained.

I found some large fish splashing in a shallow riffle, observation showing that they were spawning salmon, but that there were also some biggish fish that were not salmon. I caught one of these on an orange leaded bug: it was a rainbow trout and its stomach was full of salmon eggs. I watched further and saw up to seven rainbow trout rushing in simultaneously, sucking down the eggs just shed by one hen fish before she had time to cover them. Both cock and hen salmon chased one of the intruders, but this left the redd unguarded from the other interlopers who fed greedily on the unguarded, exposed eggs. There appeared to be three or four pairs of salmon using that particular riffle for spawning and it seems likely that not one of them completed a redd containing eggs. No doubt the anglers who introduced those big rainbow trout blame high seas netting for the decline of salmon in the Severn! Anglers should be most careful about introducing potential predators to wild rivers (see also Predators, below).

Other by-products of man's interference with the river may result in massive egg losses. In areas where rivers are used for the transport of logs (usually in rafts) redds may be gouged out as logs smash their way through shallows.

Salmon eggs need a constant throughflow of water if they are to develop. Damage to the surrounding countryside by logging, land drainage operations and disturbance of the river bed upstream of redds (for example, by pile driving for new bridge supports or putting a pipeline through a river bed) may release vast amounts of silt into the water. This silt may clog the spaces between the gravel redd and prevent throughflow of water. I was able to investigate this silting up of redds on two stretches of my own water. Following land drainage the bed of the River Wenning became covered with fine silt and in January I excavated two redds on a patch of gravel below Clapham bridge: the eggs in both were dead. Following excavation of the upper Lune for a gas pipeline the river bed was again smothered in fine silt. I carefully exposed one redd, disturbing vast amounts of silt with every stone, and again found that all the eggs had suffocated.

Excessive water abstraction can lower the level of a river so that redds become exposed. In 1979 two pairs of salmon spawned in a Hodder tributary downstream of an abstraction point. During a January hard frost the gravel bank was completely exposed and in February I carefully investigated: the eggs were all dead.

The combination of land drainage and water abstraction can so greatly reduce flow rate that what was formerly clean, bright, loose gravel and ideal for hen salmon to cut redds becomes a dark concreted mass into which they cannot cut. And if they do manage to cut, the redd silts up and the eggs suffocate. I have observed this at two places on the Ribble, where two gravel riffles were commonly used by several pairs of spawning salmon, successfully in the late 1970s, unsuccessfully in the early 1990s. Salmon still attempt to cut there in November, but by February the redds are completely smothered and, from my investigations, fail to produce a single fry.

The deterioration of the redds, consequent to the combined effects of low flow rates, low water levels and an increase of silt deposition in the gravel, is, I believe with no doubts at all, the greatest threat to a thriving, 100 per cent efficient river smolt factory – especially in rivers flowing through intensively farmed valleys or close to vast urban conurbations that need the abstracted water. The problem has received little attention from salmon fishery biologists (who work mostly on upland rivers). Yet it was a problem that Frank Sawyer identified as long ago as 1957 on trout chalk streams (which were also salmon rivers). Speaking of trout redds, Sawyer noted (in Sidney Vines, *Frank Sawyer: Man of the Riverside*, 1984) that the greatest loss occurred while the eggs were still in the redds. Actually the eggs were fertilised, the mortality occurring after the first three weeks of incubation. I arrived at the figure of 99 per cent loss after thoroughly examining many redds in different parts of the fishery, and came to the conclusion that the cause was the lack of oxygen.

Sawyer set to improving the redds, by raking them and adding loose chalk gravel, and thereby raised the hatch rate. But this work was discontinued because of the expense.

If we could invest time and money into improving redds it would certainly increase the wild-bred fry and parr stocks of most rivers and do away with the need for raising them artificially in hatcheries.

Density-dependent mortality in rivers

Estimates of river mortality, at or around 99 per cent between egg and smolt, appear to be very high. Yet such mortality is bound to be high in a well-stocked clean river simply because the river can support a maximum number of parr and produce a certain maximum number of smolts. Surplus over and beyond that maximum must die. In most animal species, populations have an underlying regulatory mechanism known as a density-dependent control. If parr stocks are lower than the river is capable of sustaining, density-dependent pressures are eased, allowing the population to increase. If parr stocks are very high and greater than the river is capable of sustaining then density-dependent pressures increase, causing the population to fall. What this means is that in a well-stocked river parr populations will tend to fluctuate around a mean or average optimum density that the river can support.

It goes without saying that to attempt to increase production in a well-stocked river by introducing fry or parr from a hatchery will be a waste of time and money, for density-dependent mechanisms will reduce the artificially raised population. By contrast, in a river where the population has been brought low (perhaps by pollution) then the parr produced by the surviving stock of fish will be in such low density that their mortality is relatively low, the density-dependent regulatory mechanisms tending to increase the population automatically.

We often attempt to help nature by adding hatchery-raised fry or parr to the river, though if the river is in good working order there should be no need to continue doing this for more than two or three salmon generations. By then the numbers of salmon returning to the river should be producing enough eggs to give the optimum number of parr that the river is capable of supporting.

The fact that so many rivers appear to require continued artificial stocking implies that there is something intrinsically wrong with those rivers as smolt factories.

The abundance and availability of food is usually the prime density-dependent control and, in salmon parr as in many other animal species, this acts through territorial behaviour. Territory size is based on the production of food in the river and also the nature of the river bed: the more food and/or the more uneven the river bed the smaller the territories (pp. 64–5). Each parr holds its own territory and, if all territories are occupied, surplus parr are forced out and die. This is a gradual process, for parr enlarge the size of their territories as they grow, which means that surplus parr (those unable to keep their territories in the face of more dominant parr) are being squeezed over a long period of time. Thus we do not find large numbers of dead parr at the waterside: mortality is spread out.

It is likely, from what information is available, that these surplus parr are more readily taken by predators than parr holding territories, so that they are rapidly culled. Perhaps parr with a territory find it much easier to hide when a predator approaches, whereas a parr that has no territory and is being bullied by parr with territories is easy for a predator to catch. There have also been some detailed reports of parr that have been starving to death. A parr without a territory cannot feed, for wherever it goes it will be moved on by the antagonistic territory holders. Rapidly its carbohydrate stores will be depleted, then its muscle fat and proteins will have to be used to provide energy. In this weakened state it is easy prey for predators, or is more likely to be infected by disease and die.

That those parr unable to gain or hold a territory rapidly disappear was confirmed in an experiment by the Freshwater Fisheries Laboratory at Pitlochry. In summer, when the parr had all established territories and the surplus had died, the laboratory scientists removed the parr from a section of one small stream but found that these now vacant territories were not refilled. The remaining parr had already fixed their territories and there were very few 'floaters', parr without territories, to fill the vacancies.

Predators

In natural environments it is true to say that predators have no long-term deleterious effects on their prey populations. And in fact, as we have just seen, predators do a great service in a well-stocked salmon river by consuming those surplus parr that cannot gain a territory. However, many (perhaps most) salmon rivers are not stocked to maximum capacity. The redds may be so poor that egg survival is dreadfully low because of the effect of human activity on the river. In these cases predators may cause real damage to the salmon parr populations. To suggest that predators be controlled is not, in today's parlance, a politically correct solution. And I suppose that it is not politically correct to suggest that mankind should return the river to the quality it was before he started ruining it!

Few mammals devour significant numbers of salmon, either immature parr and smolts or adults, in the river. Otters *Lutra lutra* certainly take a few fish, but it seems likely that many of them are weak or diseased fish. My own observations, in northern England and southern Scotland, suggest that the otter finds it much easier to catch slower-swimming fish, such as chub and eels (of which otters seem inordinately fond), than salmon. Of 29 otter kills that I have examined, only two were salmon, and one of these was a kelt in December that may have been already dead when the otter found it. Mink *Mustella vison* likewise seem little match for the fast-swimming salmon, preferring eels, frogs and toads, crustaceans and waterside birds and mammals.

There is perhaps more cause for concern when it comes to predation by mammals in the sea (though the impact of dolphins and toothed whales is likely to be negligible). B.B. Rae and W.M. Shearer estimated that grey seals *Halichoerus grypus* and common seals *Phoca vitulina* took 148,000 salmon and sea trout around the Scottish coast between 1959 and 1963, an average of 30,000 per year. W.M. Shearer and K.H. Balmain estimated that 2.8 per cent of salmon caught in Greenland waters had some seal damage, whilst in 1986 it was reported that 4.3 per cent of the North Esk salmon catch exhibited some seal damage. These salmon had escaped the attack by seals; most do not. Seals do not eat all that they catch and kill; many observers have reported salmon killed by seals but with just one bite taken from the body and the rest discarded. Many seal populations (especially those around the British Isles) have increased greatly in recent years, and by the 1970s sufficient evidence had accumulated to suggest that some culling was desirable to maintain seal populations that did less damage to commercially important fish stocks. Some culls were carried out, but then media pressure resulted in their being discontinued, despite the advice given by Professor Hewer, in Chapter 14 'Conservation of British seals', in his book *British Seals*. It is alarming, to those of us concerned about our salmon stocks, to read reports, in the autumn of 1994, of harbour seals following salmon up the Thames and catching them at the head of the tide below the weir that denies them free and easy access to fresh water. This, when we are trying to encourage the salmon stocks of the Thames to increase!

Birds take many salmon in the fry, parr and smolts stages. Kingfishers, herons, cormorants, terns, gulls and some duck (notably the 'sawbills') have all been recorded eating salmon. The sawbills, which include mainly the goosander *Mergus merganser* and red-breasted merganser *Mergus serrator*, cause especial concern where salmon populations are already fairly low. On the North Esk W.M. Shearer calculated that if the goosander and merganser populations were strictly controlled the number of returning adult salmon would increase by approximately 35 per cent. On the Miramichi, H.C. White calculated that it takes 50lb of fish for a merganser to rear her brood, 46 per cent of this fish being immature salmon, and that a cull of 1200 mergansers would increase parr production by 1.9 million. In a similar study on the Restigouche, a three year merganser control programme increased smolt production by 170,000, equivalent to 840 returning adult salmon. P.F. Elson studied the effects of mergansers and belted kingfishers on the 10 mile Pollett River, New Brunswick. Over five years, production averaged 3000 smolts per year, but in four subsequent years when the avian predators were controlled (no attempt was made to exterminate them), smolt production varied from 13,600 to 24,300 per year. I have been studying the growth of the goosander population on the Eden, Lune and Ribble in northern England: three rivers that are certainly not producing the optimal number of smolts or returning adult salmon. Here the population of goosanders grew from seven pairs in 1981 to at least 47 pairs in 1994, and in 1990–3 they took 32,000 immature salmon, equivalent to about 8000 returning adult salmon. I examined the stomachs of 11 female goosanders in late spring: they contained between three and 14 salmon smolts that were migrating seawards at the time.

Increasingly of concern in European rivers is the recent tendency of the cormorant *Phalacrocorax carbo* to seek food in fresh water (perhaps because overfishing has reduced the inshore fish stocks – we are not dealing with truly natural systems, for man has grossly changed them). Several studies are in progress, but if J.M. Anderson's research on Northern Ireland's tiny River Bush is anything to go by it is clear that cormorants can make serious inroads into salmon stocks. He found that they take up to 2500 smolts per day when the smolts are migrating to sea (i.e. over about a 28-day period). Again, management of the river ecosystem would suggest that there are sound reasons to control these predatory birds to enable maximum escapement of smolts from the river. But the media-supported bird lobby is stronger than the fish lobby and, although some legal control under licence is permitted, many fishery organizations feel unable to carry this out because of public opinion and the risk of reprisal by animal rights fanatics.

Other fish devour many salmon fry, parr and smolts, though it is likely that a large proportion of these would not have survived, being parr unable to secure territories (see above). In fresh water species that will eat salmon fry these include pike *Esox lucius*, perch *Perca fluviatilis*, ruffe *Gymnocephalus cernua*, roach *Rutilus rutilus*, chub *Leuciscus cephalus*, eel *Anguilla anguilla*, brown trout and rainbow trout and large salmon parr. In the sea, salmon have been recorded in the stomachs of Greenland shark *Somiosus microcephalus*, porbeagle *Lamna nasus*, skate *Raja batis*, cod *Gadus morhua*, pollack *Pollachius pollachius*, saithe *P. virens*, ling *Molva molva*, whiting *Merlangius merlangus*, halibut *Hippoglossus hippoglossus*, bass *Dicentrachus labrax* and sea trout.

Pike may be a major predator, especially in lakes in spring when smolts are passing through the lake from feeder streams to the sea. In Irish loughs pike have also been reported feeding on grilse: Fred Buller recorded a 32lb pike taken from Lough Conn that had an 8½lb grilse in its stomach. Ferox trout, which usually feed on charr and whitefish in lakes, also take smolts migrating through lakes. Large river trout are also predators of salmon fry and parr: a 5½lb brown trout that I caught on the Spey had 14 parr in its stomach and one that it had not swallowed still in its throat when it took my big parr-imitating 'fly'; and W.M. Shearer records trout weighing up to about one pound, 'with the remains of up to 20 smolts in their stomach', from the North Esk.

Earlier I expressed concern at stocking salmon rivers with large rainbow trout, for I have observed them taking salmon eggs. Both large rainbow and brown trout will eat any small fish, but no Atlantic salmon river naturally contains rainbow trout and most salmon rivers contain relatively few big trout. Yet there is a tendency for rivers to be stocked with large trout from fish farms to satisfy trout anglers who get bored with catching small wild trout. Such introductions are tantamount to pollution, for there is no doubt that these fish will eat salmon fry, parr and smolts, as well as the small wild trout. In 1976 many rainbow trout escaped from a fish farm in the Ribble Valley. I caught 27, 22 of which had the remains of small fish in their stomachs, including salmon parr. And I have caught brown trout that were of farm origin, weighing between one and three pounds, in the rivers Eden and Ribble with salmon parr and smolts in their stomachs. There can be no doubt that heavy stocking with big trout, especially in spring when smolts are migrating downstream, will result in a significant loss of young salmon. I am sure that many of those anglers who enjoy catching large hatchery-bred trout in their river in spring will be complaining in autumn, when they are not catching salmon, that the net fisheries are taking too many fish!

It is policy, in many rivers that have a poor salmon run, to supplement wild salmon stocks with fry, parr or smolts raised in a hatchery. However, there is some evidence that hatchery-bred young salmon are highly predated until they have grown accustomed to living in the river. J. Hult and A. Johnels reported on an experiment which showed that 11 per cent of planted fry were devoured by fish (in this case mainly perch) within 24 hours of release.

Disease

With a few exceptions, fish parasites and diseases are difficult for the amateur to identify. Sometimes the effect of the parasite or disease may be apparent, but the bacteria or whatever it is that cause the disease may require great expertise to identify them. The following are those that the angler may easily notice on either the catch or on dead and dying fish. There are many more that may cause illness or death but that will not be apparent: the fish may show no outward symptoms (they might just as easily have died from pollution or old age). It is only when there is a major epidemic, when large numbers of salmon are found dead and dying, that disease seriously reduces the salmon populations. However, the effect is generally short lived, numbers recovering rapidly (within two or three generations).

UDN (Ulcerative Dermal Necrosis) is the best known of salmon diseases, mainly through the pandemic of the 1960s and 1970s. This major outbreak began in Ireland in 1964, reached the rivers of north-west England and south-west Scotland in 1966, and most other British rivers by the end of 1968. Thousands of salmon died, and many thousands still alive but showing symptoms of the disease were removed from some rivers and buried in lime-pits. In one 12-month period (March 1967 to February 1968) 41,234 salmon that were suffering from UDN were removed from Scottish rivers, while in 1967–9 up to 70 per cent of salmon in some of the rivers of northern England showed some UDN symptoms.

During the 1970s the incidence of UDN declined and, though there are still occasional reports of fish exhibiting signs of UDN (which may not, in fact, be UDN; see below), the disease has little, if any, effect on current population levels. This pandemic, which many of us are old enough to remember vividly, was not the first major outbreak of UDN. For the disease was rife in many British rivers during the 1870s and 1880s, in some rivers into the early 1900s. That the disease may break out once more in sufficient amounts to cause concern is borne out by reports of a high incidence of UDN from some Spanish rivers in the late 1980s.

Most anglers are likely to notice salmon infected with UDN only when the disease is well advanced, and the fish, covered with a white fungal growth, are lying in shallow, still backwaters close to the bank. But occasionally a salmon will be caught showing the earlier signs. The first sign of UDN is pale blue-grey, almost white, patches on the head, sometimes also back and tail. These pale patches of skin then become a mushy blue-grey ulcer, the centre of this mushy patch sometimes being lost to reveal red raw bare flesh. The ulcerated patches enlarge to cover an increasing area of the head, back and tail region. Finally the ulcerated skin becomes invaded by a white fungus *Saprolegnia* which itself may spread over much of the body. This secondary fungal infection is consequent to UDN, not a symptom of it. The fact that a salmon is seen with white fungoid patches on its body (as many kelts are) does not indicate UDN, for *Saprolegnia* will infect any damaged area of fish skin.

If the white fungus does not cause UDN, then what does? During the 1960s and early 1970s outbreak several fish pathologists examined the ulcers and suggested several bacteria, which they had identified in the ulcers, that might be responsible. However, these bacteria are commonly found on the skins of healthy salmon, and the pathologists could not demonstrate experimentally that any bacterium was capable of causing the UDN ulcers. Another theory is that a virus is the cause of UDN. But as yet no one has been able to isolate, with any certainty, the true cause of the disease. Although salmon may be infected with UDN throughout the year, the highest incidences appear to occur in the winter months, between late October and February, in fish that are about to spawn or that have spawned. The disease has thus been linked to cold water conditions. However, it is at this stage of their life cycle that salmon are perhaps more vulnerable to disease, so the link with cold water may be coincidental.

Curiously UDN rarely affects fry, parr and smolts. Furthermore, if an affected fish manages to spawn successfully, the eggs are viable and progeny unaffected. It thus seems logical to leave affected fish in the river in the hope that they will spawn, for the fact that they may infect other fish is probably irrelevant, the disease being already in the water.

Furunculosis is a disease caused by the bacterium *Aeromonas salmonicida*. Symptoms are boils (or furuncles), usually close to the dorsal fin, which may spread over the body as bleeding ulcers, bleeding from the vent, and an accumulation of blood in the fins. Other bacteria (and fungi) may invade the ulcers, causing septicaemia (blood poisoning) and death. It is a highly infectious disease of salmon, occasionally causing large numbers of deaths especially in hot, low water conditions in summer when large concentrations of fish might occur in deep, slow pools.

A rather similar disease is called vibriosis, but in this case most bleeding spots or sores occur on the belly or close to the vent. Vibriosis is very common in eels, hence the specific name given to the bacterium causing the disease, *Vibrio anguillarus*.

Columnaris is another disease that has been reported causing ulcers on the skin of salmon. This, too, is caused by a bacterium, *Chondrococcus columnaris*. It is far more commonly seen on members of the carp family.

Inflammation of skin, congestion of the fins with blood, bleeding from the vent and also blood spots in the muscle due to haemorrhaging of blood vessels can be caused by a variety of bacterial and viral infections. Most serious of these in salmon is the so-called 'Dee disease' which was first identified from the Aberdeenshire Dee and is caused by a bacterium, *Cornebacterium*. Detailed examination of the internal organs is necessary to confirm Dee disease.

If you find many fish that seem to be suffering from one of these conditions immediately inform local or regional fisheries departments (in England and Wales, at the nearest National Rivers Authority office; in Scotland, Northern Ireland and the Republic of Ireland, the regional freshwater fisheries office). If possible provide samples.

Parasites

Parasites are very rarely the cause of death in salmon, though when present in large numbers they may weaken them or damage the skin to allow the entry of bacterial or fungal infection that may result in death.

The best-known salmon parasite is the sea louse, a small crustacean *Lepeophtheirus salmonis* that infests salmon and sea trout at sea, but which falls from the fish within days of return to fresh water (the presence of sea lice is a good indication of a fresh-run salmon or sea trout). Female sea lice are especially conspicuous, being up to 0.7in in length with a pair of long, thin egg sacs; they are usually found close to the vent or on the flanks of the salmon. Sea lice are a major pest of salmon farms (where they must be controlled by chemicals) and the collapse of many coastal sea trout populations has been blamed on infestation by huge numbers of these parasites. Although there have been some earlier reports of salmon with huge infestations, happily they seem not to be infested by sea lice from salmon farms, possibly because they do not linger close inshore near fish farms. Sea lice eat away the skin of salmon and it is possible that these damaged areas may be susceptible to fungal, bacterial or viral infections.

The gill maggot *Salmincola salmonea* is another parasitic crustacean that infests adult salmon in fresh water, usually just before, at, or after spawning when the fish are at their weakest and most vulnerable. Up to 0.4in long, they attach themselves to the gill filaments on which they feed. Because they are never found on salmon parr and smolts and only rarely on fresh-run salmon, their presence can be taken to be a good indication of a kelt; but some kelts may lack gill maggots and some fresh-run fish (notably those spawning for a second or third time) may have gill maggots. They have never been known to cause death in salmon.

The freshwater or carp louse *Argulus* is a very common parasite found on the skin of a wide range of fish species such as carp, bream, minnow, trout and pike. Since 1983 I have caught eight adult salmon in the Ribble that were infested by this parasitic crustacean and also noticed, in this river and the Eden, an increase of freshwater louse infestation on brown trout and salmon parr (one parr had 17 freshwater lice clinging to it). I put this down to extremely low water (owing to excessive abstraction) linked with warm water temperatures. Up to 0.4in (occasionally 0.5in) in length, when attached to the skin of the fish it resembles a flattened disc which, when removed and the underside examined, reveals tiny legs and tail. The lice can swim and move from fish to fish and feed by piercing the skin and sucking body fluids. When present in large numbers they may weaken fish (especially small ones) while skin infections may invade through wound.

Most species of flukes (members of the class of flatworms known as the Trematoda) live in the bodies of fish: some in the eye lens causing blindness, some in the gut, some in the liver, depending on the species of fluke. Most flukes have two or three hosts in their life cycle. One that is currently a major cause for concern has only one host – the salmon – and lives attached to the skin: *Gyrodactylus salaris*. Though *Gyrodactylus* is only very tiny, less than 0.04in in length, it can multiply extremely rapidly parthenogenetically (without the need for eggs to be fertilized) so that, in a few days, one becomes many thousands.

Gyrodactylus has traditionally never been a problem. However, a possibly virulent strain developed in some Swedish hatcheries and was transferred, with salmon fry, to Norwegian hatcheries from where it has escaped into some rivers and infested the wild parr stocks. There are reports of parr having thousands of these on their bodies, the wounds caused by *Gyrodactylus* (which eats into the skin) being infected by bacteria and fungi resulting in very high mortality. So rife has *Gyrodactylus* become in some Norwegian rivers that the parr stocks have collapsed, the number of smolts produced fallen to very low levels, and the numbers of returning salmon become a tiny fraction of what they were. So much so that some rivers have been closed to angling. Successful attempts have been made to eradicate *Gyrodactylus* with the poison rotenone, but this also kills all the fish in the treated river so that restocking, which is a slow process, must be carried out. Eventually this major problem in Norway will be overcome, but it does highlight the folly of transferring fish from one place to another without being absolutely sure that disease or parasites are not also being transferred.

Tapeworms lack a gut, food being absorbed through the skin. When adult they resemble long (often up to 1.6ft) segmented ribbons with a small round head that may have suckers and/or hooks that hold on to their host's tissues, usually inside the intestines. Heavily infected fish may be very thin. Acanthocephalan worms are also worms with a spiny head that attaches to gut wall, a narrow neck, and body up to 4in in length. Again heavily infected fish are usually very thin. Occasionally numbers of roundworms, simple, unsegmented, slender worms, are found in salmon. They are usually up to 0.8in long. Some occur in the gut, others in the liver and muscles.

Leeches are related to garden earthworms, and have a short body, distinct segments, and strong suckers at mouth and anus. They feed by sucking blood and are occasionally found on the skin of salmon, especially around the mouth and vent or gills. The sea lamprey *Petromyzon marinus* is also a parasite of the salmon that feeds by attaching itself to its host with its toothed sucker-like mouth, digesting and sucking body tissues and fluids. It is not uncommon to catch a salmon with a round sore, made by a sea lamprey, usually on the side of the fish. Like the salmon the sea lamprey is an anadromous fish, spawning in rivers and migrating seawards to feed and grow. Dying adult sea lampreys, that have finished spawning can be seen in some of the big, clean salmon rivers such as the Spey and Aberdeenshire Dee in July and August. None of these parasites has been shown to cause many deaths or to affect populations.

The spread of diseases and parasites is often caused by anglers. Careless handling may remove scales and protective slime and provide a point of entry for viruses, bacteria and fungi. Handle all fish that are to be returned to the water carefully, preferably without touching them with the hands. Use a wet net or cloth to hold the fish whilst unhooking them and use knotless nets that are less likely to damage the fish's skin.

The transfer of fish from one water to another has sometimes introduced a parasite or disease that has affected native fish populations (*Gyrodactylus* is a classic example) of the stocked lake or river. Also, disease organisms are easily transferred in slime or fish scales on landing-nets.

- Do not take part in haphazard stocking because you might introduce parasites and diseases with the fish; check with a fishery biologist first.

- Rinse nets regularly in a weak solution of mild disinfectant, especially when a fish disease is particularly prevalent.

Exceptionally high river or lake temperatures

Very occasionally it is reported, usually during a prolonged summer drought, that many salmon have died because of high river water temperatures. Certainly if water temperatures rises much above 71–73°F the fish show signs of distress, moving into rougher, better oxygenated pool necks and riffles, or in lakes into deeper, cooler water. When the temperature reaches 77°F or more some may die. Fortunately such high water temperatures are rarely encountered in the salmon's geographical range: it is probably this factor that limits the southern limits for salmon rivers.

Such an effect is more likely in rivers that have greatly reduced flows because of excessive water abstraction and land drainage, where large supplies of cool water from deep underground are no longer feeding the river during long hot summer periods.

Mortality caused directly by man

Without mankind's interference, every river in the natural range of the Atlantic salmon would have a thriving population of fish. Predators, parasites and disease, together with the occasional high mortality due to high water temperatures, would have no effect in the long term. The numbers of salmon returning to the rivers from the sea would produce enough smolts to perpetuate the bountiful runs despite predation, outbreaks of disease and parasite infestations.

We have already seen that mankind's actions, through the drainage of the river catchment area, damage to the river and by water abstraction, can reduce the effective size of the river and cause high egg and parr mortality (p. 172). Such effects should not be underestimated.

Damming salmon rivers, whether with weirs that have no fish pass and over which salmon cannot leap or with a reservoir dam that excludes salmon from areas of the river in which they traditionally spawned, has been a major cause of death in many rivers. The salmon cannot pass upstream; they cannot breed where they used to before the dam; the river upstream of the dam ceases to produce smolts; the population crashes. We saw instances of this when we discussed salmon distribution in Chapter 1; another instance is described on p. 206.

Two more obvious causes of mortality are pollution and fishing.

Chemical pollution

On a beautiful spring day, 8 April 1993, Graham Britton, Dave Evans and I went to fish one of our beats on the Eden. We arrived at the bridge and, as do all anglers when they reach a bridge, we looked over into the water. Water height was perfect; the river was as clear as crystal. A good day was in prospect. Alas, it was not to be. It was Graham who first spotted the signs of what had happened: a chub lying dead on the bottom. Then we suddenly became aware that the chub was not alone, for the river bed was strewn with dead fish. In a daze we walked upstream for a short distance, noting dead trout, grayling, salmon parr, minnows, miller's thumbs, even brook lampreys, which normally live in the mud, and eels, the fish most tolerant of pollution – and four salmon.

Having notified the authorities of the disaster and learning that there was no sign of pollution five miles downstream, we drove down the valley and then started to walk upstream to see if we could find the pollution front. By this time flies were hatching from the water surface and trout were rising. We had walked about a mile when I suddenly had a whiff of ammonia and saw, upstream, dead fish. Opposite me fish were rising to the surface and then expiring. We walked back downstream, following the slow progress of the pollution, which we couldn't see but could pinpoint accurately by the dying fish. A salmon rose, thrashed on the top and then ran so rapidly across the surface that it literally smashed its snout on a rock on the other bank: when Dave retrieved it, its snout was a mass of congealed blood. A little further downstream we saw another salmon lift in the water, make three or four thrashing movements, and then float downstream, quite dead. It took the pollution front about half an hour to move 200yd downstream, through the deep, fairly slow pools. And in this time we watched every fish that had been alive in that short length suffer and die. Altogether, all the fish in about 18 miles of what is usually pristine river were killed, including salmon to 30lb. The pollution eventually lost its effect through being diluted by a major feeder stream.

What had happened? A tanker carrying 180,000 litres of concentrated ammonium hydroxide was transferring its load into a farm tanker (apparently it is common practice to inject ammonia into the soil as a fertilizer). It crashed over into a small stream and its contents were lost. Was it a 'one-off accident'? No, it was a one-off incident caused by sheer negligence on the part of the tanker driver and farmer, but also on the part of a government that allows vast quantities of dangerous chemicals to be transported by accident-prone road transport.

I am writing this almost two years later, and the river has still not recovered. Will it recover? Eventually, unless another accident happens. And one nearly did in 1994 when a tanker carrying toxic chemicals crashed on the A66 road which runs near to the river. The bottom 10 miles of the river had not fully recovered from an earlier accident, three years before, when a dairy inadvertently released polluting waste into the river and killed all the fish.

Every year 'one-off' pollution incidents poison many miles of river: tanker crashes, accidental discharges of untreated sewage or industrial or farm effluent, or accidental spillage of chemicals from water treatment plants. A few years ago a tank containing creosote was accidentally allowed to pour its entire contents into a river: 40 miles of river was killed. I once arrived at a riverside car park and started to tackle up. A police car arrived with siren blazing and lights flashing: 'Don't fish today! Some cyanide has been accidentally released into the river!' The police car sped off to pass the message to other anglers and to warn farmers to keep their livestock from the water.

Though no one can legislate against human error, legislation could greatly reduce the risks of such environmental catastrophes. If the penalties that courts were required to impose on such polluters were colossal, and included mandatory prison sentences for the directors of companies that pollute, potential polluters would take greater care to ensure that it could not happen.

Organic pollution

Sewage, waste from paper mills, dairies and food processing plants, seepage from farm silage clamps and slurry pits – these can all pollute our rivers. They may be one-off incidents or long-term pollution.

Organic pollutants are those containing a high concentration of carbon-containing compounds, usually derived from animals or plants, or animal (including human) faeces and urine. When these enter the water, bacteria feed on them and the numbers of bacteria multiply at a tremendous rate. These bacteria remove oxygen from the water and the resulting lack of oxygen kills the fish.

The effect is strongest close to the source of pollution, the effects diminishing further downstream as the organic content and bacterial population in the water decline. In areas most likely to be affected by such pollution in the long term (for instance sewage works, paper mills and factories manufacturing dairy products) weirs have often been constructed downstream; the weir oxygenates the water and hastens the bacterial breakdown of the pollutant.

Salmon, like trout and grayling, are intolerant of even small amounts of

185

organic pollutant and they will run quickly through stretches of river that are permanently affected by small amounts to reach cleaner water upstream. I used to fish one river beat immediately downstream of a sewage works that discharged fully or partially treated effluent. Salmon rarely rested in the half mile of water between the sewage works and the weir, or in or below the weir pool, other than for a few minutes when they were running through. The three pools immediately above the sewage outfall had major resident and running lies. It was over a mile downstream of the weir to the next resident lies, at a point where the pollution never reached. Thus that mile and a half beat never held salmon (we rarely caught more than five in the season), though hundreds passed through it; it did, however, hold shoals of dace and chub, which are less susceptible to the effects of low-level, long-term organic pollution.

On many other, long river systems (such as the Trent and Ouse in Britain and many rivers of Germany, Holland and France) the lower reaches are clean enough and have a high enough oxygen content to support a 'coarse fish' population, but the oxygen content of the water is too low for salmon to pass through to the cleaner upper reaches. If, as is currently happening on many such rivers, the organic pollutants are reduced and oxygen levels raised by only a small degree, salmon may be able to pass through these lower reaches, find resident lies in cleaner water upstream and re-establish thriving populations. This has happened on the Thames (pp. 204–5), Ribble (pp. 205–7), Tees and Tyne in recent years. No matter how perfect the spawning areas and nursery streams are, if salmon cannot pass upstream nor smolts downstream the river will never have a salmon population.

It ought to be the policy of all governments to enforce legislation that insists that all organic effluents be treated before they are poured into a river or lake.

Acid rain

Acid rain is the most insidious of all long-term pollutants, for it appears unseen and comes and goes as the wind changes direction. Furthermore, the pollution is often carried vast distances (often across international boundaries) from polluter to the region polluted.

When fossil fuels are burnt, waste poisonous gases containing nitrogen and sulphur are pumped into the atmosphere, from car exhausts, urban fires burning coal and coke, and from coal- or oil-fired power stations. When these gases dissolve in water they become acids: nitric acid and sulphuric acid. In towns and cities the effect of these acids is quite marked, for they corrode buildings and monuments, especially those built of limestone or marble, which are especially vulnerable to acid attack. Power stations attempt to prevent these acids falling on nearby towns and cities by releasing them through tall chimneys. The gases thus rise in the air and dissolve in the water droplets of clouds. The wind blows the clouds away, and eventually the droplets of acid fall to the ground as acid rain.

Regions of high rainfall are most susceptible to falls of acid rain: in Britain, north and central Wales, the Lake District, south-west Scotland; in mainland Europe, the mountainous region of south-west Norway. All are regions with major salmon fisheries. The gases that give rise to the acidity of the rain falling in these regions originate mainly in the heavily industrialized parts of south Wales, midland and northern England, Germany, Poland and the Baltic States. The amount of acid rain falling in these susceptible areas has increased greatly since 1950. A report published in 1990, *Acid Waters in Wales*, demonstrated that each year 10 kilograms of sulphur in sulphuric acid and 5 kilograms of nitrogen in nitric acid fall on every hectare of the Welsh uplands.

Acidity is measured on the pH scale, where pH7 is neutral, pH1 the most acid, and a decrease by one pH unit means a ten-fold increase of acidity, a decrease of two pH units a hundred-fold increase of acidity. In Wales the pH of the River Ystwyth fell from pH6.5 in 1970 to pH5.5 in 1980: it became ten times more acid. In the River Conwy the pH fell from 6.8 to 6.0 in the five years 1975–80: a six-fold increase in acidity. Another report, by University College London (Department of the Environment 1988), demonstrated that mean pH of many upland waters has declined by between one and one and a half units in the past 50 years, indicating an increase of acidity of between ten-fold and thirty-fold.

These are long-term changes. However, during a fall of extremely acid rain there may be a sharp, sudden fall of pH which is often lethal for salmon. In 1984–5 Bill Arnold of Knott End Estate recorded rainfall with a pH as low as 3.4 falling in the Lake District, the acid component of which had originated from places as diverse as West Germany, south Wales, and the regions of northern, north-eastern, central and southern England (in Falkus and Buller's *Freshwater Fishing*, 1988). These falls resulted in the death of salmon and sea trout in the Esk. A similar fall of pH in a September 1984 downpour in the Glaslyn Valley resulted in the immediate death of 117 fresh-run salmon and sea trout; those fish surviving were diagnosed as suffering physiological damage. In 1981, 1500 salmon parr were stocked into the upper Tywi; there was a fall of acid rain and they were all dead within four weeks.

But it is not just the increase of acidity that causes mortality. Increasing acidity of water flowing through soil, especially in areas afforested with conifers, results in an increasing solubility of aluminium (which is normally held in an insoluble state in the soil). Aluminium is poisonous, causing the gills to become congested with mucus and damaging internal organs such as the kidney and liver.

Both the increase of acidity and the increase of aluminium in the water cause death of adult and immature salmon and a failure of salmon eggs to hatch. The effect is, however, of even greater impact on the entire river ecosystem. By comparing surveys carried out before acid rain began to have an impact on the rivers (in the 1940s and 1950s) with more recent surveys, it is clear that the invertebrate stocks of streams in areas prone to acidification have collapsed, both in the number of species and in overall population sizes. These invertebrates are food for many species of waterside bird. So, in such areas species like the dipper have declined: in some rivers from 10–12 pairs to 1–2 pairs per six miles of river. Even if salmon themselves were unaffected by acidification, there would no longer be enough food to support the optimal numbers of smolts that the river produced before acidification.

In the worst-affected areas of Wales, north-west England, Scotland, Sweden and Norway, lakes that had thriving fish stocks in 1945 had none by 1990, and in some rivers stocks had declined by 80 per cent or more in the same period. In the 10-year period from 1976 to 1985, salmon catches on the Welsh rivers Dysynni, Glaslyn, Clwyd and Conwy were only 37 per cent, 38 per cent, 49 per cent and 58 per cent respectively of the 1966–75 catches. The Welsh report laid the blame for this decline firmly at the door of acidification. In the years between 1970 and 1990 the formerly massive runs of sea trout and big runs of salmon in many rivers of west Cumbria and south-west Norway collapsed: where there were hundreds of salmon in the 1960s, by the late 1980s there were only tens. Such is the effect of acid rain.

Since about 1990 governments of the pollution-producing regions have begun to insist that the major producers of acid rain (mainly fossil-fuel-burning power stations) incorporate 'scrubbers' that will remove the bulk of the pollutants. But such a policy is expensive and many old power stations have yet to fit them. In 1994 one English power station, which has been shown to cause acidification in Wales, Scotland, north-west England and even Norway, actually failed to use the scrubbers already fitted on the grounds of cost. Immediate and positive action is urgently needed to impose the legal necessity of scrubbers, and to reduce the emissions of acidic gases from all sources by developing alternative forms of energy. The argument, so often given by industry and government, that this is too expensive is deplorable. For the cost of acidification on our environment is too great to be measured in financial terms.

Farm fertilizer pollution

It has become policy, of both national governments and the European Union, to urge farmers to produce the maximum amount of food by whatever means, even though much of this will be surplus and sent into store. To this end farmers are encouraged to dose the land with subsidized inorganic fertilizers. A large proportion of these is leached into rivers and lakes. This might appear, initially, not to be a bad thing, for the fertilizers cause an increase of aquatic plant growth which in turn will cause an increase of invertebrates (fish foods) and result in larger populations of fish. However, it is not so simple. One plant that thrives in artificially high nitrate and phosphate levels is the alga *Cladophora* (or blanket weed). This chokes the river or lake bed and, during warm summer evenings, removes large amounts of oxygen from the water. Clean-water invertebrates (e.g. stoneflies, some upwinged flies and crayfish) may be exterminated and where the pollution is very bad fish stocks (especially of salmon and trout) may suffer. In warm springs, when *Cladophora* may coat the river bed from April onwards, it may choke alevins and fry still in the redds.

There are efforts being made to reduce this waste of fertilizers and pollution of water, but mainly because of the high level of nitrates and phosphates in the drinking water that has been abstracted from rivers. Surely, if the concentration of these in the water is too high for safe human consumption, it is too high for the river ecosystem!

Industrial poisons

These poisons may be of several types: metals such as cadmium, lead and mercury, or noxious compounds such as PCBs (polychlorinated biphenols), cyanide and acids from industry; agricultural herbicides and insecticides used to kill pests (they also kill fish); oil and products of the oil refining industry.

During the last two hundred years or so many rivers have become dumping grounds for industrial and urban waste, especially in or just above the estuary where most industry tends to be concentrated. Thus rivers like the Rhine and Meuse and Mersey have become so polluted in their lower reaches and estuaries that these reaches are fishless and the pollution acts as a barrier that prevents migratory fish such as the salmon passing from sea to cleaner upper areas. This pollution is 'traditional': it began during the Industrial Revolution and in the economic post-war boom of the 1950s, before groups such as anglers had a strong enough voice to oppose it. Such pollution continues today because of both the economic and the political difficulties of pursuing a major clean-up. The effects of a clean-up can be seen in rivers where this has been possible. For example, the River Tyne was a thriving salmon and sea trout fishery until the cities and towns of Newcastle upon Tyne, Tynemouth, Gateshead and North and South Shields began using the estuary as a waste receptacle. By the 1960s salmon and sea trout runs had been almost eliminated. In the years from about 1975 efforts were made to clean up the pollution and by the late 1980s the river had quickly reverted into one of England's major salmon and sea trout fisheries. Likewise the Tees, the estuary of which is a mass of chemical industrial plant. Well into the 1980s the lower reaches were highly toxic, and anyone falling in there would have been lucky to survive. But by the early 1990s pollution had been reduced to a level through which salmon and sea trout could pass to cleaner water upstream. (See also the Thames, pp. 204–5.)

The insidious effects of some poisons, especially heavy metals, organohalides and PCBs, has recently been illustrated by a disease affecting Baltic salmon, known as M74. 'It has been speculated that the symptoms of M74 are the result of high levels of PCBs or heavy metals building up in adult females [salmon], and being passed on to the eggs, causing an estimated 90 per cent of mortality at the alevin stage' (*Salmon, Trout & Sea-Trout*). Such a mortality rate seriously threatens the future of the Baltic race of Atlantic salmon.

Fishing

Fishing is no more than taking a crop from the surplus salmon that every river *ought* to be producing. If the river is functioning at 100 per cent efficiency as a smolt factory then the crop can be quite large. Alas, most rivers are not functioning at 100 per cent, and it may well be that the river has no surplus and that no crop should be taken at all until the population has recovered.

Commercial fisheries

There are three major classes of commercial salmon fisheries: high seas fisheries, which catch salmon from their marine feeding grounds; offshore fisheries, which catch salmon migrating back from their marine feeding grounds to the rivers of their birth; and estuary-river fisheries, which take fish that are beginning their journey upstream in their natal river.

The high seas fisheries, driftnetting off Greenland and long-lining around the Faroes and off northern Norway, are of fairly recent origin. Although a few salmon were caught off Greenland in the first half of the twentieth century, this fishery really developed from 1959, when the extent of the salmon stocks feeding in this region was fully appreciated. Between 1960 and 1965 the Greenland catch increased dramatically, from less than 100 tons to over 1500 tons per annum, and by the early 1970s it had risen to over 2500 tons (Fig. 26). International concern resulted in quotas being set and thereafter the catch declined. It is of interest, however, that in later years fishermen were unable to catch their quota, perhaps because there were not enough salmon (potential multi-sea-winter fish) feeding there.

The Faroe fishery was fairly insignificant, at up to 40 tons per annum, until 1979 when the catch rose to 191 tons, 1980 544 tons, and 1981 1009 tons (Fig. 26). Quotas were then imposed and the catch delined.

The Norwegian sea fishery commenced in the mid-1960s, peaked at almost 980 tons in 1970, but was closed down in 1984 (Fig. 26).

Anglers considered the advent of these high seas fisheries to be almost the last nail in the coffin of the Atlantic salmon. These fisheries were blamed, in part at least, for the demise of the spring runs and, in the case of the Greenland fishery, the decline of large multi-sea-winter fish (though the spring runs and the numbers of big salmon were declining before these fisheries began operating: see Chapter 4). It should be noted, however, that the impact of these high seas fisheries on the numbers of salmon returning to the rivers was greater

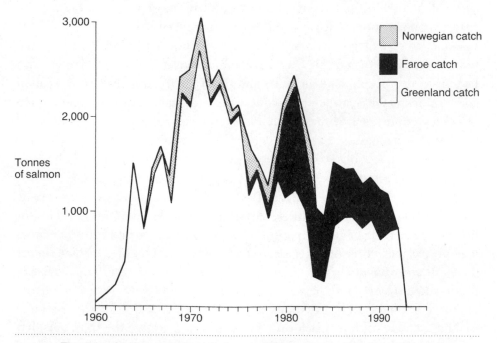

Fig. 26 – High seas catches of salmon off Greenland and the Faroe Islands and in the Norwegian sea

than the tonnages of salmon landed by the fisheries. For the salmon caught on their feeding grounds were feeding and growing fish. They had not reached their full size before being caught. Thus, had they been caught in or close to their natal rivers after they had completed their growth, the total weight would have been far greater. Calculations by W.M. Shearer indicated that every ton of salmon caught off Greenland would have weighed 1.29–1.79 tonnes had that ton eventually returned to European rivers, and 1.47–2.00 tons had the one ton continued to grow and returned to North American rivers. In other words, harvesting a ton of salmon in the high seas was potentially equivalent to removing up to two tons from the river fisheries.

In 1992 Orri Vigfusson, chairman of the North Atlantic Salmon Fund (NASF), successfully completed negotiations for a cessation of commercial fishing for salmon in Faroese waters, and in 1993 he succeeded in negotiating a moratorium of the commercial fishery in Greenlandic waters. Both agreements are on short-term bases, and will have to be renegotiated in future years. But that is a good start, and may eventually result in a completed protection of salmon on its marine feeding grounds. The deal agreed by Orri includes compensation being paid to the former salmon fishermen. Magnificent! This means that thousands of salmon that would have been captured on the high seas will return to their rivers, increase the bag for anglers and bolster the spawning population. The only sad thing is the lukewarm contribution made by some European governments, most notably the Irish and British whose rivers have most to gain (Dr David Solomon calculated that this buy-out will benefit anglers in Scotland alone by an extra 10,000 multi-sea-winter salmon and an extra 30,000 spawners). By contrast the Icelandic, Canadian and United States governments gave maximum, high-level support to Orri Vigfusson and the NASF initiative.

The true impact of offshore fisheries is difficult to judge, mainly because evidence suggests that the true catch is far greater than the declared catch. Also, because these fisheries are scattered around the coastlines and fish can be landed in a large number of different harbours, they are far more difficult for fisheries protection boats to monitor. This is especially the case in some areas (e.g. off Ireland) where drift nets are fished mainly at night. In Canadian waters the numbers of migrating salmon that are caught offshore are carefully regulated. It is in the eastern Atlantic, especially around the coasts of the British Isles, that excessive netting is still carried out.

The declared offshore catch (mostly by drift net) around the Irish coast has varied from about 800 to over 2400 tons per annum. And although fishery consultants have made proposals to the government of the Republic of Ireland to reduce this catch, the government has made no attempt to do anything at all other than nothing! At their peak, the Greenland catch was 2500 tons and the Faroes catch about 1000 tons: the declared Irish catch is in the same league and the true catch probably much greater. Most of the Irish catch consists of grilse, heading for British and Irish rivers. If the average weight of these grilse is $6^1/_2$lb, then a catch of 1000 tons is equivalent to about 350,000 fish that fail to make their home rivers.

Another offshore fishery that is causing concern is the drift net fishery that operates off the north-east coast of England, for its declared catches have generally varied between 40,000 and 90,000 salmon per annum since the late 1960s. Most of these salmon are destined for Scottish rivers, so that if the fishery were closed the effect on Scottish rivers would equal or exceed the effect caused by the cessation of high seas fishing as calculated by David Solomon (see above). Proposals have been put to the British Ministry of Agriculture, Fisheries and Food, but the apathetic response has been that the fishery might be phased out in the future.

When one considers the positive steps to conserve salmon stocks by the Icelandic, Canadian and US governments, supported by the Greenland and Faroese, and by the Norwegians in closing their high seas fishery, it is a sad reflection on Britain and Ireland whose irresponsible and apathetic governments are too weak to act.

Of course, it may be argued that high seas and offshore fisheries are simply taking some of that surplus that a thriving salmon river will be producing. What is wrong with that, provided that there are quotas preventing overfishing?

The problem is that both high seas and offshore fisheries do not differentiate between rivers, for the salmon that they catch come from different rivers, often from different countries. They will catch salmon from the relatively small number of thriving river systems and from many rivers where either the river stocks need some careful conservation because they are not producing a huge excess that may be cropped or where the runs of fish are so low that they need 100 per cent protection. Such random catches should have no part of modern salmon fisheries conservation. The amount of crop that may be taken must be decided river by river. For that reason, the only good way to crop salmon is by commercial netting in the estuary and by rod-and-line fishing upstream.

Such a policy would greatly benefit not only salmon stocks, but also the estuary fishermen and anglers. It could therefore be regarded as a selfish policy. It is only right, therefore, that those who would benefit pay compensation to those who do not. Anglers often consider that the salmon caught out at sea are *their* salmon or salmon belonging to *their* rivers. True! Our rivers produce the smolts. But the smolts gain their weight by feeding on lesser fish, crustaceans, squids and so on in Greenlandic, Faroese and arctic Norwegian waters. What we catch owes much of its weight to their, not our, rivers. It is only right and proper, therefore, that we compensate those who have the rights to fish those waters: we must do this through the NASF.

The final argument in the debate is between anglers and the commercial fisheries at the river mouth. The commercial cropping of salmon in estuaries (and, in many rivers until fairly recently, far upstream: in the late nineteenth century there were salmon nets in the Lune as far as 35 miles from the sea) is of ancient origin. In bygone days, before pollution and water abstraction and damming of rivers and before netting at sea, huge numbers of salmon were removed from even fairly small rivers by estuary nets: see the Foyle system (pp. 207–9) and Ribble (pp. 205–7). The rivers as smolt factories could withstand such depredation, for they were often working at or close to 100 per cent efficiency. As the salmon stocks declined in most rivers, and sometimes in rivers where no decline could be noticed, so netting seasons became shortened and the number of hours each week when the nets could operate was reduced. Such restrictions gave times when salmon could pass upstream without hindrance in addition to the times when the netsmen could not operate (perhaps at low tide, or during a spate). But even these restrictions were never considered enough by rod anglers. The sight of a haaf-netsman taking a salmon from the Nith estuary at Glencaple, or a trammel-net catching a fish in the Lune, or a sweep-net being brought in with a dozen sea trout and couple of grilse on the Spey made most anglers shake with rage!

Estuary netting *is* the most logical way of harvesting the surplus salmon crop. But for effective cropping, which allows enough fish to pass upstream for the rod-and-line fishery to get good sport and to leave a healthy spawning stock, it is essential to know what that surplus is. In a properly managed river these four factors are known (or at least a fairly accurate estimate can be made): how many fish are likely to run in the year; how many fish must be left to spawn; how many fish must there be in the river to give anglers good sport and to guarantee the income from anglers; how many should be cropped by netting. Unfortunately there are very few well-managed rivers (one is described, the Foyle, on pp. 207–9).

In recent years the angling lobby has made much of the value to the local economy of netted salmon and of the profit from estuary netting stations compared with a salmon caught by an angler. This is a valid argument.

The following is from *Hansard* accounts of questions in the House of Lords, 26 May 1993:

The Earl of Kimberley asked Her Majesty's Government: How many salmon and sea trout were caught by the Crown Commissioners at Speymouth each year for the last five years?

Lord Fraser of Carmyllie: The following information has been supplied by the Crown Commissioners from their records of catches of salmon, grilse and sea trout by the Spey sweep nets:

Year	Salmon	Grilse	Sea Trout
1988	1132	4090	6931
1989	2267	6712	7589
1990	1791	2970	5339
1991	587	1985	3015
1992	1650	5905	2807

The Earl of Kimberly asked Her Majesty's Government: What is the gross and net income derived by the Crown Estate Commissioners from netting operations in Scotland and what percentage of such income is derived a) directly and b) from leasing?

The Earl of Caithness: The gross income derived by the Crown Estate Commissioners from netting operations in Scotland was £120,120 in the financial year ending 31 March 1993. The net income during the same period was £11,449. In percentage terms, the gross income derived directly was 82% with 18% from leasing.

Note that the answer to the second question related to all the Crown Commissioners' netting stations in Scotland, and not just the Spey, and that the profit from the netting of these thousands of fish in 1992–3 amounted to the grand sum of £11,449. A profit of barely £11,500 for all that effort and all those salmon! The following year the nets at Speymouth were discontinued.

When it comes to the value of an individual salmon there is a great difference between a netted salmon and one caught on rod and line. A netted salmon may be sold for £10 on the market, that £10 being circulated into the local economy by the netsman and his employer. A rod-caught salmon is worth far more to the local economy. Let me illustrate this. In 1993 I caught four small salmon and two sea trout in a typical summer week's fishing on the Aberdeenshire Dee: their market value would have been about £50. But to catch them I spent:

Cost of fishing (used in the management of the estate)	£193
Contribution to the Dee Fisheries Association	£10

Hotel (and thus suppliers and employees of the hotel)	£350
Bar drinks (thus supporting the whisky industry!)	about £30
Food (we barbecue by the river and the money goes to shops in the town of Banchory)	£60
Petrol (divided between petrol stations in Dundee, Banchory and Stirling)	£45
Miscellaneous	£20

The total cost, to me, of those fish was over £700, 14 times the value to the local economy of the same fish had they been netted.

The difference can be even more marked. I was once given a piece of rod-caught salmon weighing about 1lb. A rough calculation indicated that that small piece had yielded the local economy approximately £1500, which is about 500 times its value as net-caught salmon. It tasted delicious.

Which reminds me of the tale of the English angler who went for a week's fishing in Ireland. In the last hour of the last day of his holiday he caught his one and only fish. A small grilse, weighing barely 4lb.

Holding it up, he protested to the gillie, 'That fish has cost me more than two thousand pounds!'

'Ah! To be sure,' replied the gillie. 'Isn't it a grand thing ya didn't catch two of 'em!'

We should note that not all of the fish that now run the River Spey, instead of being cropped in the estuary, are taken by rod-and-line anglers. Taking the 1992 catch statistics for the Spey, had the 10,362 salmon, grilse and sea trout not been netted but run the river, it is likely that somewhere in the region of 2500 of them would have been caught by anglers. At less than one extra fish per rod per week, this would make no noticeable difference to the anglers' catch. What it would do is to greatly increase the breeding stock. And it did, for the reports that I received from Spey correspondents on the populations of salmon on the redds in November 1993 (the first year without estuary netting) were heartening. For instance: 'I have never seen so many fish in the river. When they moved, it was as though the entire river bed moved!'

There may come a point, however, when the numbers of salmon returning to the unnetted rivers is so great that it would be wrong not to take a reasonable crop from them. Going back to the beginning of this chapter, a fully stocked, thriving river will produce a large surplus of adult salmon that ought to be harvested. This harvesting is best carried out by regulated rod and line and by netting. However, if the river is clearly not fully stocked with adult salmon, then no harvest should be taken at all . . . including by rod and line. Of course, anglers imagine that they catch very few of the fish running a river, that their efforts have little overall effect on salmon populations, but . . .

Rod-and-line fisheries

The statement that rod anglers do no harm whatsoever to the salmon stocks of rivers and lakes requires some qualification. In a thriving fishery it is true, but there are some circumstances when it is not true.

Several fishery scientists (amongst them E.M.P. Chadwick, P.F. Elson, A.S. Gee, G. Gudbergsson, T. Gudjonsson, N.J. Milner and D.H. Mills) have calculated the proportion of salmon running upstream that are taken by anglers. On Ireland's Burishoole system anglers take between 5 per cent and 20 per cent of fish, with an average of 12 per cent. In four Icelandic rivers the percentage of salmon taken by anglers varies widely (from year to year and from river to river), from about 11 per cent to over 80 per cent, with averages of about a quarter and a third of fish running the river (the Blanda is exceptional, anglers taking two-thirds of the run). In some Canadian rivers catch rate ranged between 16 per cent and 38 per cent of the run.

In well-stocked rivers such a catch rate may be no problem, for enough salmon will remain to repopulate the river. If the river stocks are low and greater escapement is required to increase stocks, then these catch rates are too high. It may be desirable to stop cropping altogether until stocks have reached the maximum that the river can support.

One might imagine that the proportion of salmon taken by anglers will be fairly constant: for instance, whether the run is 1000 or 100,000 the catch will always be, say, 20 per cent of the run. This is not true: there is evidence to suggest that the smaller the number running the river, the higher the proportion of these that will be caught by anglers. So anglers may take only 10–20 per cent of a big run of fish, but more than 60 per cent of a small run.

One might imagine that the chance of catching a salmon is a fairly constant figure, but it is not. Spring salmon are more likely to be caught than autumn-run fish: one obvious reason is that they are available to be caught over a longer period. But also the larger the fish and the older the fish (in terms of sea age) the more likely is that fish to be caught: rods might catch 80–90 per cent of multi-sea-winter fish but less than 30 per cent of grilse running a river. In other words, grilse are more difficult to catch than multi-sea-winter salmon. It is because of the great decline of multi-sea-winter, spring-run salmon that angling seasons have been altered, restrictions put on angling methods, and (on the Aberdeen Dee) strict limits imposed on the number of fish that may be killed by anglers (see p. 213).

Observations from several rivers (such as Northern Ireland's Bush, Scotland's Tummel and Norway's Drammens) indicate that salmon are more readily caught below a high dam, before they have entered the fish pass or been lifted up a dam, than above a dam. It also seems that, in big rivers, a higher proportion of the salmon run is taken by anglers when low water predominates through the angling season than in a season dominated by high water.

Despite these few statistics and observations, far more work is needed on the proportion of salmon that run the river that is taken by anglers and factors that affect this proportion. Unfortunately, relatively few anglers give catch returns: in parts of Britain and Ireland as few as 5 per cent give returns. Many of those returns include lies (usually understating the numbers of salmon caught). As two very good anglers told me, 'If we tell the estate how many we do catch our rent might go up!'

How can anglers complain about commercial fisheries if they themselves are taking as many fish as they can catch, without due regard for future stocks? How can anglers complain about anything if they fail in their duty to give honest returns of the fish they have caught? Good management of every river needs accurate, honest and full returns from all anglers.

Poaching

As Andy Blezzard, the best water bailiff we have had on my local rivers, put it, the week after he had apprehended a poacher on one of our beats, 'If a river has no poachers, it has no salmon!' A sad fact, but there it is.

Poaching can take many forms. There are the rare men who sniggle the odd fish for the pot to feed their family. All criminal poachers pretend to be in this category, and unfortunately all too often urban magistrates believe them and dish out paltry penalties. Others poach for sheer bravado: I knew three of these well; all were quite wealthy fellows who enjoyed the risk of being discovered and the adrenalin-packed escape. Equally sad are the supposed anglers who use 'almost' conventional fishing tackle to foul-hook salmon. These are failed anglers, who have admitted to themselves their inability to catch fish fairly. When they walk from the river with a couple of fish their conscience is salved by a macho feeling, 'Aren't I clever to catch these!' One poacher in this category, whom I know well, is a fairly famous name in the angling world, his reputation as a catcher of salmon being bolstered by the fish that he deliberately foul-hooks. He was caught once but let off with a caution!

The fourth category of poachers are those who are in it for the money – big money. With their nets, explosives and poisons they may take a large proportion of salmon running a river and destroy parr and other life in the stream. We do not know how big an effect they have, for, like many anglers, they do not declare their catches, but there is little doubt that on some rivers, such as the Foyle (p. 208), they make considerable inroads into the spawning runs.

When calculating the salmon runs, catch statistics and resulting numbers of spawning salmon, losses to poaching must be assessed and included. A wild guess? On some rivers poachers take at least 10 per cent of the run and on other rivers the figure might well be over 20 per cent.

Salmon farming and ranching

In salmon farming, salmon are raised in a hatchery to smolt stage, and then put in netting cages in a sheltered arm of the sea (a sea loch or fjord) where they are fed to the size at which they will be marketed. Salmon ranching, which has recently begun in Norway, involves raising salmon to smolt stage in a hatchery, and releasing the smolts in a river estuary. They go off to feed in the sea and are harvested in the river on their return from the sea.

The advent of salmon farming in the late 1960s and 1970s was seen, by most salmon anglers, as a bright light on the horizon. Huge numbers of salmon would be produced. The price of salmon would fall to ridiculously low levels. It would no longer be financially viable to net wild salmon at sea or in the estuaries, and the reduced profit from poaching would not be worth the risk of getting caught. Alas, it has not worked out this way. Although a phenomenal amount of salmon is farmed (currently about 70,000 tons), mainly around the coasts of Ireland, Scotland and Norway, and the cost of salmon on the market has fallen in real terms in the last 20 years, wild salmon is still in sufficient demand to make commercial netting and poaching worthwhile.

Unfortunately salmon farming and ranching have produced major problems for our wild salmon and sea trout stocks, and our wild river and lake salmon fisheries. Wherever there are salmon farms in the sea, there the wild sea trout stocks have collapsed. The reason for this is that the salmon farms regularly have very high infestations of sea lice. The salmon farmers treat their stock with chemicals, but the sea trout feeding close to the fish farms become heavily infested with sea lice. They either die or, as some recent research suggests, quickly head back into the river (where the sea lice die) and remain there as small brown trout.

Farmed salmon are carefully selected for a fast growth rate to the size demanded by the market (usually about 7lb). Farming involves selective breeding in which the genes that are useful to the farmer are selected at the expense of the genes that best favour a wild population. Thus the farm salmon, though it looks similar to a wild salmon (there are differences, and a farmed salmon can easily be picked out from a bag of wild fish by its malformed fins and blunted snout), is not the same as a wild fish, any more so than an Aylesbury duck is a wild mallard or a farmyard goose a wild greylag. And as salmon farming progresses and selection intensifies, so the genetic differences between farmed and wild salmon will become wider.

Unfortunately a large number of salmon escape each year from fish farms. They have been located in the marine feeding grounds and have been reported returning to many rivers with native wild salmon. Farmed salmon have been reported running many Norwegian rivers, including the Alta and Namsen. They have been recorded from many rivers in Ireland and the west of Scotland (one informant told me that 'There is not one Scottish river between the Mull of Kintyre and Cape Wrath that is not affected by farm escapees'). In 1994 one was caught on the Cumbrian Derwent and another on the Aberdeenshire Dee, two rivers that are far away from salmon farms.

These farmed salmon will interbreed with the native population. This may have two major effects. Firstly, the genetic purity of the salmon in each river is likely to become altered. This important point is discussed below. Secondly, it is quite likely that the parr and smolts from farmed fish or from hybrids between wild and farmed fish are less adapted for living and growing in the river than pure wild fish. The outcome of this could be a decline of the salmon populations of affected rivers. To allow farmed stocks to escape and to interbreed with wild salmon is a form of pollution – biological pollution – and steps ought to be taken, immediately, by Irish, British and Norwegian governments to prevent its happening.

Artificial stocking of rivers

Salmon farmers select fish that become smolts at one year old and raise them to marketable size in the hatchery. Parr that do not smolt at the end of their first year are often sold on to managers of wild salmon rivers to increase the wild salmon stocks.

This, however, is wrong! The only correct method of artificially propagating salmon in order to stock a river is to use the river's own strain of salmon. Eggs and milt should be taken from the wild stock and transferred to the hatchery. Here the eggs and fry from each river should be kept isolated. These can then be later introduced into their own river. Each river, or tributary of each river, has its own genetic strain that has evolved over the last 10,000 years. Its genetic structure makes each salmon perfectly adapted to its own river; nothing should be done that might damage that genetic integrity.

If a river is clean and accessible to migrating salmon, and if the degree of cropping by commercial fishermen and anglers is carefully regulated, there should be no need for hatcheries. If a river needs a hatchery to support the wild spawning stock, there is something intrinsically wrong with the river.

The state of salmon populations

I mentioned earlier some of the problems of using catch statistics as a measure of salmon populations and fluctuations (p. 105). Briefly these are that many anglers and commercial fishermen fail to give an accurate catch return; that fishing seasons and methods have varied over the years and have thus affected catch statistics; that returns for many regions are lacking when one goes back more than about 40 years; that catch returns are not an accurate measure of true salmon populations. But there is no real alternative to catch statistics. Indeed, there is little hope of obtaining good statistics of salmon runs in future years unless a high proportion of rivers have a modern fish-counter installed, ideally just above the tideway. Nevertheless, in spite of the inaccuracies of catch statistics, they do show certain trends that can be used in our examination of population fluctuations.

I am often asked whether salmon populations have declined, and the answer is undoubtedly yes. This 'yes', however, demands some qualification. The salmon population of *some* rivers may not have fallen appreciably in modern times (say, from 1850). On the other hand, the salmon populations of *many* rivers have certainly declined. Several British rivers, such as the Yorkshire Ouse and Trent, the Mersey and Clyde, and several North American, Finnish and Swedish rivers, and most of the salmon rivers between the Bay of Biscay and Denmark lost all their salmon in the nineteenth and first half of the twentieth centuries. So the salmon must have declined. We will look at examples of these in a moment.

But first of all, the questioner is usually concerned with the last few years. For instance, in the last fortnight three anglers have, on separate occasions, asked if the salmon stocks on certain rivers that we fish have decreased since the late 1970s and early 1980s. Each looked back through rose-tinted spectacles at years when almost every time we went near the river we caught fish. We reminisced . . . about that week in October 1981 when we had that magnificent run of fish that averaged 17lb and when we had several up to 26lb. But has there really been a decline? No! Just as, in our childhood, every summer day was hot and sunny, and every winter was blessed with deep crisp snow, so we fool ourselves into remembering the good days and forgetting the bad. Yet when I check through my diaries there were lots of blank days in that wonderful year of 1981 . . . but did I not catch six fish in five consecutive days in 1993? And what about 1988 and the 34lb fish? And so on . . .

When considering short-term trends we must remember that all wild animal populations fluctuate from year to year, and the salmon is no exception. So the fact that runs may be extremely low over three, four or five years is not necessarily cause for concern. Mortality at sea may be high (don't forget that this mortality is about four times more variable than river mortality) in those years. Again, this is not something to worry about over the course of a few years. It is a natural feature of salmon populations. In back-end run spate rivers especially, the cause of wide fluctuations may simply reflect year-to-year climate variations. In drought autumns the run may be so late that many fish enter the river after the angling season has closed. This happened on many rivers in parts of Ireland, northern England and Scotland in 1994 when there was prolonged low water and few fish ran the rivers. Few fish were caught and the run appeared to be tiny, as judged from fishing returns, but by late November the rivers were stuffed with fish! Next year may be completely different: low mortality on the high seas feeding grounds linked to perfect running conditions when the fish arrive back in the estuary may result in the runs of a lifetime!

Even on the greatest of salmon rivers, in the halcyon days of the 1960s when the spring run of multi-sea-winter fish dominated our catches, it was possible to have a blank week's fishing. I think it was Arthur Oglesby who, writing in that period, declared that if an angler visits one of the best beats in the same week over five years he or she will have one great week, three moderate to mediocre weeks and one dreadful week.

Since the spring run declined in the late 1970s and early 1980s and has been replaced by a summer or autumn run it can be even more difficult. The demise of the spring run on so many rivers has led many anglers to believe that the salmon has declined in those rivers: the fact that a later run has compensated to some extent is overlooked, especially when one considers the often erratic nature of back-end runs. In spring the rivers are often ideal for salmon to run. In the back-end the exact timing of the run depends on the amount of water and it is much easier to miss out and believe that there are few fish about. I fish the Nith for a week in late September, some years also in November. As good a time as any! Often there is either no water (it invariably pours down the day I return home) or too much water (the river is just fining off the day I return home). On two other rivers that I fish the autumn run is now so late that 60 per cent run after the salmon fishing season is over. In October we are moaning about the decline of the salmon; in November the rivers are stuffed with them!

Always be cautious, therefore, when considering a very few years' statistics, or your own memory or general impressions. One trait of the human psyche is to look for disaster where there is none. Do you recall the panic engendered by the media following the series of dry hot summers in the mid-1970s and early 1980s? Global warming and the hole in the ozone layer caused by aerosols were blamed. But then, in the mid-1980s we had a series of cold winters. This time we were warned of an impending ice age!

Many anglers, again looking at short-term trends, consider that the runs of salmon are cyclical, where the population peaks every so many years. This view has had some scientific support. A.S. Gee and N.J. Milner have suggested a ten-year cycle, others a cycle of between eight and eleven years (one suggested a six-year cycle). One argument goes along these lines: 1988 was a bumper 2SW salmon run, therefore (the eggs laid at the end of 1988 will hatch in 1989, three years in the river as a parr and two years away at sea) 1994 should be a great 2+SW run. It does not work like that! If you examine carefully the graphs given in this part of the book you will find it impossible to trace predictable cyclical fluctuations unless a great deal of imagination is used. This is to be expected because the factors that affect the sea life and mortality of salmon – Atlantic climate and sea temperature, and the abundance of several potential food species – do not fluctuate in a set, regular pattern.

Fluctuating populations

The remainder of this chapter is given over to the examination of population fluctuations of salmon in a few selected rivers. The rivers have been chosen because they illustrate how populations have fluctuated naturally, perhaps mainly owing to variation of conditions out on the sea feeding grounds (which also affect the timing of runs; see pp. 115–18). But they also illustrate many of the features that might cause a collapse of salmon stocks or prevent a depleted stock of salmon from increasing. The only way to assess salmon populations and to make plans for the future conservation of the fish is on a river-by-river basis. Now that commercial fishing has ceased (on the high seas and in some estuaries), and what commercial fishing remains is threatened with closure or tighter controls through the lobbying of the NASF and other organizations, the real future of the Atlantic salmon lies in the individual rivers.

Icelandic rivers

We will begin with Icelandic rivers for they suffer little pollution and the only problem, if it is a problem, is high seas netting (which, we have seen, has recently been phased out). Figure 27 gives total salmon catches from 1974 to 1993. This shows that the population, as measured by catches, has fluctuated, just as the population of most wild animals fluctuates from year to year. Note also that there is no sign of a regular cycle over this 20-year period, there being peaks in 1978, 1986, 1988 and, to a lesser extent, 1992. It will be interesting to see, now that high seas netting has been stopped, whether the Icelandic catches increase significantly in the near future. Only time will tell.

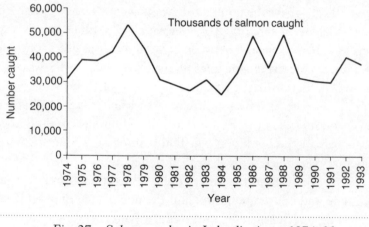

Fig. 27 – Salmon catches in Icelandic rivers, 1974–93

Thames

'Though some of our northern counties have as fat and as large [salmon] as the river Thames, yet none are of so excellent a taste,' wrote Izaak Walton in *The Compleat Angler* in 1653, for the Thames had been famous for its salmon from Roman times. Big salmon too, averaging 16 pounds. A century later, in 1754, the salmon catch from the Thames around London was so great that the price fell to sixpence per pound and the Lord Mayor was asked to use his good offices to reduce the amount of netting, perhaps not so much as a salmon conservation measure as to keep the price high on the market. Even at the end of the eighteenth century the Thames supported at least 400 netsmen (who caught other species as well as salmon) but the numbers of fish were declining. From 1810, when the catch totalled about 3000, the Thames salmon population collapsed, the last being taken in about 1833.

It was argued that overnetting was a major cause of the extinction of salmon in the Thames, but although this pressure was undoubtedly great it had been so for centuries. The death knell for the Thames salmon was undoubtedly pollution by industry and with raw sewage. The Thames stank so badly that on warm summer days members of Parliament were almost suffocated by the stench of the river oozing by.

Since the 1960s attempts have been made to clean up the Thames so that by the early 1970s many species of sea fish were living once more in the tidal water downstream from London. But in *Anglers Mail* in April 1973 Alwyne Wheeler could hold out little hope for an early return of the salmon, announcing that 'I cannot see salmon running up the Thames for 50 years, given that the river improves at the same rate as it has lately.'

In November 1974 a salmon, weighing 8lb 4½oz, was caught, alive, in the Thames and today, 20 years later, a small run has developed.

Any river that has lost its salmon mainly because of pollution will see some salmon colonizing the river when the pollution ceases.

Ribble

Though not a famous salmon river, the Ribble (with its two major tributaries, the Hodder and Calder) has been thoroughly studied by A.T.R. Houghton in his *The Ribble Salmon Fisheries* for the years up to and including 1950; recent statistics have also been provided by the Ribble Fisheries Committee. Through these sources we can see the impact of three major problems affecting salmon populations. Catch statistics (rod and commercial estuary nets combined) are shown in Fig. 28.

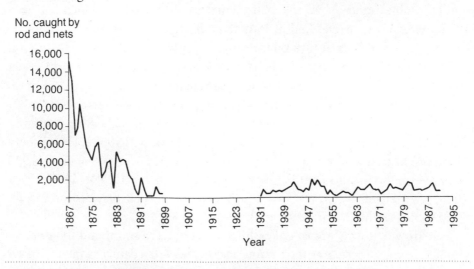

Fig. 28 – Salmon catches on the Ribble, 1867–1995

From the first published catch statistic it is clear that the Ribble was a prolific salmon river in the mid-nineteenth century, for a net catch of over 15,000 salmon from a small river indicates a most healthy state. However, it was not thus a century earlier, for unscrupulous landowners in the estuary and just above the tide had virtually blocked the entire river in their attempts to trap salmon, to such an extent that smolts could not migrate downstream, nor salmon upstream to the spawning grounds. The worst of these obstructions, Bessow Caul, just downstream of where the M6 bridge crosses the river today, was finally demolished in 1811, allowing salmon to return upstream, and during the 1860s permanent baulks and stake nets in the estuary were made illegal and removed. This action allowed the mid-nineteenth century population to flourish. But even so there were other weirs, some that the salmon could pass in high water, and one that salmon could pass only on certain days when the fish pass was opened by the owner. But the river was clean, and, as Frank Buckland reported to the *Preston Chronicle* on 10 September 1867, 'The Ribble is a most valuable salmon river; there were very good breeding grounds, and it had a fine estuary. There was a great nursery above for the fish to breed in . . .'

But then, in the 1860s, an impassable weir was constructed across the upper Ribble close to the market town of Settle. This cut off the salmon from a large proportion of their upper river spawning grounds. The size of the 'smolt factory' was immediately reduced: the salmon run declined. 'But', Houghton pointed out, 'the spectacular collapse of the Ribble salmon fisheries between 1867 and 1895 was not due to any one cause but to several causes all working together to one end.'

The Ribble estuary became canalized making drift-netting, which began in 1872, extremely effective. And in 1861 the industrialized, urban Calder Valley began spewing industrial filth out into the lower Ribble. By 1900 the salmon run on the Ribble had more or less been wiped out; so much so that from then to 1930 no catch statistics are available . . . it is likely that there were no salmon to catch. Efforts were made to propagate salmon and resurrect the run, but pollution from the Calder continued to be a problem, especially during summer thunderstorms that pushed a plug of fetid water into the Ribble. The Fishery Board's reports give all too frequent gloomy statistics: for instance, 4 July 1942 'Salmon and sea trout killed below Calder Foot'; 10 June 1943 'Thick black sludge; fish killed'; 16 June 1947 'Fish killed and turned black'. But despite these problems the Board persevered.

The growing townships of Lancashire required clean water and the pristine Hodder, being so close, was the obvious target. In 1930 a dam was finally closed that flooded the headwaters as Stocks Reservoir and excluded salmon and sea trout from their upland breeding streams. Then a series of abstraction points were developed along the Hodder from which extra water was taken and piped away.

In recent years the Calder has been greatly cleaned up, so much so that salmon and sea trout run that once filthy stream. Also the lower Ribble, which was so greatly affected by the Calder, holds salmon throughout the year. But the loss of the headwater streams for spawning, and the excessive abstraction of water and intensive land drainage over most of the catchment, which have reduced flows and led to the exposure of extensive areas of former river bed and the concreting of gravel redds, have reduced the potential of the Ribble as a smolt factory. Instead of returning to a run that would enable a catch of 5000 or more salmon each year, with over 15,000 in exceptional years, the run (as measured by declared catch) now fluctuates around a mean of about 1000. I know this river well, and, taking into account the widespread damage to the entire system, I doubt if it would be possible to increase the run to 2000 fish (as measured by declared catch).

Foyle

The Foyle is an extensive river system that flows into the sea at Derry. In the 22 miles from Strabane to Derry the river is a wide estuary and used by commercial netsmen and poachers. At Strabane two rivers join to make the Foyle, the Finn (which is still dominated by a spring run) and the Mourne (which is dominated by a summer and autumn run); the Finn and Mourne fish are thus two distinct genetic populations. The headwaters of both Finn and Mourne are crystal clear, with abundant invertebrate food for salmon parr; and, while there has been some land drainage in the catchment, it is not excessive nor is there significant abstraction. The only barrier to running fish is a big weir at Sion Mills, downstream of the Finn–Mourne confluence, which has an antiquated, though effective, fish pass. Two other rivers are part of the Foyle system, the rivers Roe and Faughan which enter Derry Lough below the city of Derry. The entire river system is regulated by the Foyle Fisheries Commission (FFC).

The Foyle system is a splendid smolt factory, but the problem faced by the river and the FFC is ensuring that enough adult salmon manage to reach the redds to spawn (it is estimated that 8000 is the required number). The first problem is the extent of legal, commercial netting in the estuaries and at sea off the estuaries. As can be seen from Fig. 29 the catch is enormous, and possibly greater than any commercial catch made anywhere else of similar size in the world. What is so incredible is that the commercial fishing season is a short one: barely six weeks from 15 June to 31 July (up to and including 1992 the season was 21 June to 31 August – three weeks or 50 per cent longer). Also,

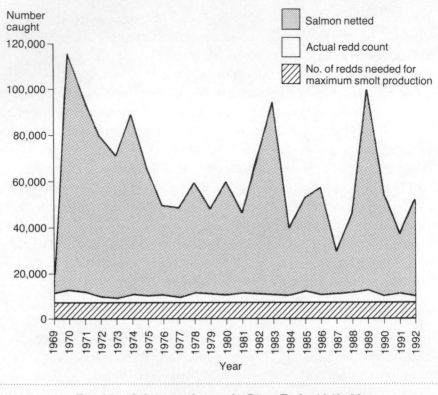

Fig. 29 – Salmon catches on the River Foyle, 1969–92

netting in the sea in, and off, Lough Foyle is restricted to the hours 6 a.m.–6 p.m. on just four days each week (Monday to Thursday) and in the river estuary between the hours of 6 p.m. on Monday and 6 p.m. on Friday (the nets here being able to fish only at certain stages of the tide). These commercial fishing seasons and times when fishing is permitted are regularly reviewed. There are also, in the tidal Foyle, extensive sanctuary areas where netting is prohibited. Can the Foyle system withstand such pressure? Certainly, at nights and weekends during the fishing season, and before and after the season, there is ample opportunity for fish to run the river system above the netting areas. But there are two other problems.

The first is the extent of poaching, mostly at night, especially on the Foyle itself. During the winter the local poachers make their own poaching boats out of bits of plywood, string and six-inch nails, filling the gaps with putty or rubber solution, so that they have a good supply just in case they are arrested and a boat confiscated. They brave the dangerous Foyle, in the dead of night, in these 'coffins'! And through the winter they lay up a stock of monofilament nets so that they will not run out of gear during the summer. The extent of the problem can be seen from the numbers of illegal boats and nets seized: in 1992, 559 nets and 63 boats. I spent one July morning out with the Foyle Fisheries Commission: in the space of two hours we seized a net and a boat. But, although the numbers of salmon taken illegally must be very large, no one can put a figure on it. As Gerald Crawford (Secretary of the FFC) explained in a paper to the 1986 Atlantic Salmon Symposium, 'At least we know that if illegal fishing were to cease there would be an increased spawning escapement. That is the major impact that illegal fishing has on salmon stocks . . . If there were no illegal fishing the increase in population would have a multiplier effect on succeeding generations. If it were possible to increase the potential spawning stock each year by even 10 per cent this would, in the course of a few generations, have a very marked effect on the stock level.'

But the anglers don't help. For the FFC to manage the river properly they need accurate returns from anglers. Only about 5 per cent of around 5000 anglers purchasing licences to fish the Foyle system send in a return, and between one- and two-thirds of these returns declare a nil catch. I don't believe these nil returns at all, for even the most incompetent novice could not fail to catch at least one salmon in a year of fishing here!

Evidence for my doubts comes from a recent incident where an angler sent in a nil return but then had his photograph in the local newspaper being presented with a club trophy for having caught the biggest salmon of the season! In the 1988 FFC Report, Ian Small attempted to calculate the true rod catch of salmon using quite complex mathematical calculations: in 1987, when the declared catch was a mere 390 fish, Ian reckoned the true catch to be in the order of 2600. Such under-recording of catches is highly significant when, as was stated earlier, the system needs a spawning head of 8000 fish. How stupid anglers are sometimes!

Figure 32 also shows the estimates of the numbers of redds each year in the Foyle system. Eight thousand adults or at least 4000 redds are needed for maximum production by the river. In many years the number of redds is below optimum, but the continued efforts by the FFC to curb poaching, supported by honest anglers, could remedy this in future years to maintain the Foyle's status as the world's most prolific Atlantic salmon river.

Nith

The Nith is a river of moderate size, some 50 miles long and draining 440 square miles of moorland. It flows from hills in Ayrshire, past the villages of Sanquhar and Thornhill and the town of Dumfries, to the Solway Firth.

Up to about 1954 the river suffered greatly from pollution. In the upper valley are considerable coal reserves, and mined coal was washed using stream water that fed a thick, black sludge into the main river. It was reported that, in places, the river bed was coated with up to a foot of glutinous coal waste, and every spate brought down treacly, black water. There was also a thriving tweed industry in the valley, and several tweed mills had weirs (locally called caulds) to provide a head of water. These caulds were impassable for salmon, save in high water. And, as we have seen, the high water was contaminated with coal sludge. Then, at the head of the estuary, Dumfries had a most primitive sewage system that released raw or only partially treated sewage into the river. This caused the death of salmon stranded downstream in low water; salmon could pass through this sewage-laden stretch only during a spate.

In 1934 the Nith Fishings Improvement Association was founded. In the following 20 years they persuaded the National Coal Board to stop using the streams for discharging coal waste. They persuaded the mill owners to pull down their caulds. And they persuaded Dumfries Town Council to build a modern sewage works that would release only fully treated effluent into the river. Up to 1948 commercial netting took place at the head of the tide at Dumfries. This was stopped in 1948. Also, the amount of haaf-netting in the estuary was reduced from 1962 to allow for greater escapement of running salmon. In 1949 a stocking policy was adopted, where eggs were raised to eyed ova stage in a hatchery and then put out in the river headwaters.

The effect of these actions resulted in a marked improvement in the runs of salmon (grilse are included with salmon), as can be seen from the following five-year average declared catches by anglers:

1935–39	1940–44	1945–49	1950–54	1955–59	1960–64
289	205	289	432	1307	2322

1965–69	1970–74	1975–79	1980–84	1985–90*
1862	1552	1382	1947	3386

*Six years' data

Note that the decline in catches in the late 1960s was due, in part at least, to the ravages of UDN, which reached the Nith in 1966, and the catches of the late 1970s were affected greatly by the drought years of 1975–6. Note also that the true catch will be significantly higher than this because many anglers do not report their true catches. Also, poachers take an unknown quantity of fish from the river.

Earlier I described how the number of grilse has increased as a percentage of the catch on many rivers, especially from the 1960s, but that this increase of grilse appears to be independent of the runs of multi-sea-winter salmon (pp. 112–13). This has happened on the Nith: in the years 1951–4 15 per cent of the catch were reported as grilse, in the years 1986–1990, 26 per cent. But in terms of numbers of fish, both age categories have increased, the grilse from an average of 52 per year to 908 per year, the multi-sea-winter salmon from an average of 284 per year to 2603 per year. We have also seen a decline, in many rivers, of the spring run. This too has happened on the Nith: in the 1960s about 25 per cent of salmon ran the Nith in spring, 35 per cent in summer and 40 per cent in autumn. By the 1980s only about 5 per cent ran in spring, 30 per cent in summer and 65 per cent in autumn.

Dee

The Aberdeenshire Dee has long been one of the world's great salmon rivers, most notably for its spring run. It is a clean river, rising in the Cairngorm Mountains and flowing through a valley that is only lightly farmed, mostly as pasture, and with small towns and villages that produce insignificant quantities of pollutants. In recent years the numbers of salmon running the Dee have declined dramatically, especially those fish that run the upper, western beats above Banchory (Fig. 30). What has happened is that the fish that run the river in 'spring' (i.e. from December through to May and that are caught by spring anglers) have virtually disappeared. Rod-and-line catches in spring have

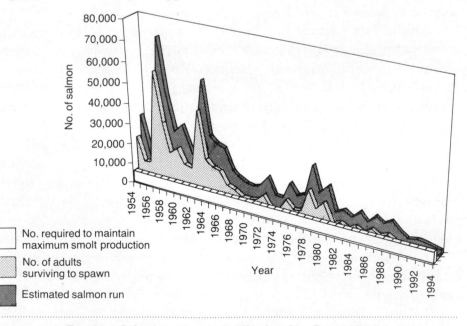

Fig. 30 – Salmon catches on the Aberdeenshire Dee, 1954–94

211

declined on the Dee from between 5500 and 6000 per year in the 1950s to close to 2000 in the early 1990s.

This decline of the spring run is not special to the Dee, for the spring catches on the Spey have declined, in the same period, from 3000–3500 per year in the early 1950s to barely 1000 in the early 1990s and on the Tweed from 4000–4500 in the 1950s to barely 500 per year in the early 1990s. But unlike most other rivers (such as the Spey and Tweed), there has not been a corresponding increase in the numbers of grilse and summer and autumn salmon running the river. Because the Dee and its problems have featured frequently earlier in this book, I will summarize the problems here and the measures being taken by the Dee Salmon Fishing Improvement Association (DSFIA) to try to resolve these problems. The catastrophe affects not just the spring salmon run. It affects the entire economy of the valley, for salmon fishing brings some £6 million in revenue to this sparsely inhabited valley and provides the equivalent of 422 full-time jobs. Thus the Dee valley economy, which depends on attracting anglers, is collapsing.

In the early 1980s it was believed by many anglers that one main cause of the salmon decline on the Dee was estuary netting, and in 1986 the last net was removed. Yet the fact that in the 10 years up to the end of netting the Dee rod fishery caught an average of 5878 but an average of only 3174 in the 10 years after the cessation of netting (W.M. Shearer) indicated that the problem was far greater than was at first thought.

Scientific data released by the DSFIA in *Newletter 3* (autumn 1994) demonstrated that 5800 spring salmon must survive to spawning to generate enough young salmon to maintain a thriving spring run. Since 1980 this number has only just been achieved in four years, and in no years at all since 1988. Consequently on the major nursery streams, the Clunie, Ey and Gairn, the populations of parr have declined in the years from 1989 to 1994 by between 50 per cent and 80 per cent. These important nursery streams for immature fish that should eventually return as spring salmon are thus producing relatively few smolts. Of the smolts that go to sea, it appears that, whereas up to 40 per cent returned as adult salmon in the 1960s and 1970s, only 20 per cent have returned since the 1980s. That is 20 per cent of an already reduced smolt run.

DSFIA suggests that the problem lies primarily at sea, implying that climatic changes over the North Atlantic have led to changes in the marine feeding areas that have caused a higher mortality of the spring-run fish. Other important factors, the DSFIA argue, are the drift net fishery off north-eastern England (p. 193), other fishing operations in the North Sea, and perhaps predation by seals. Although these factors are undoubtedly important inroads into the Dee salmon runs, I do not think that it is so simple. Spring runs have declined on many rivers, as we saw in Chapter 4. But in most rivers the overall run has not declined: it has changed from a spring into a summer–autumn run and is likely to revert to a spring run sometime in the future.

In most rivers, smolts are being produced as they always have, but they are coming back at different times. In the Dee, smolts are not being produced! And I suspect that there is something intrinsically wrong with the river. But that is my opinion; the DSFIA might be right, yet only time will tell.

Nevertheless, the efforts being made to promote the Dee salmon runs by the DSFIA are to be applauded, for they involve careful monitoring of the river, allowing an increased escapement of spring salmon for spawning, an improvement of the river as a habitat for parr, and the use of artificially rearing salmon parr from the river's own genetic strain of salmon.

From 1995 the angling season will commence on 1 March rather than 1 February and the method throughout the river will be fly only (salmon are less easily damaged and easier to return unharmed to the water when caught with fly compared with spinner). Anglers are allowed to kill only one spring fish in a week's fishing (why even one?) and in summer and autumn only fresh-run silver fish may be kept, though there are added restrictions depending on the size of fish and part of the river being fished. Without such constraints, the only other solution would be to stop angling altogether.

The DSFIA are also taking action to improve the river by encouraging farmers (through compensation) to fence off a buffer strip of land up to 10yd wide along the river. This will prevent sheep and cattle eroding the banks, and encourage lush growths of riverside vegetation that will increase the insect populations by the water and thus contribute to the summer foods of parr. And the DSFIA has also been a major contributor to the building of a hatchery at Glen Tanar that can hatch 420,000 salmon eggs taken from the remnant salmon stocks and raise 120,000 of them to parr stage.

It will be interesting to see if the efforts of the DSFIA are rewarded by an increased run of spring salmon. Anglers who have fished this most lovely fly river will all hope that they do succeed.

Stop press! Though not of the quality 20 years ago, the 1995 spring run was the best for years. Also, it seems the fish counter was grossly underestimating the run of fish for 1994! This all points to the fact that we still do not fully understand the intricate nature of salmon populations.

Connecticut

It is likely that the Connecticut River was the most prolific Atlantic salmon river in North America for, up to at least 1792, salmon penetrated its entire 11,000 square mile watershed. In 1798 a impassable dam was constructed across the river, some 105 miles above the tide, and in the following years to about 1814 other impassable dams were built downstream and across all the major tributaries. These dams exterminated the salmon so quickly that, when a salmon was accidentally caught in the estuary in 1872, no one could identify it (Anthony Netboy, *The Salmon*, 1974). Following the passage through US Congress of the 1965 Anadromous Fish Act, investigations began into the feasibility of reintroducing salmon to the Connecticut and other similarly ruined rivers. In a 1986 report, R.A. Jones, of the Bureau of Fisheries of the State of Connecticut, described how attempts had to be made in improving water quality, for there had been no need to constrain polluters once the salmon runs had been exterminated. Then the dams had to be fitted with fish passes: this was at great expense for three 'fishways' cost (in the 1980s) $25 1/2 million. Finally, because the Connecticut's own stock of salmon had been lost, it was essential to import brood salmon from elsewhere and propagate from them with a hatchery (the initial cost of the hatchery was $100,000). The first juvenile salmon were released into the river in 1967 and in 1976 the first salmon to return to the Connecticut, a cock fish, was trapped and its milt used to fertilize 41,000 eggs taken from salmon in the Penobscot River. In the first 10 years of the project only 13 salmon returned, but since then numbers have slowly increased with a run, currently, of over 1000 fish. In 1986 cash terms, this programme was costing $200,000 annually.

Many former salmon rivers in Finland, Sweden, the Baltic States and from Portugal to Jutland have lost their salmon primarily because of the damming of rivers. The Connecticut experience shows that it is possible, given sufficient time and funding, to turn them all, once more, into salmon rivers.

Awe and Orchy

The River Awe is a short river, barely four miles long, that drains from the fresh water of Loch Awe to the salt of Loch Etive. The River Orchy is the main feeder of Loch Awe, flowing from Loch Tulla and Rannoch Moor to enter Loch Awe near Dalmally. The Awe was once famous for its great salmon, 30 pounders once being fairly common and several over the 50lb mark having been taken there in bygone years (pp. 119–22). But then, in 1964, a hydroelectric dam was constructed at the head of the River Awe, destroying seven major pools that were major resident lies and spawning grounds. Also, through the winter, so much water was retained by the dam that much of the remainder of the River Awe dried up, leaving eggs to rot in the exposed gravel banks. The Awe salmon stocks were thus exterminated. The genetic strain of salmon special to the Awe was destroyed.

The hydroelectric dam has a fish lift that carries migrating salmon, destined for the Orchy, into Loch Awe. We do not know the numbers of salmon that ran into Loch Awe and then into the Orchy before the dam was built, but in the years immediately following the construction of the dam the number was about 6000 salmon and this has fallen steadily ever since, reaching an all-time low of 1600 in 1994. Why have these numbers declined if there is an efficient fish pass? Firstly, the Orchy catchment has been affected by forestry, which has ploughed up and drained the moorlands. These moorlands held and slowly released into the Orchy vast amounts of water, so that flow rates were always good, even during droughts. The forestry schemes have turned the Orchy into a spate stream where high rainfall is followed by a quick and violent spate, the river quickly falling to much lower levels. Thus the spawning gravels and nursery areas have been greatly reduced. Also, there is a great loss of smolts migrating downstream through the Awe hydroelectric dam. Research by Alan Black of the Institute of Aquaculture has shown that 38 per cent of smolts are killed as they pass downstream through the turbines of hydroelectric dams. Such a mortality seems bound to result in a declining salmon population (hydroelectric dams, even where there is a fish pass, have decimated salmon stocks on many other Scottish, Irish, mainland European, US and Canadian salmon rivers). Efforts are being made to increase the salmon run into the Awe–Orchy system by the raising of fry in a hatchery. However, this is unlikely ever to result in a thriving wild-bred salmon population as occurred before the dam and forestry developments.

These few selected rivers demonstrate that the decline of the salmon in many rivers is due almost entirely to the ways by which mankind has mistreated those rivers. Where we still have clean rivers, unaffected by land drainage, damming and water abstraction, and where there is some control of the amount of cropping in the river, then there remains a thriving salmon population. Where a river is polluted, or there is excessive water abstraction or land drainage, or some of the headwaters are lost through building impassable weirs, or the river dammed, especially for hydroelectric purposes (even with a fish pass), the salmon stocks invariably suffer. Yet the salmon is a resilient fish. Reduce or remove the causes of the loss or major decline of salmon in a river and the salmon will return and numbers build up. We have seen this on the Thames, also the Tyne and Tees in recent years. Only very recently (16 January 1995) an angler from Derby told me of a salmon caught in the River Trent: another river where a salmon run seems to be starting to develop after the ruination of the Industrial Revolution.

Dear reader, look at your own rivers. Have the numbers of salmon running them declined? Are they working at 100 per cent efficiency as smolt factories? Why not? You too should be able, with a little research (sometimes a walk along the entire river with a detailed Ordnance Survey map will reveal much), to identify the major problems. The hard work is then getting these problems resolved through the lobbying power of your fishing club, the river's fishery management organization (all rivers should have such a body), and through national and international salmon conservation organizations. If all salmon anglers did this, besides simply going out to catch salmon, we would revolutionize the conservation of rivers and the salmon.

Conservation measures and the future of salmon stocks

I am very optimistic about the future of our salmon populations. But this optimism depends on the continuing impetus in conservation measures. It is important that the following problems that have faced our salmon populations for so long continue to be lessened:

- A reduction of pollution in our rivers, lakes and the sea: anglers ought constantly to be lobbying their governments to legislate against all pollution and to impose severe penalties on polluters and make them bear the full cost of removing and repairing the effects of pollution.
- A rational attempt should be made to reduce the excessive abstraction of water from river systems: from boreholes, from the river directly and by the construction of new reservoirs on river systems. In Britain it is a ghastly fact that between one-third and a half of the water abstracted never reaches its destination; it is lost in leaking pipes, dripping taps or simply poured away to no purpose. That water should be flowing down our rivers and held in our lakes.

  Anglers ought constantly to be lobbying their governments to enforce water conservation measures and to legislate against such wastage.
- Rivers, throughout the range of the salmon, should all be accessible to salmon. Anglers ought constantly to be lobbying governments to legislate that either impassable dams and weirs are removed or effective fish passes are installed.
- Commercial fishing on the high seas feeding grounds and the netting of salmon migrating between their feeding grounds and home rivers should be banned internationally. This is the most haphazard and ineffective way of harvesting the surplus salmon. Anglers should support unanimously the North Atlantic Salmon Fund in their efforts and lobby governments (most especially the dilatory British, Irish and European Union governments) to this end.
- Salmon farming should be more tightly controlled and the escape of salmon

from farms be treated as a form of pollution – which it is. Governments must be made aware of the problems of salmon farming and be lobbied until they act.

- Poaching, whether at sea or in the rivers, can make great inroads into salmon stocks. The penalties for poaching are too small and often not fully imposed by the courts. We should lobby governments to increase penalties and insist that the courts impose these penalties.

- Every salmon river is unique. For this reason we ought to know, for each major salmon river, what is its optimum smolt-producing capacity, what is the number of adult salmon needed to produce that smolt population, and what surplus stock of adult salmon (which may then be harvested) that smolt run will generate. Also, the timings of the runs of returning salmon should be known. Salmon anglers should be prepared to fund this research through their fishing licences.

  When this information is known, then fishing seasons and catch limits should be imposed that guarantee that the estuary net fishery (if there is one) or rod-and-line fishery leaves enough adult salmon at the end of each season to generate the optimum smolt run. If the salmon stocks are not great enough (as currently on the Aberdeenshire Dee) then fishing should be stopped or a catch-and-release policy adopted until stocks recover.

- To control the sale of illegally caught salmon (whether by poachers or by anglers taking more than their quota) a tag system, as applies on some Canadian rivers, should be introduced. Each angler receives a certain number of tags when he or she purchases a fishing permit. When a salmon is caught and killed, the tag (which cannot be removed other than by cutting) must be immediately attached to the fish. It would be illegal to have a salmon in one's possession or to buy or sell a wild salmon that is not so tagged.

  Critics of this system argue that a black market in tags would develop, or that an unsuccessful angler might give or sell tags to a more successful angler. But there is no other way of telling a legally caught fish from one taken illegally. It works in Canada. Can the critics of the tag system come up with a better solution?

- Bolstering the stock of smolts produced in the river with hatchery-raised fry, parr or smolts should be unnecessary in a healthy river where cropping of surplus salmon is controlled. But where it is to be carried out, every effort should be made to ensure that the ova and milt used in the hatchery come from the river's own salmon population. It should be illegal to randomly release the progeny of unidentified salmon into a river.

- The *Gyrodactylus* problem (p. 181) has damaged over 30 Norwegian rivers to date, and was caused by importing the parasite from another country (Sweden). There is no need at all for such movements of fish. To risk any wild salmon population by importing fish that might carry some disease or parasite is grossly irresponsible. It should be made illegal in all countries having a wild salmon population.

- Anglers are responsible for the water that they fish: they are responsible for the quality of the water, and the plants and animals (including the fish) that live in or by the water. Certainly, if it were not for anglers of previous generations we would not have as many salmon rivers and lakes to fish as we have now. It is our responsibility that we pass on, to future generations, angling that is at least of the quality that we have enjoyed – and preferably better. We should constantly be trying to improve the quality of our sport.

There are two sides to this responsibility:

a) a personal responsibility – nothing that we do as individual anglers should harm the other animals and plants with which we share the water and waterside, and nothing we do should bring the sport of angling into disrepute. There is a growing anti-blood sports and anti-angling lobby in Europe; we should ensure that we, as individuals, do not provide them with any ammunition which they could use against our sport.

b) a collective responsibility – to bring to task those other anglers who shirk their own personal responsibility; to pursue with vigour, through our national angling organizations and by lobbying our elected national and local government representatives, those who pollute or seek to damage our lakes and rivers; to ensure that we give correct returns of the fish that we catch and that we fish fairly, with due regard for the fish, the river and other anglers.

Personal angling behaviour

Killing fish

One of the great joys of angling is to take home a salmon to eat. This necessarily involves killing the fish.

If you are going to kill fish then always carry a 'priest', the right instrument for the job. Kill the fish immediately it is landed by tapping it hard on the top of the head.

To leave a fish flapping about in a boat or on the bank, or to carry the fish until a suitable stick or stone has been found, is wrong. It is inhumane; it brings the sport of angling into disrepute.

Overfishing

Anglers complain loudly about overfishing of salmon and sea trout stocks at sea and in estuaries, but they rarely think about the numbers of salmon and sea trout that they themselves kill. Gone are the days when anglers should permit themselves to kill more than a brace of salmon in one day or dozens in one year, even if salmon may seem, on a few occasions, superabundant and prepared to grab the fly eagerly.

What will you do with those that you cannot eat? Sell them to subsidize your fishing or your regular income? Fishmongers sell fish; anglers ought not to do so! Perhaps you like to give them away to non-angling friends? By all means give your nearest and dearest a piece of a fish that you have caught. But to give them away just because they are surplus to your needs, to people who themselves do not contribute to the upkeep of our fisheries as anglers, is a waste of fish. The cost of farmed salmon is so low that they can go and buy one of those.

Some anglers consider it clever to catch and kill big bags of salmon. You can see this in their eyes when they sit or stand next to the row of fish that they have caught. But no one need boast about killing salmon. When it is in a net a fish cannot hit back! It is far harder, and therefore a mark of character, to put a fish back, unharmed, into the river.

I am not advocating a blanket policy of catch-and-release, for that is just as wrong, morally, as killing as many salmon as possible. A catch-and-release policy is a licence to play with living creatures for sheer pleasure. The pleasure of angling is the pleasure of a hunter: that of catching something to eat.

Enjoy catching fish, not killing them. Do not aim to catch your limit; instead limit your kill to the minimum you need for the table. And, let me suggest, take a crop from the grilse or smaller salmon, and put back the bigger ones that will produce more eggs, and perhaps encourage a run of the multi-sea-winter fish that have declined so drastically in recent years.

Carelessness at the waterside

- Remember that monofilament does not rot; it accumulates and sooner or later some animal is going to become entangled in it and die a slow, lingering death. Discarded monofilament and baited hooks kill hundreds, if not thousands, of wild birds, amphibians, reptiles and mammals with which we share the waterside every year. Take home all waste monofilament and old hooks and burn them.
- Besides being unsightly, empty bottles and cans are lethal traps for small waterside animals that might creep in but cannot escape. Broken bottles and sharp metal can cut and seriously injure wild animals, farm livestock and small children paddling at the water's edge. Take them home.
- Discarded food and food wrappers are unsightly, but they also attract rats. Someone may contract the deadly Weil's disease (easily picked up from

ground contaminated by rat urine) because of the careless angler who has attracted rats by discarding waste food. Take all litter and waste food home.

- Do not flatten and trample waterside vegetation, or kick or dig a more comfortable seat in the bank. Damage may result in bank erosion which may ruin a good riffle. It will also make the owner of the land that has been eroded less likely to welcome anglers in future. Waterside vegetation provides many birds with nest sites, food and shelter. Many anglers find the flowers, reeds and sedges of the waterside aesthetically beautiful; we don't want them destroyed.

When you see an angler who displays a lack of personal responsibility, say something! Thoughtless people need to be encouraged to think for themselves.

Enjoy being at the waterside and being a salmon angler – *and when you leave the waterside after a fishing session leave only your footprints.*

INDEX

THE LIFE CYCLE OF THE ATLANTIC SALMON

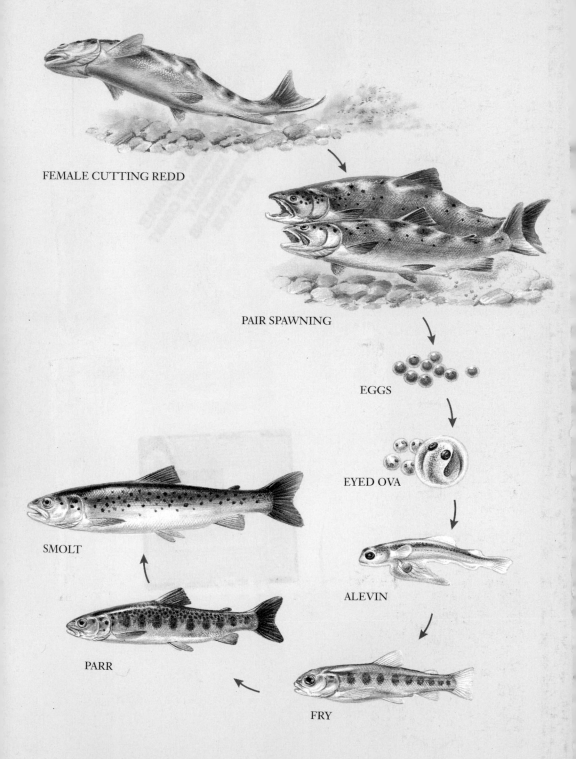

FEMALE CUTTING REDD

PAIR SPAWNING

EGGS

EYED OVA

SMOLT

ALEVIN

PARR

FRY